JESUS IN EXODUS

Michael Esses, D.H.L.

LOGOS INTERNATIONAL
PLAINFIELD, NEW JERSEY

Scriptures quoted herein are a mixture of Esses' own
translation and paraphrase from the Hebrew Masoretic
text. Special acknowledgment is made of the use of
portions of the Amplified Bible, copyright 1965 by
Zondervan Publishing House.

To my dear friend, Corrie ten Boom, who in her life, like Moses in the Exodus from Egypt, always had the choice to either stop at the "Red Sea" of difficulty or to go through by faith, totally trusting and relying upon Jesus for His divine protection as she helped to deliver my people Israel.

No greater love has anyone than that he would be willing to lay down his life for his fellowman. Praise the Lord!

Preface

ISRAEL, O ISRAEL

A people hated, a people discriminated against, a people in bondage, a people in slavery, yet these people clung to the fact that God had spoken to their fathers, saying He was their God and they were His people.

He stated to Abraham, the father of the people of faith, that they would dwell in bondage for four hundred years in a land not their own, but in the end of the fourth generation—to the exact day, the minute, the hour—they would leave Egypt in a miraculous deliverance unheard of in the history of man.

God would take his people from the midst of another people and separate them to Himself forever.

They would stand, all four and a half million of them, at Horeb and hear with their own ears God thunder to them from Sinai, "I AM the Lord *Thy God* which brought thee up out of Egypt."

Jesus still speaks to us this day saying, "I AM the Lord *Thy God* who brought you up out of your Egypt, your bondage, your sin, your slavery.

"I have taken your sin upon Myself and I have set you free from the bondage of sin. By My stripes, you have been healed in every area of your life—spiritually, physically, emotionally, financially—and whom I have set free is free indeed—in deed!"

Rev. Michael Esses, Ph.D., D.H.L., M.A.

Contents

Other books by Michael Esses:
Michael, Michael, Why Do You Hate Me?
The Phenomenon of Obedience
Jesus in Genesis
The Next Visitor to Planet Earth

JESUS IN EXODUS

Michael Esses, D.H.L.

1

Introduction

The Book of Exodus is the second book of the Bible written by Moses. The Book of Genesis was written by him from existing documents, from tradition handed down to him, and from divine revelation, but Exodus is Moses' diary.

This second Book of Moses was originally called, in the Hebrew, the Book of the Going Out of Egypt. That is its oldest name. At a very early date, however, it came to be known as the Book of Names, because it starts out by saying, "These are the names. . . ."

The name Exodus comes from the chief event recorded in it, the departure of the children of Israel out of Egypt. Exodus was a term used in the Septuagint, meaning *seventy*, the Greek translation of the Old Testament made by the seventy rabbis who were commissioned to go from Jerusalem down into Alexandria, Egypt, to translate the Old Testament into Greek.

Exodus is a natural continuation of Genesis. Genesis describes the lives of the fathers of the Hebrew people; Exodus tells the beginning of the people itself. It records Israel's enslavement in Egypt and their deliverance from bondage. It describes the institution of the Passover, the covenant at Mount Sinai, and the organization of public worship that was to make Israel into a kingdom of priests and a holy nation.

Israel was told by the Lord, "I have chosen you, not because you're the greatest, but because you're the least. If I can show the world that I can take you and make a people out of you through My miraculous saving power, they will know that nothing is too hard for Me. I will transform you into a people who can stand up and walk in the Spirit of God."

The Book of Exodus is full of the murmurings and the backslidings of Israel as well as the divine guidance and instruction committed to Israel by God that they might bring His word to all the heathen of the world. God made an everlasting covenant with the people of Israel that they might share Him with heathen nations so that they, too, might know His reality and believe. Believers in the living God have somebody to turn to in time of distress, in time of need, in time of trouble, in time of joy, and in time of peace. He is the source of all life.

In Exodus we see the apostasy of the golden calf and the revelation of God as merciful, gracious, long-suffering, abundant in goodness and truth, keeping mercy unto the thousandth generation, forgiving iniquity and transgression and sin. He will by no means clear the guilty. Those who refuse to repent will never be forgiven. But the Lord says, "If you will come to Me in total repentance and ask for My forgiveness, I will look into your heart. I will see that you are sincere, and I will forgive you. All you need to do is to open your mouth and say, 'Lord, I'm sorry.' "

Did you ever see an argument between a husband and a wife or between a girl and her boyfriend? One stands in one corner and pouts, and the other stands in the other corner and pouts. Until one of them humbles himself and makes the move to say, "I'm sorry," there can be no reconciliation.

It's the same way with us and the Lord. Until we go to Him and say, "I'm sorry for the sin I have committed; I have examined myself and have found that I can't live without You; Lord, I need Your help," He will not help us. But when we turn to Him in repentance, He gives us the power to be overcomers over all circumstances.

The Jewish New Year, Rosh Hashanah, begins with a ten-day period of self-examination for all Hebrew people who do not know Jesus Christ. They have to look into their hearts, souls, and spirits to find out what they've done during the past year that they have to confess to the Lord. They have to ask His forgiveness for everything on the Day of Atonement.

Before the destruction of the temple in A.D. 70, while the sacrificial system was still being practiced, we see that once a year, the high priest had to go into the holy of holies to atone for himself, his family, and for all the rest of the people. He had to go in with a blood sacrifice. And the atonement he made with the blood of the slain animal was good for only one year. But for those who know Jesus, the atonement has been taken care of once and for all. Praise God that the atonement He has made for you and me is from everlasting to everlasting. The work of Jesus is for all generations of mankind.

In the Book of Exodus, we have the foundation of Jewish and Christian life in the Ten Commandments. In the Hebrew, they are called the Ten Living Words. They are words that are alive, and they were given to us by the Word Himself. These Ten Commandments, spoken at Sinai, form the Magna Charta of religion and morality, linking them for the first time and for all time in a perfect union. Five of the commandments show us how one ought to live with God; the other five show us how to live with one another.

In the New Testament, Jesus tells us that He never did away with the Ten Commandments but that He came to fulfill them (Matt. 5:17-19).

The Book of Exodus is an epic account of Israel's redemption from slavery, in which mankind learns that God is a God of freedom. Even as in Egypt He stood up for the brick-making slaves against the royal tyrants, God ever exalts righteousness and freedom; He always humbles iniquity and oppression. If you know the Lord and love Him with all your heart, soul, and mind, pray that the Lord will have mercy on any person who comes against

3

you. The promise that God made to Abraham is still good: "I will bless those who bless you, and I will curse those who curse you." No nation on the face of this earth has continued to grow and flourish that has persecuted either Christians or Jews. They all go into a decline the minute they start persecuting the children of God.

Some years ago, I bought the separate components for a stereo outfit. I started to read the instructions for assembling it, but they were so complicated I figured I would try to put it together without the instructions, just using my own common sense. Well, $340 and some six frustration-filled months later, I telephoned the manufacturer and complained about his product.

"Why don't you read the directions?" they advised me.

Well, I read the directions, then, but I'd already made such a mess of things that I finally had to have them come out and do the job.

Exodus contains some important directions for successful living for us. Let's look at them before we regret our delay.

2

The Israelites Increase and Multiply

(EXODUS 1)

These are the names of the sons of Israel who came into Egypt with Jacob, each with his household: Reuben, Simeon, Levi, and Judah, Issachar, Zebulun, Benjamin, Dan, Naphtali, Gad, and Asher. And all the souls that came out of the loins of Jacob were seventy souls. Joseph was already in Egypt. (Exod. 1:1-5)

Actually, only sixty-six Israelites went down into Egypt, because Joseph was already there, together with his wife, who was the daughter of the priest of On, and Joseph's two children, Ephraim and Manasseh.

And Joseph died and all his brethren, and all that generation. But the children of Israel were fruitful, and increased abundantly, and multiplied, and waxed exceedingly mighty, and the land was filled with them. And there arose a new king over Egypt who knew not Joseph. (Exod. 1:6-8)

There's a time lapse of four hundred years between the closing of Genesis and the beginning of Exodus. The Pharaoh in power at the time that Joseph went into Egypt was of the Hyksos dynasty. The Hyksos were a Semitic people, related to the Hebrew people. They had come in from Canaan and conquered the land of Egypt. They were in agreement with the people of Israel. According to Hebrew oral tradition, Joseph won the Pharaoh to the living God, causing him to give up his idolatry.*

By the time the Book of Exodus began, however, the original ruling class was back in power again. The new Pharaoh said, "I never heard of this fellow Joseph, and I don't want to hear of him. As far as I'm concerned, there was never any such person." And the Pharaoh commanded that Joseph's name be removed from every pylon in Egypt, that every statue of Joseph be destroyed, and that everything that made mention of Joseph be wiped out, just as if he had never existed.

> And the new Pharaoh said unto his people, Behold, the people of the children of Israel are too many, and they are too mighty for us. They outnumber us both in people and in strength. (Exod. 1:9)

The rise of anti-Semitism expressed itself in the Pharaoh's desire to get rid of the Jews. In the world today, there are only thirteen million Jews, and yet people will stand up and say, "They are too mighty; they're too great; let's get rid of them." This exaggeration about their numbers is caused by hatred, jealousy, and fear, the same emotions that were at work among the Egyptians. It seemed to them that the land was full of Israelites, that they were everywhere. "They filled the theaters; they filled the places of amusement," is the comment of the Talmud.

Their increase was the Israelites' only crime. They were not rebellious against the ruling powers, and there was no fault with which the unfriendly Pharaoh could charge them except that they were being obedient to the Lord's command that they be fruitful and multiply. God had said, "I will put you in this furnace, but I will bring you up as a mighty nation. I'll take down twelve tribes, but I'll bring you up as a congregation of people."

The supposed "crime" of the Israelites was really the Lord's blessing in action. But the new Pharaoh did not know God, and so he stirred up trouble against the Israelites, saying,

> Let us deal craftily with them, lest they multiply, and it come to pass that when there befalls us any war, they will join

6

themselves unto our enemies and fight against us, and so get themselves up out of the land. (Exod. 1:10)

For high reasons of state, the Pharaoh made it a national policy to deal unfairly with the people of Israel. "Wherever you find them," he said, "if you can take advantage of them in some way, go right ahead. It's one hundred percent kosher with the Egyptian government for you to do it."

From that day until this time, the same policy has existed. But every time the Egyptians have come against God's chosen people, they have bumped their heads against the wall. No one can afflict God's people and get by with it forever.

The Egyptians set over them [the Israelites] taskmasters to afflict them with increased burdens. (Exod. 1:11a)

The Hebrew word for *taskmasters* means *gang overseers, gang masters*. The appointment of the taskmasters was the first move by Pharaoh in the scheme to check the increase of the Israelites. The free and independent settlers of Goshen who had been invited to Egypt as guests were subjected to the basest kind of slavery. They were compelled to labor on public work projects without pay. This labor was a sort of tribal tax which they had to render, and for which their own leaders were held responsible. Egyptian and Assyrian monuments which still stand today show gangs of slaves working as brick masons, stone breakers, and at other hard labor under the lash of overseers from among their own people.

The Pharaoh was out to break the spirit of the people of Israel. If he could break their spirit, he'd have a broken people, and he could do anything he wanted to with them. But as long as their spirit was alive, there was still hope for them to escape the tyranny.

You can never break the spirit of a Christian, because his hope is in the Lord Jesus Christ. The early Christians went into the lions' dens, and into the arenas, singing songs of thanksgiving and hymns of praise. Their spirits were unbroken. Their hope couldn't be taken away from them because they knew that to be absent from the body is to be present with the Lord Jesus Christ.

With the taskmasters over them,

The Israelites built for Pharaoh the store-cities of Pithom and

7

Raamses. But the more the Egyptians afflicted them, the more the Israelites multiplied and spread abroad. (Exod. 1:11b-12a)

The Lord was multiplying them so exceedingly that the land of Goshen couldn't hold them all. They began to spread from border to border, over the whole land of Egypt.

And the Egyptians were grieved because of the children of Israel. And they made them to serve with rigor. They made their lives bitter with hard service, in mortar, in brick, and in all manner of service in the field. All their service, wherein they made them serve, was with harshness and severity. (Exod. 1:12b-14)

The Israelites were subjected to crushing oppression in an effort to annihilate their physical energy and their spirit. The Egyptians calculated to break them completely by breaking them physically and spiritually.

And the king of Egypt spoke to the Hebrew midwives, of whom the name of one was Shiprah and the other Puah. And he said, When you do the office of a midwife to the Hebrew women, and see them upon the birthstool, if it is a son, then you shall kill him; if it be a daughter, then she shall live. (Exod. 1:15-16)

Because of God's revelation to Abraham, Isaac, and Jacob that He would send a deliverer to Israel, Satan had knowledge of Moses. Satan revealed this knowledge to Pharaoh's magicians, and they in turn told Pharaoh. Pharaoh now knew that a deliverer was coming, just as Herod knew that Jesus was coming and sought to destroy Him. The Pharaoh sought to destroy the deliverer of the people of Israel by telling the midwives to kill the newborn male children of the Israelites.

But the midwives feared God more than they did the king of Egypt, and they did not do as the king of Egypt commanded them, but they saved the men children alive. (Exod. 1:17)

The fear of the Lord is the beginning of wisdom, and if we have enough wisdom to fear the Lord, we won't transgress against His laws. The midwives were not about to put themselves in a position to violate the future commandment that would say, "Thou shalt not murder." Although the commandments had not been written down yet, the people knew right from wrong.

And the king of Egypt called for the midwives, and said unto them, Why have you done this thing? Why have you saved the men children alive?

And the midwives said unto the Pharaoh, Because the Hebrew women are not as the Egyptian women. The Hebrew women are lively. Before we even get there, they have already had their babies. (Exod. 1:18-19)

The midwives explained to the Pharaoh that the Egyptian women were spoiled and vain. "The Egyptian women need us to help them deliver their babies, and they call for us as soon as they feel the first little labor pain. But the Hebrew women are strong and vigorous. They don't wait for anything, and the Lord takes care of the delivery for them before we can even get there. We can't help it that we don't make it on time."

And God was pleased that the midwives honored Him instead of Pharaoh. The midwives were well aware that the Hebrew mothers knew of the edict that their male children were to be killed if they called the midwives to attend them, so the Jewish women endured their birth pains without help in order to save their babies.

Therefore, God dealt very well with the midwives. And the people multiplied, and waxed very mighty. And it came to pass, because the midwives feared God, that He made them houses of their own. (Exod. 1:20-21)

God built up the families of the midwives. He increased their prosperity, and they multiplied and increased abundantly.

And Pharaoh charged all his people saying, Every son that is born to the Hebrews, you shall cast into the river, and every daughter that is born, you shall save alive. (Exod. 1:22)

When he saw that the Hebrew midwives were not doing the job of killing the Hebrews' male babies, Pharaoh told his own people to do it. And he made it an actual commandment that Hebrew male children were to be killed. He wrote it on a scroll and made it

9

irrevocable, and there was a death sentence for anyone who broke the law. The Hebrew male babies were to be thrown into the Nile.

Egypt is a rainless desert which the Nile converted into a fertile garden by flooding once a year. Since most of the Israelites lived away from the Nile, and the Pharaoh's savage decree could not have been strictly carried out by the Israelites themselves, the people of Egypt searched the land for the little children and cast them into the river. Impractical and inhumane as it was, we know, by Hebrew oral tradition, that this edict was actually enforced for three years.

Ultimately, however, the Lord's will is the only will that will be done, the only will that will win out in the long run. And His will was that He was going to deliver the people of Israel in a mighty deliverance, just as He had promised Abraham, Isaac, and Jacob. And the whole deliverance, the whole story of the Exodus, is a picture prophecy of what Jesus would come to do for us.

---

* The *Midrash Rabbah* on Genesis (p.831) says that when the Pharaoh told the Egyptians to go to Joseph and do what he told them to do (Gen. 41:55), the Pharaoh was referring to "circumcision—i.e., conversion to belief in the true God."

The Deliverer's First Forty Years
(EXODUS 2:1-15)

> And there went a man of the house of Levi, and took to wife a
> daughter of Levi. (Exod. 2:1)

Even at that time, the Jews knew enough not to marry outside of
their tribe, because it would mess up the laws of inheritance.

> And the woman conceived and bore a son. And when she saw
> him, that he was a goodly child, she hid him for three months.
> (Exod. 2:2)

How could anyone hide a baby for three months when the
Egyptians were out scouting around for little boy babies to cast into
the river? When the Scripture says that he was a "goodly child," it
means, among other things, that he didn't cry. The Lord moved
upon him and made him understand that he had to keep his mouth
shut. It was a life or death matter, and he didn't cry until the Lord
told him to open his mouth. A baby can understand and obey God's
Holy Spirit much more readily than we can, and the child heard and
was obedient to the Lord.

After three months, however,

> When the child's mother could no longer hide him, she took
> for him an ark of bulrushes, daubed it with slime and pitch,
> and put the child therein and laid it in the flags by the river's

brink. And his sister Miriam stood afar off to see what would be done to him. (Exod. 2:3-4)

After Miriam's faithfulness in standing by the water, the Rock, Jesus Christ, stood by the children of Israel throughout forty years in the wilderness and supplied water for all their needs. And later, another Miriam (Mary) gave birth to the One who was God in the flesh, the One from whom come the springs of living water.

And the daughter of Pharaoh came down to the river that particular day to bathe at the river. (Exod. 2:5a)

This was contrary to all Middle Eastern customs and traditions. The daughter of Pharaoh would naturally have had her own private pool for bathing. But that day, by divine appointment, she went to bathe in the river.

And her maidens walked along by the riverside. When she saw the ark among the rushes, she sent her handmaid to fetch it. And when she opened it, she saw the child. And behold, the baby wept. (Exod. 2:5b-6a)

When the ark was opened, the Lord gave Moses permission to cry. "Moses, now you can cry and scream and yell all you want to. You've been holding it in for three months like a goodly child, and now you can let it loose." Believe me, Moses cried.

Pharaoh's daughter had compassion on him from that cry.

She said, This is one of the Hebrews' children. (Exod. 2:6b)

She knew he was a Hebrew child because of the clothes in which he was wrapped. They signified that he was from the tribe of Levi. Each tribe had its own colors, its own design.

Then said his sister to Pharaoh's daughter, Shall I go and call you a nurse from the Hebrew women, that she may nurse the child for you? (Exod. 2:7)

Because the baby was only three months old, he needed to be breast-fed for a while yet.

And Pharaoh's daughter said to her, Go. And the maid went and called the child's mother. (Exod. 2:8)

The Lord was going to allow Moses to be raised in two cultures, two traditions. He would be brought up as a general, a prince, a leader in the court of Egypt for forty years. But while he was small, his Hebrew mother would also bring him up in the nurture and admonition of the Lord, in the tribe of Levi, the only tribe that still believed God would bring forth a great deliverance, a great miracle, a great exodus. Moses' mother taught him about the God of Abraham, Isaac, and Jacob, the living God. When the time came for a showdown, Moses would have to choose between the two cultures in which he had been raised.

There comes a time in your life and mine when we have to come to terms with the Lord, when the Lord says, "Choose this day whom you will choose." He talks to your flesh and my flesh, saying, "If you're going to choose your own way, stay right where you are. But if you're going to choose My way, take a step forward by faith." Joshua said, "As for me and my house, we will choose the Lord." That's what I say, too.

When the maiden, Miriam, had brought the child's mother, Pharaoh's daughter said unto her, Take this child away, and nurse it for me, and I will give you your wages. And the woman took the child and nursed it. And the child grew, and she brought him to Pharaoh's daughter, and he became her son. And she called his name Moses, for she said, Because I drew him out of the water. (Exod. 2:9-10)

By means of the wages, the Lord would supply all the material needs of Moses' mother. She was feeding and taking care of her own baby, and she loved doing that, but she was being paid for it by Pharaoh's daughter.

And it came to pass in those days, that when Moses had grown up, he went out unto his brethren, and looked on their burdens. And he saw an Egyptian smiting an Hebrew, one of Moses' brethren. And he looked this way and that way, and when he saw that there was no man, he smote the Egyptian, and hid him in the sand. (Exod. 2:11-12)

Moses had made his choice. He could have been the next Pharaoh of Egypt, but he chose instead to side with the abominable Hebrew people, the people of Israel. Surely Moses must have had a glimpse of Jesus in the future, a glimpse of life everlasting. Instead of settling for a fleeting moment of material possessions, wealth, and glory, he sought the glory of the next world by serving the Lord (Heb. 11:24-26).

And he went out the second day, and behold, two men of the Hebrews were striving together, and he said unto him that did the wrong, How come you smote your fellow Israelite? And he said, Who made you a ruler and a judge over us? Do you think now to kill me as you killed the Egyptian? And Moses feared and said, Surely the thing is known.

Now when Pharaoh heard the thing, he sought to slay Moses. But Moses fled from the face of Pharaoh, and dwelt in the land of Midian where he sat down by a well. (Exod. 2:13-15)

4

Moses in Midian

(EXODUS 2:16—4:26)

As Moses fled from Egypt to Midian, he was beginning the second forty years of his life. The Lord was going to make him a pastor of sheep. And He was going to teach Moses more through the sheep than Moses taught the sheep. When the sheep came bleating and crying and murmuring and griping, he was going to learn the patience to stand and see the salvation of the Lord.

The place of Moses' first pastorate was Midian, located in the southeastern part of the Sinai peninsula, beyond Egyptian jurisdiction, on the east side of the Gulf of Aqaba.

> Now the priest of Midian had seven daughters, and they came and drew water and filled the troughs to water their father's flock. (Exod. 2:16)

It's not uncommon in the Middle East even today for water to be drawn for the cattle by the girls or the women instead of the men. It's hard work, but they do it, and it's not considered to be degrading at all.

> And the shepherds came and drove the girls away so they could water their own flock, but Moses stood up and helped the seven daughters. He watered their flock for them. When they came to Reuel, their father, the old man asked, How

come you got through so early? And they said, There was a man who helped us. An Egyptian delivered us out of the hand of the shepherds. Moreover, he drew water for us, and he watered the flocks.

And he said unto his daughters, Where is he? What kind of hospitality have you shown him? Why is it that ye have left the man? Call him, that he may eat bread with us. Let us break bread together. (Exod. 2:17-20)

With our Arab brethren, to this very day, the minute we break bread and eat salt together, we're considered to be bound as brothers. They will never betray us; we will never betray them.

Moses, being called, went in, ate the meal with Reuel, and Moses was content to dwell with the man. And Reuel gave Moses Zipporah, his daughter. (Exod. 2:21)

Why did Reuel not give Moses one of the other seven daughters instead? Because Zipporah was the one chosen by the Lord. She was the only one who could put up with a man like Moses. The whole thing was done by divine appointment. Moses was a man of fire, a man with a hot temper. His wife would have to be a calming influence in his life, and Zipporah had a gentle spirit.

The Lord always gives us the proper mate. He gives us a perfect balance when He says by His Holy Spirit that a man shall leave his father and his mother and cleave unto his wife and they shall become one flesh. Check your own life and you'll see that together, you and your spouse are perfectly balanced in the Lord Jesus Christ.

Moses' wife bore him a son, and he called him Gershom, which means in the Hebrew, I have been a stranger in a strange land. (Exod. 2:22)

In the Hebrew, even today, every name has a meaning. I was named after the archangel Michael who received his name because he stands by the throne of grace and says, "Who is like unto Thee, O Lord? Who is like unto Thee, O Lord?" He constantly praises the Lord, and all of us are supposed to do just that.

And it came to pass in the course of those many days, almost forty years, that the king of Egypt died. And the children of

Israel sighed by reason of their bondage, and they cried, and their cry came up unto God by reason of their bondage. (Exod. 2:23)

The Lord had heard their cry before this, but He'd shelved the entire situation until the appointed time. "At the appointed time," He had said, "I will deliver you. In the meantime, I have you in a furnace, in a fire. I am working with you, I am taking the garbage out of your life, and I am making of you a nation, a congregation of people."

And God heard their groaning, and remembered that He had a covenant with Abraham, with Isaac, and with Jacob. (Exod. 2:24)

"Now," the Lord had said, "now is the appointed time that I have designated. Now I will start My big deliverance that I showed Abraham when I put him into that deep sleep and told him, 'Know for a surety that your descendants will go and sojourn in a strange land, but I will bring them up with wonders, with signs, and with miracles, that all the earth will know that I am the Lord.' Now is the time when I will bring judgment against all the gods of Egypt."

And God saw the children of Israel, and He knew their condition. (Exod. 2:25)

God had never closed His eyes to the suffering of the children of Israel, but He chose His own time for the promised deliverance. In the meantime,

Moses was keeping the flock of Jethro, his father-in-law, the priest of Midian. And he led the flock to the farthest end of the wilderness. (Exod. 3:1a)

Moses was in the depths of obscurity. He was living as a total nobody. God never gives any exalted office to a man unless He has first tested him in small things. I have a dear pastor friend in the northern part of Oregon. He told me that many years ago, he went to work for some Jewish people in a clothing business. It was the first job he'd ever had, and on the first day, he found a nickel in a pair of trousers. Right away, he was concerned, and he took it to the owner.

"I found this nickel," he said.

The owner of the business looked at his brother and nodded his head. Neither of them said anything, however.

My pastor friend had remained puzzled by this experience, but being a Jew, I was able to explain it to him.

"You passed the test," I said.

"I passed the test? What do you mean?" he asked me.

"Well, they were testing you to see what you would do. If you could be trusted with a nickel, they knew you could be trusted with the store, the whole business. But if you had chosen to think that a nickel was not important, and if you had put it in your pocket without mentioning it to them, they would have known that you were dishonest."

The Lord was testing Moses while he was keeping the flock of Jethro. By oral tradition we have it that Moses saw a little lamb stray from the flock, and when he followed it, he found himself at a little brook where the lamb was quenching its thirst. And Moses turned to the little lamb and said, "Had I known that you were thirsty, I would have taken you in my arms, and I would have carried you to the water."

Then Moses heard a heavenly voice speak to him:

"You are now fit to be the shepherd of Israel because you went out after a little lamb."

Moses did for the little lamb exactly what Jesus does for you and me. He leaves the ninety-nine that are secure, and He goes out to find us and bring us back to the flock where He gives us wells and springs of living water that never run dry.

Moses was at the farthest end of the wilderness, where the vegetation was very scanty. There were very few shrubs, and it was an exceedingly solemn, dreary desert.

> And Moses came to the mountain of God, Horeb. (Exod. 3:1b)

Horeb was called the mountain of God because, later on, the glory of God would be manifested there. Actually, the mountain itself was called Horeb, and the summit of it was called Sinai.

> And the Angel of the Lord appeared unto him in a flame of fire out of the midst of a bush. (Exod. 3:2a)

18

The Angel of the Lord was the Redeeming Angel, Jesus Christ Himself, the pre-incarnate Christ.

And Moses looked, and behold, the bush burned with fire, but the bush was not consumed. And Moses said, I will turn aside now, and see this great sight. I will see why the bush is not burning. And when the Lord saw that he turned aside to see, God called to him out of the midst of the bush and said, Moses, Moses. (Exod. 3:2b-4a)

The Angel of the Lord, who is Jesus, was in the midst of the bush. He and God are one and the same forever, and in these passages, the Bible confirms that.

And Moses said, Here am I. (Exod. 3:4b)

Moses answered God's call in the same way that Abraham, Isaac, and Jacob had done. "Here am I" means, "Here am I to do Your will, O Lord. You command me, and I will do it."

And God said, Do not come near. Put off your shoes from off your feet, for the place whereon you stand is holy ground. Moreover He said, I am the God of your father, the God of Abraham, the God of Isaac, and the God of Jacob. And Moses hid his face because he was afraid to look upon God.

And the Lord said, I have surely seen the affliction of My people that are in Egypt, and I have heard their cry because of their taskmasters, and I know their pain. And I have come down to deliver them out of the hands of the Egyptians and to bring them up out of the land of Egypt unto a good land, a large land, unto a land flowing with milk and honey, unto the place of the Canaanites, the Hittites, the Amorites, the Perizzites, the Hivites, and the Jebusites. And now, behold, the cry of the children of Israel is come unto Me. Moreover, I have seen the oppression wherewith the Egyptians oppress them. Come now, therefore, and I will send you unto Pharaoh that you may bring forth My people, the children of Israel, out of Egypt.

And Moses said unto God, Who am I that I should go unto Pharaoh and bring forth the children out of Egypt? (Exod. 3:5-11)

JESUS IN EXODUS

In his youth, Moses might have felt himself worthy to serve the living God. He might have said, "Okay, God. I am able, and I will do it for You," but with age and maturity, Moses could think only about his unfitness for the gigantic undertaking set before him.

And the Lord spoke to him and said, Certainly I will be with you. And this shall be the token, the sign, that I have sent you: When you have brought forth the people out of Egypt, you shall serve God upon this mountain. (Exod. 3:12)

When the Lord said, "I will be with you; I will never leave you or forsake you," Moses should have known he had nothing to fear, but he still argued with the Lord. And God gave him a sign, but Moses wasn't satisfied.

And Moses said unto God, Behold, when I come unto the children of Israel, and I shall say unto them, The God of your fathers hath sent me unto you, and they shall say unto me, What is His name? what shall I say unto them?

And God said unto Moses, I AM THAT I AM. (Exod. 3:13-14a)

In the Hebrew, this means that God said, "I am self-existent; I am the eternal God. I am the Father, the Son, and the Holy Spirit, the exact opposite of all forms of idolatry." And He further declares, "I am the cause of all things. I shall be what I shall be. I will cause to be what I will cause to be. Nothing happens by accident, but only by My divine wisdom, My divine will, My divine permission. You may think of Me as God the Father; you may think of ME as God the Son; you may think of ME as God the Holy Spirit. I AM THAT I AM. No man will ever be able to comprehend or fathom Me."

Later, we see Jesus saying, "Before Abraham was, I AM." And Jesus repeated "I AM" seven different times when He said, "I AM the resurrection. I AM the way. I AM the bread of life. I AM the truth. I AM the life. I AM the light of the world. I AM the first and the last." Jesus is constantly who He says He is, and He never changes.

When Moses asked how he should answer the children of Israel, the Lord said,

You shall say unto the children of Israel, I AM has sent me to you. (Exod. 3:14b)

And Moses wondered, "What kind of a crazy name is that? 'I AM sent me to you.' If I tell them that, they'll think I'm nuts!"

And God knew what Moses was thinking. He knew his heart better than Moses knew it himself. Moving by His love, His grace, and His mercy,

God said moreover unto Moses, You shall say unto the children of Israel, The Lord God of your fathers, the God of Abraham, the God of Isaac, and the God of Jacob, has sent Me unto you. This is My name forever, this is My memorial unto all generations. (Exod. 3:15)

I believe that at this point, the Lord revealed the true name of the living God to Moses—"Yeshua," which is "Jesus." And Moses knew the true name of God, not the unpronounceable name of God which is YHWH, but he knew the full name of God, the name Jesus, the name we can call upon. Scripture tells us that no man has ever seen God and lived, so it was surely Jesus Himself who appeared unto Moses.

Then God told Moses,

Go, gather the elders of Israel together, and say unto them, The Lord God of your fathers, the God of Abraham, of Isaac, and of Jacob, has appeared unto me, saying, I have surely remembered you, and I have seen that which is done to you in Egypt. And I have declared that I will bring you up out of the affliction of Egypt to the land of the Canaanite, the Hittite, the Amorite, the Perizzite, the Hivite, and the Jebusite, to a land flowing with milk and honey. And they will listen to your voice. And you shall go, you and the elders of Israel, unto the king of Egypt, and you shall say unto him, The Lord, the God of the Hebrews, has met with us. And now let us go, we pray thee, three days' journey into the wilderness, that we may sacrifice to the Lord our God.

And I know that the king of Egypt will not give you leave to go, except that I reveal My mighty hand, saith the Lord. (Exod. 3:16-19)

The Lord was acknowledging that He knew Pharaoh would not let the people go until He had dealt with him in a mighty way.

And I will put forth My hand, saith the Lord, and I will smite Egypt with all My wonders which I will do in the midst thereof. And after that, he will let you go. And I will give this people favor in the sight of the Egyptians. And it shall come to pass, that, when you go, you shall not go empty-handed. Every woman shall ask of her neighbor, and of her that sojourns in her house, jewels of silver, jewels of gold, garments, raiment. You shall put them upon your sons and upon your daughters, and you shall despoil the Egyptians. (Exod. 3:20-22)

The Lord said, "I'm going to pay you for the four hundred years you spent in slavery, and I'll give you favor in the sight of the Egyptians. Mrs. Goldberg, Mrs. Epstein—all the women—will knock on the doors of the houses of the Egyptians and say, 'Let me have your jewels, and your gold, and your silver, and your clothes.' And the Egyptians will say, 'Take them already.' "

God was giving Moses every promise that He was planning to fulfill, but Moses was still not satisfied.

Moses answered and said, But behold, they will not believe me. They will not listen to my voice, but they will say, The Lord has not appeared unto you. (Exod. 4:1)

The Lord had said, "Go down into Egypt, Moses. I will be with you, and later, you will serve Me upon this mountain. I'll give you a whole bagful of signs and wonders, and I'll even let the Israelites carry away some of the riches of Egypt." Instead of saying, "Oh, boy! When do we start?" Moses said, "But—but—but—" because he was standing in his own righteousness, pride, and arrogance. He was not trusting God. He was not believing His promises.

And the Lord said unto him, What is that you have in your hand? And he said, A rod. (Exod. 4:2)

Moses, being a shepherd, had a shepherd's staff with him.

And the Lord said, Cast it on the ground. And he cast it on the ground, and it became a serpent, a deadly serpent, and Moses ran from before it. (Exod. 4:3)

Moses took off like someone scared to death.

And the Lord said unto Moses, Put forth your hand, and take it by the tail. I'll prove to you who's Lord. (Exod. 4:4a)

If you and I were going to pick up a deadly snake, we'd grab it by the head so we wouldn't get bitten and die. But the Lord told Moses, "Take it by the tail so it can turn around and strike at you. But I'll show you My divine protection. I am with you always. And when I am with you, nothing can hurt or harm you in any way. There is a wall of fire around you protecting you. It is My Holy Spirit, and it is I who am with you."

Moses put forth his hand and laid hold of it, and it became a rod in his hand once again. And the Lord said to him, I give you this sign, this miracle, that they may believe that the Lord, the God of their fathers, the God of Abraham, the God of Isaac, and the God of Jacob, has appeared unto you.

And the Lord said furthermore unto him, Put now your hand into your bosom. And he put his hand into his bosom, and when he took it out, his hand was leprous, as white as snow. And He said, Put your hand now back into your bosom. He put it back into his bosom, and when he took it out of his bosom, behold, it was turned again as his other flesh. (Exod. 4:4b-7)

The Lord was going to give Moses three signs to overcome the three difficulties he expressed: that the Israelites would not believe his message; that they would not believe the Lord sent him; and that they would not believe the message of freedom. The first sign was the rod, the second sign was the hand of leprosy, and the Lord giving him the power to heal in the name of the Lord. Now He would give him a third sign.

Then God said, And it shall come to pass, if they will not believe you, neither will they listen to the voice of the first sign, that they will believe the voice of the latter sign. And it shall come to pass that if they will not believe even these two signs, neither will they listen to your voice, that you shall take of the water of the river and pour it upon the dry land. And the

23

water which you take out of the river shall become blood upon the dry land. (Exod. 4:8-9)

There was only one tribe in Israel that still believed in the Lord, and that was the tribe of Levi. The rest of the tribes were worshiping the Nile as a god, just as the Egyptians did. And the Lord was saying that the third sign would be that the god that they worshiped, a fertility god, would be turned into blood. Nothing can live in blood except bacteria.

And Moses said unto the Lord, O Lord, I'm not a man of words. Neither before nor since You have spoken to Your servant, for I am slow of speech, and I have a heavy and awkward tongue. (Exod. 4:10)

Moses was complaining, "I'm not a preacher. How can I talk to three million rabble-rousers and make them listen? As a matter of fact, I stutter, and I've never been able to persuade anybody of anything. They'll never listen to me."

Still showing His love, His grace, His mercy, and His unending patience,

The Lord said to him, Moses, who made man's mouth? Who makes a man dumb? Who makes a man deaf? Who makes a man to see? Who makes a man to be blind? Is it not I, the Lord? Go, and I will be with your mouth, and I will teach you what you shall say. (Exod. 4:11-12)

Notice the words of Jesus when His disciples, who had noticed a man blind from birth, asked Him, "Was this man born blind because of the sins of his ancestors or his own sins?"

Jesus answered, "Neither. It was not that this man sinned, or his ancestors, but that the works of God might be made manifest in him."

Everything is done by God's divine love. Nothing happens by accident. God said, "Moses, it is I who made your mouth exactly the way I wanted it. It is I who caused you to be slow of speech. It is I who caused you to stammer. And everything I do, I do for My glory."

And Moses said, O Lord, I pray You, send by the hand of some other whom You will send. Send somebody else.

And the anger of the Lord was kindled against Moses. And the Lord said, Is there not Aaron your brother, the Levite? I know that he can speak well. Behold, he's coming forth to meet you. And when he sees you, he will be glad in his heart. (Exod. 4:13-14)

Aaron was very fluent in speech. He could outtalk anybody. And God went on to say to Moses,

You shall speak unto him. You shall put the words in his mouth. I will be with your mouth, and with his mouth. And I will teach you what you shall do. (Exod. 4:15)

"I will speak to you personally," the Lord said to Moses, "and you can convey the message to Aaron. Let him do the talking."

And he shall be your spokesman unto the people. It shall come to pass that he shall be to you a mouth, and you shall be to him in God's stead. (Exod. 4:16)

Today in our families, the Lord Jesus Christ makes the man the prophet and priest in his home, and he stands in God's stead. The Lord Jesus talks to him and he conveys the message to his wife and family.

And God said, Moses, you shall now take in your hand this rod, wherewith you shall do the signs that I have shown you. Then Moses went and returned to Jethro, his father-in-law, and said unto him, Let me go, I pray thee, and return unto my brethren that are in Egypt, and see whether they be yet alive. And Jethro said to Moses, Go in peace. Shalom. (Exod. 4:17-18)

The Lord had prepared the heart of Moses' father-in-law, so he was willing to let Moses go.

And the Lord said unto Moses in Midian, Go, return into Egypt, for all the men are dead that have sought your life. And Moses took his wife and his sons, and set them upon an ass, and he returned to the land of Egypt. And Moses took the rod of God in his hand.

And the Lord said unto Moses, When you go back into Egypt, see that you do before Pharaoh all the wonders which I have put in your hand. But I will harden his heart, and he will not let the people go. And you shall say unto Pharaoh, Thus saith the Lord, Israel is My son, My firstborn. And I say unto you, Let My son go, that he may serve Me, and if you refuse to let him go, behold I will slay your son, your firstborn.

And it came to pass on the way at the lodging place that the Lord met Moses and sought to kill him. (Exod. 4:19-24)

The Lord had just commissioned Moses, and now He was seeking to kill him! Why? Remember that Moses was married to Zipporah, the daughter of the priest of Midian. Zipporah was an Arab, and the Arabs do not circumcise their children until they are thirteen years old because that was the age of Ishmael when he was circumcised. But Jews are commanded by the Lord to circumcise their male children on the eighth day of their lives.

When Moses' little boys were born, Zipporah had said to him, "Sweetheart, let's do it my way, according to the customs and traditions of my father's house." And Moses had agreed to go along with her.

The Lord had never said anything to Moses about circumcising his boys before he knew the Lord. But after he met Him personally, his first obligation was to be obedient to the Lord to circumcise his children immediately so they would be included in the everlasting covenant.

But Moses had listened to his wife when she said, "No, let's keep on waiting until they're thirteen years of age, and then we'll do it in the Arab tradition, instead of doing it the way you think the Lord wants you to do it." Moses had listened to her at the time, but, meanwhile, the Lord was dealing with her, too. And she suddenly had the discernment of spirit to know that the Lord was out to kill Moses for his disobedience, and she must have felt partly to blame about it.

So Zipporah took a flint and cut the foreskin of her son and cast it at the feet of Moses, saying, Surely a bridegroom of blood are you to me because of the circumcision. (Exod. 4:25-26)

Zipporah had called him a bridegroom of blood because circumcision is the symbol of the covenant between God and the child, and the child was referred to as the "bridegroom of the covenant."

After the circumcision had been performed, the Lord was no longer seeking to kill Moses. And Zipporah took the two boys and went back home to her father. Moses headed for Egypt, ready to be obedient to the Lord in all things. He had learned his lesson.

5

Bricks without Straw

(EXODUS 4:27—5)

And the Lord said to Aaron, Now go into the wilderness to meet Moses. And he went, and he met him in the mountain of God, at Mount Sinai, and he kissed him. And Moses told Aaron all the words of the Lord, wherewith he, the Lord, had sent him and all the signs with which he had charged him. (Exod. 4:27-28)

The Lord, knowing the heart of the people of Israel who had been in captivity and slavery for four hundred years, realized that they would find it hard to believe that the time of redemption was finally upon them, that this was the acceptable day of the Lord, that it was the day of their long-awaited salvation. And the Lord knew that Moses and Aaron were going to have to use signs and wonders to prove that it was the Lord who had sent them.

And Moses and Aaron went and gathered together all the elders of the children of Israel, and Aaron spoke all the words which the Lord had spoken unto Moses and did the signs in the sight of the people. And the people believed. (Exod. 4:29-31a)

In the New Testament, Jesus said, "If you don't believe anything else, believe the signs, believe the works that I do. If you can't believe anything else, believe that which you have seen with your own eyes."

> And when the people heard that the Lord had brought them to their appointed time, the children of Israel bowed their heads and worshiped, because they knew the Lord had seen their affliction. (Exod. 4:31b)

After the confidence of the people of Israel had been restored by means of the miraculous signs that the Lord gave, Moses and Aaron were ready to approach Pharaoh on behalf of the people. It was necessary for all the people, not just the tribe of Levi, to believe that the Lord was about to deliver them. There had to be an act of faith and an act of belief for them to receive what God had already done for them. He had already accomplished the deliverance, but Israel would have to receive it. They would have to stand and see the salvation of the Lord and march forth in victory.

But how could Moses and Aaron enter into the court of Pharaoh to speak to him? Where would the permission come from? Who would prepare the way? Again, it was all done by divine appointment. The Lord had said, "I will go before you. As long as you are in My will, I will go before you, I will go behind you, and I will go on each side of you." And God did prepare the way, and Moses and Aaron found themselves confronting Pharaoh exactly as God had told Moses.

> Standing face-to-face, toe-to-toe with Pharaoh, Moses and Aaron said unto him, Thus saith the Lord God of Israel, Let My people go, that they may hold a feast unto Me in the wilderness.

> And Pharaoh said, Who is the Lord that I should listen to His voice and let Israel go? I know not the Lord, and moreover, I will never let Israel go. (Exod. 5:1-2)

"This God you are talking about, who is He?" Pharaoh was saying. "We've got our own gods here. We've got the golden calf and the bull, the frogs and the jackals, the camels, the Nile, the moon and the stars. What do we need of another god? We've got plenty of them already. Besides, I never heard of the God you're talking about.''

Pharaoh was openly contemptuous because He did not know the Lord, he did not acknowledge His right to command him to do anything.

In the Talmud, the rabbis state that Pharaoh turned to his seventy scribes who knew all the tongues spoken on the earth, and he asked them, ''Have you ever heard of a God called YHWH or Jehovah, the God of eternity?''

They answered, ''We have sought in all the books of all the people among all the names of all the gods, but we have not found one by the name of YHWH in any of our books.''

They spoke the truth, because the name of the Lord as He had revealed it to Moses was a new revelation. None of the heathen rulers of old knew the God of freedom, the God of holiness, and the God of righteousness. He was not in their thinking or in their dictionaries.

Then Moses and Aaron said to Pharaoh,

The God of the Hebrews has met with us. Let us go, we pray thee, three days' journey into the wilderness, and sacrifice unto the Lord our God lest He fall upon us with pestilence or with the sword.

And the king of Egypt said unto them, Wherefore do you, Moses and Aaron, cause the people to break loose from their work? Get you to your burdens. And Pharaoh said, Behold, the people of the land are now many, and you make them rest from their burdens. (Exod. 5:3-5)

''You're causing the people to do something which is against our law,'' Pharaoh said. ''The Israelites are supposed to work twenty hours a day. Why are you unsettling them from their work with all this talk of a pilgrimage, of a feast, of a sacrifice? Get back to your labor, all of you. You're causing unrest in the land. My slaves can't be allowed to go out and sacrifice unto the Lord. They have to keep on sacrificing their lives to serve me.''

And the same day, Pharaoh commanded the taskmasters of the people, and their officers, saying, You shall no more give the people straw to make brick, as before. (Exod. 5:6-7a)

After his encounter with Moses and Aaron, Pharaoh had decided to make things tougher than ever on the Israelites. From now on, they would not be given straw to use as part of the raw material in making their bricks. The straw was necessary for holding the clay together to prevent it from cracking. What would they do now? Pharaoh said,

Let them go and gather straw for themselves. And the number of bricks which they did make before, their quota, you shall lay upon them. You shall not diminish any of their quota, for they are idle; therefore they cry, saying, Let us go and sacrifice to our God. (Exod. 5:7b-8)

Pharaoh claimed that it was because they didn't have enough to do that the Israelites were saying, "Let us go sacrifice to our God." They were working twenty hours a day, but Pharaoh thought they had too much leisure time on their hands. That's why they were dreaming up mischief saying they wanted to go sacrifice to their God. Pharaoh would knock that foolishness out of them, he thought, and he issued a new edict:

Let heavier work be laid upon them that they may labor therein. And let them not regard lying words. (Exod. 5:9)

When he said, "Let them not regard lying words," Pharaoh was implying that Moses was a liar and that there was no such thing as a living God, a God of freedom, of holiness, and of righteousness.

"They're getting their quota of whatever garbage they eat, and they all have good steady jobs, working twenty hours a day," Pharaoh said. "They're living in the mud, and they're getting beaten regularly. What more could they possibly want—social security already yet?"

Whatever they wanted, Pharaoh was determined not to give them anything but trouble.

And the taskmasters of the people went out, and their officers, and they spake to the people, saying, Thus saith Pharaoh, I will not give you straw. Go yourselves, get you for yourselves straw where you can find it, for nothing of your work will be diminished. So the people were scattered abroad throughout all the land of Egypt to gather stubble for straw. (Exod.

5:10-12)

Can you imagine what a back-breaking job that was? Modern archaeologists have found evidence of the stubble in the bricks which were made without straw. It actually took place exactly as the Book of Exodus says it did.

And the taskmasters were urgent, saying, Fulfill your works, your daily tasks, as when you had straw. And the officers—the foremen—of the children of Israel, whom Pharaoh's taskmasters had set over them, were beaten and asked, Wherefore have you not fulfilled your appointed task in making brick both yesterday and today, as before?

And the officers of the children of Israel came and cried unto Pharaoh, saying, How come already yet? Wherefore do you deal thus with your servants? We have been your faithful servants. We have sold out to you. We have been traitors to our own people. How come you're beating us? There is no straw given unto your servants, and they say to us, Make bricks, and behold, your servants are beaten, but the faults are in your own people. (Exod. 5:13-16)

"It's not our fault," the officers were saying to Pharaoh. "If you'd give us the stuff, we'd make the quota of bricks. But without the raw materials—you expect us to make something out of nothing?"

But Pharaoh said, You are idle. Therefore you say, Let us go and sacrifice unto the Lord. Go therefore now, and work; for there shall no straw be given unto you, yet you shall deliver the full quota of bricks. And the officers of the children of Israel saw that they were set with mischief when they said, You shall not diminish in the least your full daily quota of bricks.

So they met with Moses and Aaron, who stood in the way as they came forth from Pharaoh. And the foremen said unto them, The Lord look upon you and judge because you have made us to stink in the eyes of Pharaoh, and in the eyes of his servants, and you have put a sword in their hand to slay us. (Exod. 5:17-21)

What could Moses do? He was only obeying orders from the Lord. Where could he go to complain? The buck has got to stop someplace. There was only one place he could turn, and he did it.

And so Moses returned unto the Lord and said, Lord, how come already yet? Wherefore have You dealt ill with this people? Why did You ever send me? Didn't I tell You in the very beginning that You ought to send somebody else? For since I came to speak unto Pharaoh in Your name, we've had nothing but problems. He has dealt ill with this people. Neither have You delivered Your people at all. (Exod. 5:22-23)

I admire the courage and sincerity and honesty in Moses. The Lord wants you and me to speak to Him in the same forthright manner. If we petition Him for something, He wants us to come right to the point, just as Moses did.

At this point, Moses did not realize what the future held. He did not realize that the Lord had planned a great deliverance, that He was going to bring His people out through a crucible of fire, through a furnace of silver, refining them as gold. Moses didn't realize that God was actually going to bring them up as a nation and a congregation of people. He didn't know all the great miracles that the Lord would do to demonstrate to the world that He is the living God. Moses didn't know that God was about to bring judgment upon all the gods of Egypt. It was natural that he would be discouraged. But God wouldn't leave him in that state forever.

6

Reminders of God's Promises

(EXODUS 6—7:7)

Then the Lord said unto Moses, Now you shall see what I will do to Pharaoh. For by a strong hand shall he let them go, by a strong hand shall he drive them out of his land when I get through with him. (Exod. 6:1)

"You'll not have to ask him if you can go," God said to Moses. "When I get through with him, he'll be begging you to leave."

And God spoke to Moses and said, I am the Lord. When I appeared unto Abraham, unto Isaac, and unto Jacob, they did not know Me by My name YHWH, but by My name El Shaddai. (Exod. 6:2-3)

The Hebrew name for God is the unpronounceable name of YHWH. Translators of the Bible added vowels to make God's name pronounceable and came up with Yahweh or Jehovah. But Abraham, Isaac, and Jacob knew God only as El Shaddai. El is the singular name of God, referring to His mighty power. Shaddai would be translated from Hebrew into English as "a full-breasted woman." God is saying here that the patriarchs did not know Him in the fullness of His power but His mercy in which He was revealing Himself to Moses and the children of Israel. They knew Him as more than just a Father figure, however. When the *Father*

35

nature of God had just about reached the point of spanking His disobedient children to the point of no return, the *Mother* nature of God came forth and took them to His bosom and nurtured them. God had pity and mercy and didn't wipe them out even when they richly deserved it.

"I'm more than just a Father," God says. "I'm a Father and a Mother. I'm everything you need in every area of your life."

And I have also established My covenant with them, to give them the land of Canaan, the land of their sojournings, wherein they sojourned. And moreover, I have heard the groanings of the children of Israel whom the Egyptians keep in bondage, and I have now brought forth the appointed time of My covenant. (Exod. 6:4-5)

God had made a covenant with His people, an everlasting covenant. The *appointed time* was the time concerning which God had promised Abraham that He would bring the children of Israel up in a mighty deliverance.

Wherefore say unto the children of Israel, I am YHWH. I will bring you out from under the burdens of the Egyptians. I will deliver you from their bondage. I will redeem you with an outstretched arm and with great judgments. (Exod. 6:6)

The Lord was going to redeem His people. He would buy them back with a blood sacrifice, the blood of a Perfect Lamb.

I will take you to Me for a people. I will be to you a God. And you shall know that I am the Lord your God, who brought you up from under the burdens of the Egyptians. (Exod. 6:7)

The gospel of the Old Testament is right here, with God saying, "I shall be your God, and you shall be My people." The people of Israel were supposed to go out and spread that gospel to all the nations of the world, to show them that there is a God of freedom, a God of holiness, and a God of righteousness who would say to anybody who would believe, "I will be your God, and you shall be My people."

The Lord went on to say,

I will bring you in unto the land, concerning which I lifted up My hand to give it to Abraham, to Isaac, and to Jacob. And I

will give it to you for an heritage because I am the Lord.
(Exod. 6:8)

He would not be giving them the land because they deserved it,
but because He had given His word which could not be broken.
The Lord never goes back on His word.

Here we can see two covenants coming into existence—the big
"if" covenant, and the big "but" covenant. The Lord says, "*If*
you will be obedient and keep My commandments, this land will
be yours as a heritage forever." Then Israel says, "Yeah, *but*—"

And Moses spoke in this manner to the children of Israel, but
they refused to listen to Moses because of their impatience of
spirit and because of their cruel bondage. (Exod. 6:9)

The people were so utterly crushed by their disappointment that
they paid no heed to the promise of redemption. They were already
having to break their backs by going out to dig up stubble, and now
this troublemaker, Moses, had the gall to tell them that things were
going to turn out all right eventually. This God he kept talking
about—who was He anyway? And where was He?

And the Lord spoke unto Moses saying, Go in and speak to
Pharaoh king of Egypt, that he let the children of Israel go out
of his land.

And Moses spoke before the Lord, saying, Behold, the
children of Israel have not listened unto me. How then shall
Pharaoh hear me, I who am of uncircumcised lips? (Exod.
6:10-12)

"Even our own people won't listen to me, Lord," Moses
complained to God. "What makes you think Pharaoh's going to
listen?"

And the Lord spoke unto Moses and unto Aaron, and gave
them a charge unto the children of Israel, and unto Pharaoh
king of Egypt, to bring the children of Israel out of the land of
Egypt. And these are the heads of their fathers' houses: The
sons of Reuben the firstborn. . . . (Exod. 6:13-14a)

The genealogy continues through verse 25.

These are the Aaron and Moses to whom the Lord said, Bring
out the children of Israel from the land of Egypt according to

37

their host. And who spoke unto Pharaoh king of Egypt about bringing the children of Israel out of Egypt. These are that same Moses and Aaron.

And it came to pass on the day when the Lord spoke to Moses in the land of Egypt, that the Lord spoke unto Moses, saying, I am the Lord: speak unto Pharaoh king of Egypt all that I speak unto you. (Exod. 6:26-29)

God instructed Moses not to say anything more and not to say anything less than what He instructed him to say. "That which I tell you to do," Moses understood God to be saying, "you tell Aaron. He'll say the words, and everything will go according to My will. Don't add; don't subtract; don't do anything with My word except to proclaim it."

And Moses said before the Lord, Behold, I am of uncircumcised lips. How then shall Pharaoh listen unto me? (Exod. 6:30)

Moses was still trying to squirm out from under. He didn't want the job. He didn't want the pastorate. He didn't want the responsibility of the ministry. He didn't want to have anything to do with the children of Israel. "Pick somebody else," he kept insisting. But in spite of Moses' continued efforts to wiggle out from under his assignment, the loving-kindness of the Lord toward Moses continued:

And the Lord said unto Moses, See, I have set you in God's stead to Pharaoh; and Aaron your brother shall be your prophet. (Exod. 7:1)

Moses was to stand in the place of God, and Aaron would be his prophet. God gives us the same message, the same authority. He tells us we are standing in His place when we become Christians, and we acknowledge with our lips and believe with our hearts that Jesus died for us. And Jesus has given us all authority. He has even said, "You shall do greater things than I have done, because I go to the Father."

The Lord was reminding Moses of all that so he could go ahead and do the job and stop worrying about it.

You shall speak all that I command you. Aaron your brother shall speak unto Pharaoh, and he, Pharaoh, shall let the children of Israel go out of his land. And I will harden Pharaoh's heart, and multiply my signs and wonders in the land of Egypt. (Exod. 7:2-3)

Was it cruel of the Lord to harden Pharaoh's heart? No, because He was accomplishing something by it. He was proving to the people that He is the Lord. As He poured out His love and His grace and His mercy upon Pharaoh, He was seeking Pharaoh's salvation, giving him chance after chance. Up until the sixth plague, He would keep on seeking Pharaoh's salvation before He passed him from grace unto judgment.

If you and I keep receiving the love, the grace, and the mercy of the Lord, but we keep turning away from that love and grace and mercy, we will be hardening our own hearts. We ourselves will pass from grace into judgment if we refuse the conviction of the Holy Spirit. Praise God that He is so patient with us. He works on us for thirty, forty, fifty, even sixty years to bring us to the point where we will listen to Him.

Moses was eighty years old, beginning the last third of his life with these rabble-rousers who wouldn't listen to him. Constantly, they would be saying, "Who appointed you, Moses? Who made you general over us? Who sent you? Where is this God you talk about?"

Even after all the miracles God would perform for them, they would be rebellious, crying out in unbelief, "Where is He?"

God told Moses exactly how it was going to be:

Pharaoh will not listen unto you. I will lay My hand upon Egypt, and bring forth My hosts, My people, the children of Israel, out of the land of Egypt by great judgments. And the Egyptians shall know that I am the Lord, when I stretch forth My hand upon Egypt, and bring out the children of Israel from among them.

And Moses and Aaron did so, as the Lord commanded them, so did they. And Moses was eighty years old and Aaron was eighty-three years old when they spoke to Pharaoh. (Exod. 7:4-7)

Moses and Aaron were both well past retirement age when they started out on the great assignment God had given them. We should never think we're too old to be used by the Lord God.

7

The Plagues Get Going

(EXODUS 7:8—9:12)

And the Lord spoke unto Moses and unto Aaron, saying, When Pharaoh shall speak unto you, saying, Prove your authority by a miracle, then you shall tell Aaron, Take your rod, cast it down before Pharaoh, that it may become a serpent.

And Moses and Aaron went in unto Pharaoh, and they did so as the Lord had commanded. Aaron cast down his rod before Pharaoh, and before his servants, and it became a serpent.

And Pharaoh called for the magicians and the sorcerers, and all the magicians of Egypt. They also did in like manner with their secret art. For they cast down every man his rod, and they became serpents also. (Exod. 7:8-12a)

How could Satan duplicate what God had done? How could he counterfeit a miracle like that? He could do it only because the sticks and rods were created by the Lord. There was life in them, just as in the rest of God's creation.

But Aaron's rod swallowed up their rods. But Pharaoh's heart was hardened, and he did not listen to them, as the Lord had spoken. And the Lord said unto Moses, Pharaoh's heart is

41

stubborn. He refuses to let the people go. (Exod. 7:12b-14)

There was a miracle right before Pharaoh's eyes, but his heart was hardened, and he said, "Big deal. So what if Aaron's rod swallowed up another bunch of rods. For that I'm supposed to let four million people go out of slavery? You've got to be kidding!"

Then God had further instructions for Moses:

Get yourself to Pharaoh in the morning. Behold, I know that he will be going out to the water. Stand by the river's brink to meet him. (Exod. 7:15a)

Pharaoh would be going out to worship the water. The Egyptians believed that the more they worshiped the water, the more the water would rise. The higher the Nile River got, the more it would flood over its banks and the better crops they would have. Even today, the Nile is a prime source of Egypt's fertility. In the time of Moses, there were a number of religious festivals in honor of the Nile god, festivals at which the Pharaoh himself officiated. Hymns addressed to the Nile are still in existence today.

And God said to Moses,

The rod which was turned into a serpent, you shall take into your hand. And you shall say to him, The Lord, Yahweh, Jehovah, the God of the Hebrews, has sent me unto you, saying, Let My people go that they may serve Me in the wilderness. And behold, up until now, you have not listened, Pharaoh. And thus saith the Lord, In this you shall know that I am the Lord: Behold, I will smite with the rod that is in mine hand upon the waters which are in the river, and they shall be turned into blood. And the fish that are in the river shall die, the river shall become foul, and the Egyptians shall loathe to drink water from the river.

And the Lord said unto Moses, Say unto Aaron, Take your rod, stretch out your hand over the waters of Egypt, over their streams, over their rivers, over their pools, over all their ponds of water, and they shall become blood, and there shall be blood throughout all the land of Egypt, both in vessels of wood, and in vessels of stone.

And Moses and Aaron did so, as the Lord commanded. He

lifted up the rod, smote the waters that were in the river, in the sight of Pharaoh, in the sight of his servants; and all the fish that were in the river died. And the river became foul. And the Egyptians could not drink water from the river, and the blood was throughout all the land of Egypt. But the magicians in Egypt did in like manner with their secret arts. (Exod. 7:15b-22a)

The magicians of Egypt had to go into the land of Goshen to find some unpolluted water to turn into blood. In the land of Egypt, all the water had been turned into blood already, but in Goshen, there was still pure drinking water. Nothing among the Israelites was polluted.

And Pharaoh's heart was made hard and obstinate, and he did not listen to Moses and Aaron. It was just as the Lord had said. And Pharaoh turned and went into his house. He didn't take even this to heart. (Exod. 7:22b-23)

Pharaoh paid no attention to what was happening before his very eyes. His magicians ignored the significance of everything, too.

All the Egyptians dug around about the river for water to drink, for they could not drink of the water of the river. And seven days were fulfilled, after the Lord had smitten the river.

And now the Lord spoke unto Moses, saying, Go in unto Pharaoh, and say unto him, Thus saith the Lord, Let My people go, that they may serve Me. And if you refuse to let them go, behold, I will smite all your borders with frogs. And the river shall swarm with frogs, which shall go up and come into your house, into your bedchamber, upon your bed, into the houses of your servants, upon your people, into your ovens, into your kneading-troughs. And the frogs shall come both upon you, and upon your people, and upon all your servants. (Exod. 7:24-8:4)

The Egyptians were very fussy, finicky people. If a single frog was in the house, they would have a conniption fit. And there were going to be hundreds of frogs in their houses. This plague, like the preceding plague of blood, was a miracle in accordance with the Lord's will. The land of Goshen was not touched by the plague.

43

And the plague of frogs was a miracle on top of another miracle, because the frogs came out of a dead river which had been flowing with blood for seven days.

And the Lord said unto Moses, Say unto Aaron, Stretch forth your hand with your rod over the rivers, over the canals, over the pools, and cause frogs to come up upon the land of Egypt.

And Aaron stretched out his hand over the waters of Egypt, and the frogs came up, and covered the land of Egypt. And the magicians did in like manner with their secret art, and they brought up frogs upon the land of Egypt. (Exod. 8:5-7)

Since blood has life in it, Satan was able to perform a counterfeit again. But he can never duplicate life. The frogs were not created by the devil.

At this point, Pharaoh was going yo-yo, because the frogs were on his bed, and all over the table where he wanted to eat his meals. He couldn't stand it. His magicians were no help. They could bring up the frogs just as Moses and Aaron had done, but they were powerless to get rid of them. Pharaoh was ready to call a conference with the troublemakers.

Pharaoh called for Moses and Aaron, and he said, Entreat the Lord for me that He may take away the frogs from me and my people, and I will let the people go that they may sacrifice to the Lord.

And Moses said unto Pharaoh, Have thou this glory over me. Tell me when I shall pray to the Lord for you, and your servants, and your people that the frogs be destroyed from you and your houses and remain in the river only. (Exod. 8:8-9)

Here Moses stepped beyond the bounds of his authority. The Lord never told Moses to ask Pharaoh to set a time when he wanted the frogs to disappear. But Moses did it anyway. He let Pharaoh have the glory over him in setting a time for the frogs to be gone. Moses might have been thinking that if Pharaoh set the time himself, and God heard Moses' cry, Pharaoh would have to believe that the frogs had been sent by God and removed by Him.

And Pharaoh said, Tomorrow I want it done. And Moses

said, Be it done according to your word, that you may know there is no one like unto the Lord our God. And the frogs shall depart from you, from your houses, from your servants, and from your people. They shall remain in the river only.

And Moses and Aaron went out from Pharaoh, and Moses cried to the Lord because of the frogs which He had brought against Pharaoh. (Exod. 8:10-12)

Because Moses had overstepped his authority, he had to go back to the source of all life and cry unto the Lord. In the Hebrew, the language makes it very clear that Moses cried a very strong cry. It was absolutely necessary that the Lord back him up in what he told Pharaoh He could do.

And the Lord did according to the words of Moses. He backed him up. He gave him the authority, and the frogs died out of the houses, out of the courts, and out of the fields. They gathered them together in heaps, and the land stank.

Now when Pharaoh saw that there was a reprieve, a respite, he hardened his heart again and he listened not unto them, just as the Lord had said. And the Lord said unto Moses, Say unto Aaron, Stretch out your rod, and smite the dust of the earth, that it may become gnats throughout all the land of Egypt. And they did so. Aaron stretched out his hand with his rod, smote the dust of the earth, and there were gnats upon man and upon beasts. All the dust of the earth became gnats throughout all the land of Egypt. (Exod. 8:13-17)

Gnats get in your nose and in your eyes and ears. You breathe them into your lungs. I used to go fishing in Florida, and at certain times of the year, the gnats were terrible. There was nothing you could do about them. A plague of gnats would be really awful to live through. And the plague of gnats was everywhere except in the land of Goshen. As before, the children of Israel were divinely protected by the Lord.

And now the magicians sought with their secret arts to bring forth gnats, but they could not. So there were gnats upon man and upon beast. (Exod. 8:18)

The magicians could not counterfeit the plague of gnats because

45

they could not bring life out of the dust. The Lord God is the only Creator of life, and the magicians were beginning to realize that fact.

Then the magicians said unto Pharaoh, This is the finger of the living God. But Pharaoh's heart was hardened, and he would not listen to them, just as the Lord told Moses he would not listen.

And the Lord said unto Moses, Rise up early in the morning, and stand before Pharaoh. Behold, he comes forth to the water, and say to him, Thus saith the Lord, Let My people go, that they may serve Me. Else, if you will not let My people go, behold, I will send swarms of flies upon you, upon your servants, upon your people, and into your houses. The houses of the Egyptians shall be full of swarms of flies, also the ground upon which they stand. (Exod. 8:19-21)

This would be a plague of gadflies. A gadfly's bite is worse than a mosquito's bite. And again, as the Lord had promised, the Israelites would be protected:

I will set apart in that day the land of Goshen in which My people dwell that no swarms of flies shall be there, to the end that you may know I am the Lord in the midst of the earth. (Exod. 8:22)

"I'm not up in heaven, somewhere," God tells us. "I am in the midst of the earth in My *shekinah* glory, in My Holy Spirit. I dwell in the midst of My people, in the midst of the earth. Lo, I am with you always, even to the end of the age." And the Lord went on to say,

I will put a division between My people and your people, and by tomorrow this sign shall come to pass. And the Lord did so. (Exod. 8:23-24a)

When the Lord says He will put a division somewhere, it means He will set His people apart. He puts Jesus between the saved and the unsaved. Those who believe in Him will have the Lord Jesus Christ with them. Those who do not believe will be by themselves. Those who choose darkness will have total darkness. Those who choose light will have total light. Jesus Himself forms the division, standing between His people and the plague, so that all people will know that He is the Lord of all the earth.

And there came grievous swarms of gadflies into the house of Pharaoh, into his servants' houses, and into all the land of Egypt. The land was ruined by reason of the swarms of flies. And Pharaoh called for Moses and for Aaron and said, Go and sacrifice to your God here in the land of Egypt. And Moses said, It is not suitable or right for us to do that; for the animals the Egyptians hold sacred and will not permit to be slain are those we will sacrifice to the Lord our God. Lo, if we sacrifice the abomination of the Egyptians before their very eyes, will they not stone us? (Exod. 8:24b-26)

Moses knew that he and his people were to travel three days' journey into the wilderness to make their sacrifice unto the Lord. It was not right for them to offend the Egyptians by sacrificing cows in their land. The Egyptians worshiped the cow. Later, the Israelites would make a golden calf because of the idolatry they picked up in Egypt. Moses explained to Pharaoh why they could not sacrifice cows in his land, and then he said,

We will go three days into the wilderness and sacrifice to the Lord our God as He shall command us. And Pharaoh said, I will let you go, that you may sacrifice to the Lord your God in the wilderness; only you shall not go very far away. Please entreat the Lord for me. (Exod. 8:27-28)

Pharaoh was eager to be rid of the gadflies once and for all.

And Moses said, Behold, I go out from you, and I will entreat the Lord that the swarms of flies may depart from Pharaoh, from his servants, and from his people tomorrow. Only let not Pharaoh deal deceitfully any more in not letting the people go to sacrifice to the Lord.

Moses went out from Pharaoh and he entreated the Lord. (Exod. 8:29-30)

Moses prayed for Pharaoh and for all Egypt that the flies might be taken away from them.

And the Lord did according to the word of Moses. And He, the Lord, removed the swarms of flies from Pharaoh, from his

47

servants, from his people, and there remained not one. (Exod. 8:31)

All the flies disappeared just as quickly as they had come. The Lord had sent them, the Lord took them away.

And Pharaoh again hardened his heart another time also, and he would not let the people of Israel go.

Then the Lord said unto Moses, Go in unto Pharaoh and tell him, Thus saith the Lord, the God of the Hebrews, Let My people go, that they may serve Me. For if you refuse to let them go, and you will hold them still, Behold, the hand of the Lord is upon the cattle which are in your field, upon your horses, the asses, the herds, and the flocks. There shall be a very grievous murrain. (Exod. 8:32-9:1-3)

This murrain would resemble our modern hoof-and-mouth disease, which spreads like wildfire.

And the Lord shall again make a distinction between the cattle of Israel and the cattle of Egypt. There shall nothing die at all of all that belongs to the children of Israel. And the Lord appointed a set time, saying, Tomorrow the Lord shall do this thing in the land. And the Lord did that thing on the morrow, and all the cattle of Egypt died, but of the cattle of the children of Israel, not one died. (Exod. 9:4-6)

The Lord had appointed a set time, saying to Moses, "You better tell Pharaoh that tomorrow at exactly 3:02 P.M., this plague is going to come upon his cattle. All at once, they will start dying, at the time which I have set."

And Pharaoh sent to find out, and behold, there was not so much as one of the cattle of the people of Israel dead. But the heart of Pharaoh was stubborn, and he would not let the people go.

And the Lord said unto Moses and unto Aaron, Take to you handfuls of the soot of the furnace, and let Moses throw it heavenward in the sight of Pharaoh. It shall become small dust over all the land of Egypt, and it shall be boils breaking forth with sores upon man and beast, throughout all the land of Egypt. (Exod. 9:7-9)

Moses was instructed to take the soot of the furnace and throw it toward heaven. The minute it came down again, the wind would blow it and scatter it, and it would become a boil the minute it touched a person who was not in the Lord. The people of Israel were still protected by the divine protection of the Lord, but the minute the soot hit the Egyptians, their bodies would be covered with boils.

Moses and Aaron were obedient to do what the Lord had commanded them:

> They took the soot of the furnace, and they stood before Pharaoh. And Moses threw it up heavenward, and it became boils breaking forth with blains upon man and beast. And the magicians could not stand before Moses because of the boils, for the boils were upon the magicians also, and upon all the Egyptians. And the Lord hardened the heart of Pharaoh and he would not listen unto them, just as the Lord had spoken unto Moses. (Exod. 9:10-12)

The Lord had spared the magicians before, but now they were suffering along with everybody else. And at about this point, the heart of Pharaoh had been hardened enough times that the Lord's love, grace, and mercy had passed him from grace into judgment.

8

The Plagues Intensify

(EXODUS 9:13—11)

And the Lord said unto Moses, Rise up early in the morning
and stand before Pharaoh and say unto him, Thus saith the
Lord God of the Hebrews, Let My people go that they may
serve Me. For I will at this time send all My plagues upon
your heart (signifying absolute judgment), upon your
servants, and upon your people, that you may know that there
is none like Me in all the earth. Surely now, if I had put forth
My hand in full power and I had smitten you and your people
with pestilence, you would have been cut off from the face of
the earth. But in very deed for this cause I have made you to
stand, to show you My power; that My name may be declared
throughout all the earth. (Exod. 9:13-16)

The Lord, speaking to Pharaoh, was saying, ''For this I have let
you live that you might see My salvation if you would choose to
accept it. You have seen all the miracles that I have brought upon
you, but you have refused to receive My salvation.''

And the Lord continued His message to Pharaoh through His
servant Moses:

And yet, Pharaoh, you still exalt and lift yourself up against
My people and against Me by not letting them go. Behold,

tomorrow at this time I will cause it to rain a very grievous hail, such as has never been seen in Egypt from the day it was founded until now. (Exod. 9:17-18)

Therefore send, bring in your cattle, all that you have in the field, for every man and beast that shall be found in the field and shall not be brought home, the hail shall come down upon them, and they shall die. (Exod. 9:19)

Are you wondering where the Egyptian cattle came from to be protected from the hail since, according to Exodus 9:6, all the cattle of Egypt had already died? The rabbis have an explanation. In the Talmud, they report that the cattle referred to in Exodus 9:6 were the cows, the she-cattle, and those that remained to be killed by the hail were the bulls. Another logical explanation for the presence of cattle in the land of Egypt after the plague of hoof and mouth disease is that they probably would have restocked from the herds of neighboring countries.

He that feared the word of the Lord among the servants of Pharaoh made his servants and his cattle to flee into the houses. And he that did not fear or regard the word of the Lord left his servants and his cattle in the field. (Exod. 9:20-21)

At this point, the Lord was giving the Egyptian people a chance. If they believed Him, they could be saved. If they didn't believe Him, they would die in the hail. Every Egyptian was given the chance for salvation. If he believed God's word, he could seek safety for himself, and he could bring his animals in out of the field to save their lives, too. The Lord wants to save every one of His creatures.

There were some Egyptians who took the word of the Lord seriously by this time. They knew that God was God, and that His word was truth. They brought their cattle and themselves in out of the field, and they were saved, not just from destruction by the hail, but they were saved for eternal life. Later, some of them were part of the "multitude of a mixed people" who went up out of Egypt.

So the Lord said unto Moses, Stretch forth your hand toward heaven, that there may be hail in all the land of Egypt, upon man, upon beast, upon every herb of the field, throughout all the land of Egypt.

And Moses stretched forth his rod toward heaven, and the Lord sent thunder and hail, and lightning fire rained down onto the earth. And the Lord caused the hail upon the land of Egypt. So there was hail and fire flashing up amidst the hail, very grievous, as had never been seen in all the land of Egypt since it became a nation. And the hail smote throughout all the land of Egypt all that was in the field, and broke every tree in the field. Only in the land of Goshen, where the children of Israel were, there was no hail. (Exod. 9:22-26)

Once more, Jesus Christ, the divine Separator, was standing there with His divine protection around the children of Israel.

And Pharaoh sent, and he called for Moses and Aaron and said unto them, I have sinned this time. The Lord is righteous, and I and my people are wicked. Please entreat the Lord and let there be enough of these mighty thunderings and hail. I will let you go and you shall stay no longer.

And Moses said unto him, As soon as I am gone out of the city, I will spread forth my hands unto the Lord; and the thunder shall cease, neither shall there be any more hail, that you may know that the earth is the Lord's. (Exod. 9:27-29)

Moses was going to leave the court of Pharaoh and walk out through the hail, and when he was outside the city, he would stretch forth his hand in the midst of the hail which was breaking into fire. He would entreat the Lord, and the hail would stop that the Egyptians might know that the earth belongs to the Lord and that He had sent Moses as His messenger. Moses would walk through the hail by faith, knowing the Lord was his divine protection. He wouldn't carry an umbrella.

And Moses said to Pharaoh:

But as for you and your servants, I know that you do not yet fear the Lord God.

And the flax and the barley were smitten: for the barley was in the ear, and the flax was in the bloom. But the wheat and the spelt were not smitten, for they ripen late and were not grown up yet. (Exod. 9:30-32)

Spelt is a wild sort of wheat which grows later on. Another plague would take care of it later.

And Moses went out of the city from Pharaoh, and spread forth his hands unto the Lord. The thunder and the hail ceased, and the rain no longer poured upon the earth.

And when Pharaoh saw that the rain and the hail and the thunder ceased, he sinned yet more. He hardened his heart, he and his servants. And the heart of Pharaoh was hardened, and he did not let the children of Israel go, just as the Lord had spoken by Moses. (Exod. 9:33-35)

The Lord would have to continue to deal with Pharaoh over an extended period of time. By the time the ten plagues had run their course, a full year would have gone by.

And the Lord said unto Moses, Go again unto Pharaoh. I have hardened his heart and the heart of his servants, that I might show these My signs in the midst of them. And that you may tell them in the ears of your son, and of your son's son, what I have wrought upon Egypt, and My signs which I have done among them that you may know that I am the Lord.

And Moses and Aaron went in unto Pharaoh and said unto him, Thus saith the Lord, the God of the Hebrews, How long will you refuse to humble yourself before Me? (Exod. 10:1-3a)

That's a terrible message from the Lord. When He speaks to you and me and asks, "How long will you refuse to humble yourself before Me?" we had better get on our knees and start humbling ourselves before Him. If we wait for Him to do it for us, we choose the hard way. Giving in to His will of our own accord is the easy way. If He has to do it for us, He may need to break every bone in our body to bring us to the point that He wants us. We all have to get to that point somehow, that place that is His will for us.

And Moses continued to deliver God's message to Pharaoh, saying,

Let My people go that they may serve Me. Else, if you refuse to let My people go, behold, tomorrow I will bring locusts into your border. They shall cover the face of the earth so that no one shall be able to see the earth. They shall eat the residue, that which escaped from the hail, which remains to you, and shall eat every tree which grows for you out of the field. Your houses shall be filled with locusts, the houses of all your servants, the houses of all the Egyptians, as neither your fathers nor your fathers' fathers have seen, from the day they were upon the earth to this day.

Then Moses turned himself and went out from Pharaoh. And Pharaoh's servants said unto him, How long shall this man be a snare unto us? Let the men go, that they may go and serve the Lord their God. Do you not know as yet that Egypt is destroyed? (Exod. 10:3b-7)

Pharaoh's servants realized that Egypt was destroyed, but he didn't seem to realize it yet.

And Moses and Aaron were brought again unto Pharaoh. And he said unto them, Go, serve the Lord your God. But who are they that shall go?

And Moses said, We will all go with our young, with our old, with our sons, with our daughters, with our flocks, with our herds, for we must hold a feast unto the Lord.

The Pharaoh said unto them, Let the Lord be with you if I ever let you go with your little ones! See, you must have some evil purpose in mind. Not so! You that are men, go and serve the Lord, for that is what you desire. And Moses and Aaron were driven out from Pharaoh's presence. (Exod. 10:8-11)

Pharaoh had decreed that only the men could go, that the women and children and cattle would have to stay behind. He accused Moses of lying, of having ulterior motives, and Moses and Aaron were driven out from his presence. Because the Pharaoh was still so hardhearted, the plagues would have to continue:

The Lord said to Moses, Stretch out your hand over the land of Egypt for the locusts, that they may come upon the land of Egypt, and eat every herb of the land, even all that the hail has left.

Moses stretched forth his rod over the land of Egypt and the Lord brought an east wind upon the land all that day, and all that night. And when it was morning, the east wind brought the locusts. And the locusts went up over all the land of Egypt, and rested in all the borders of Egypt. Very grievous were they; never before were there such locusts as they, nor will there ever be again. (Exod. 10:12-14)

The plague of locusts in Egypt was going to eat up everything in sight. They were going to be everywhere, even in the houses of the people. They would be so bad that the Pharaoh would be forced to call Moses again.

The locusts covered the whole face of the earth so that the land was darkened. They ate every herb of the land, and all the fruit of the trees which the hail had left. There remained not any green thing, neither tree nor herb of the field throughout all the land of Egypt.

Then Pharaoh called for Moses and Aaron in haste, and he said, I have sinned against the Lord your God and against you. Now therefore, forgive, I pray thee, my sin only this one time, and entreat the Lord your God, that He may take away from me this plague of death. (Exod. 10:15-17)

Pharaoh was finally saying the right words with his lips, but he wasn't saying them with his heart.

And Moses went out from Pharaoh and entreated the Lord. And the Lord turned an exceedingly strong west wind which took up the locusts and drove them into the Red Sea. There remained not one locust within all the country of Egypt. But the Lord hardened Pharaoh's heart, and he would not let the children of Israel go.

And the Lord said unto Moses, Stretch out your hand toward heaven that there may be darkness over the land of Egypt, even darkness which may be felt.

And Moses stretched forth his hand toward heaven, and there was a thick darkness in all the land of Egypt three days. They saw not one another; neither did they rise any one from his place for three days. But all the children of Israel had light in their dwellings. (Exod. 10:18-23)

To be separated from the Lord is to be in total darkness. And the Egyptians had a taste of hell right there. The darkness was so thick it could be felt. With it was a spirit of depression, oppression, and fear—a total darkness physically and spiritually. And no fire was able to prevail against the darkness to give them light, neither were the stars strong enough to bring forth light to them, neither was the moon or the sun. They could not even start a fire. And yet in the camp of the saved of Israel, there was total light. There is always a vast difference between God's people and the people who are anti-God.

Then Pharaoh again called unto Moses and said, Go, serve the Lord. Let your little ones also go with you. It is only your flocks and your herds that must not go.

And Moses said, You must also give into our hands sacrifices and burnt offerings, that we may sacrifice unto the Lord our God. Our cattle shall also go with us; there shall not a hoof be left behind, for thereof must we take to serve the Lord our God; we know not with what we must serve the Lord until we come there.

But the Lord hardened Pharaoh's heart, and he would not let them go. And Pharaoh said unto him, Get away from me! Take heed to yourself, take notice, that you see my face no more. For in the day that you see my face you shall die.

And Moses said, You have spoken well. I will see your face again no more. (Exod. 10:24-29)

Before Moses left the Pharaoh's presence, the Lord told Moses about the tenth plague, the plague of the firstborn.

And the Lord said to Moses, Yet one more plague will I bring upon Pharaoh and upon Egypt. Afterward, he will let you go, and when he shall let you go, he shall surely thrust you out altogether, as I said he would in the beginning.

Speak now in the ears of this people, and let every man ask of his neighbor, and every woman of her neighbor, jewels of silver and jewels of gold. (Exod. 11:1-2)

God had already promised (Exod. 3:22) that the Israelites would be permitted to despoil the Egyptians. And now was the appointed time. Mrs. Levine, Mrs. Epstein, and Mrs. Goldberg were to go to their Egyptian neighbors and say, "Let me have your jewelry already yet, and your beautiful clothing, and your garments, and your earrings.'' The Lord had told them, "The minute you ask, you'll receive,'' and they did.

So the Lord gave the people favor in the sight of the Egyptians. Moreover, the man Moses was very great in the land of Egypt, in the sight of Pharaoh's servants, and in the sight of the people.

And Moses said, Thus saith the Lord, About midnight will I, the Lord, go out into the midst of Egypt. And the firstborn in the land of Egypt shall die, from the firstborn of Pharaoh that sits upon his throne even unto the firstborn of the maidservant that is behind the mill, and all the firstborn of the beasts. There shall be a very great cry throughout all the land of Egypt, such as there has never been like it, nor shall be like it anymore. But against the children of Israel not even a dog will move his tongue, against man or beast, that you may know that the Lord does put a difference between the Egyptians and Israel. (Exod. 11:3-7)

Moses was in Pharaoh's presence still, telling him all these things that would come to pass:

And all these thy servants shall come down unto me, and bow down unto me, saying, Get you out, and all the people who follow you. And after that, I will go out. And Moses went out from Pharaoh in hot anger. (Exod. 11:8)

We have already seen that Moses had a temper. Here he displayed it to Pharaoh, and later he would display it to the children of Israel.

And the Lord said unto Moses, Pharaoh will not listen unto you, that My wonders may be multiplied in the land of Egypt.

And Moses and Aaron did all these wonders before Pharaoh. And the Lord hardened Pharaoh's heart, and he did not let the children of Israel go out of his land. (Exod. 11:9-10)

Because Pharaoh would still not let the people go, even after hearing about the plague of the firstborn, he was inviting that plague to come upon him and his people. All the firstborn would die.

9

The Passover

(EXODUS 12)

The Lord had spoken to Moses, saying there would be yet one more plague He would bring upon Egypt, the plague against the firstborn. All the firstborn in the camp and in the houses of the unsaved would die, including the firstborn among the beasts and the herds. The firstborn would be wiped out.

God being no respecter of persons, this death penalty would have fallen even upon the firstborn of Israel if they had not availed themselves of the divine protection of the Lord. Even today, among Orthodox Jews, the redemption of the firstborn must be taken care of every year on the first day of the Passover. They go through a ceremony of redemption after which they are entitled to claim that the blood of the lamb was placed upon their door until the next year, when they have to go through the whole thing again. But the yearly sacrifice isn't necessary for believers in the Lord Jesus Christ. We are redeemed once and for all by the blood of the perfect Lamb of God who takes away the sin of the world and gives us eternal life. But let us look at the sacrifice of the first Passover lamb:

> The Lord spoke again unto Moses and to Aaron in the land of
> Egypt, saying, This month shall be unto you the beginning of

months, the first month of the year to you. (Exod. 12:1-2)
The first month was called Abib. (In the modern Jewish calendar the first month is called Nisan.) Because the time of the Exodus from Egypt was to be so important in Israel's history, God changed the calendar and made the month of the Exodus the first month of the year from then on.

There are two Hebrew months in every month of our English calendar. Each Hebrew month begins about the middle of one of our months and ends in the middle of the next one. Our fourteenth day of April corresponds to the first day of the Hebrew calendar for the year, because that was the day when Israel was redeemed from the bondage of slavery and brought into the full freedom and knowledge of God.

And the Lord instructed Moses,

Speak unto all the congregation of Israel, saying, In the tenth day of this month, they shall take to them every man a lamb, according to their fathers' houses, a lamb for a household. And if the household be too little for a lamb, then shall he and his neighbor next unto his house take one according to the number of souls. According to every man's eating, you shall make your count for the lamb. (Exod. 12:3-4)

Notice the love and the grace and the mercy of the Lord here. He says if your household is too small to warrant the purchasing of a lamb, you and your neighbor can share in a lamb together, and the sacrifice will be acceptable unto the Lord. The Lord does not want to deprive any of us of any material blessing He has given us or that He has planned for us in the future. He encourages us to share with one another.

Later, in the Book of Leviticus, God says that if we cannot afford to sacrifice a lamb, a bullock, or an oxen, He will let us bring a turtle dove or a pigeon. If we cannot afford even that much, we can bring some unleavened flour, or a piece of unleavened cake, and the Lord will accept it because He sees the condition of our hearts toward Him.

For the first Passover, God told the people,

Your lamb shall be without blemish, a male of the first year.

You shall take it from the sheep or the goats. And you shall keep it until the fourteenth day of the same month, and then the whole assembly of the congregation of Israel shall kill it at dusk. (Exod. 12:5-6)

The lamb was to be taken on the tenth day of the month and kept until the evening of the fourteenth, three full days according to the Hebrew way of reckoning.

This first Passover lamb was to be sacrificed at dusk, and when the true Lamb of God went to the cross, He gave up His spirit at dusk. The Passover sabbath was coming in, and He had to be taken down from the cross before that high holy sabbath. Even at His death, He remained without sin. He gave up His spirit voluntarily, saying, "It is finished." We can understand that to mean that Jesus was conveying to us, "That which I have come into the world to do is completed. I have taken all the sin, all the transgression, all the iniquities of the people upon Myself. I have taken their grief, their afflictions, and their sorrows, and by My stripes, I have healed them. When they come to know Me, all they need to do is to lift up their hand, touch the hem of My garment, and they will be made whole in every area of their lives."

God's instructions for the first Passover went on to say,

And they shall take of the blood, and put it on the two sideposts and on the lintel above the door of the houses where they shall eat it. (Exod. 12:7)

As they were obedient to put the blood on the sideposts and on the lintel above the door, they were making the sign of the cross. And when the Lord saw the sign of the cross in blood, he would pass over them and spare the firstborn of their houses.

If any one of the people of Israel had gone out of his house where the sign of the blood was around the door, the plague would have touched him, and he would have died. Everybody had to stay inside the house under the divine protection of the blood of the lamb. In the same way today, we are sealed in Him, we are kept safe in His body and in His blood. We are under His divine protection. Without it, there's no telling what would happen to us.

And they shall eat the flesh in that night, roasted with fire, and

61

unleavened bread. And with bitter herbs they shall eat it. Eat it not raw, nor sodden at all with water, but roast with fire, its head with its legs, and with the innards thereof. And you shall let nothing of the meat remain until the morning. And the bones and inedible bits which remain until the morning, you shall burn with fire. And thus you shall eat it: with your loins girded, your shoes on your feet, and your staff in your hand. And you shall eat it in haste, for it is the Lord's passover. (Exod. 12:8-11)

The Lord was saying, "Be ready to move at a moment's notice. Have your loins girded, your knapsack on your back, your shoes on your feet, your staff in your hand ready to travel when I tell you to go.

This same readiness is required of Christians today. "I'm coming in the twinkling of an eye," the Lord says, "and I want you to be prepared. Have your knapsack on your back, your shoes on your feet, and your loins girded and your staff in your hand. Be ready to travel at a moment's notice. Have your lamps full. Be lit with My Holy Spirit."

For I—not an angel, but I, the Lord—will go through the land of Egypt tonight. I will smite all the firstborn in the land of Egypt, both man and beast. And against all the gods of Egypt will I execute judgment. I am the Lord. And the blood shall be to you a sign and a seal upon the houses where you are. (Exod. 12:12-13a)

To me, this is the most thrilling part of the Old Testament, that we are signed and sealed in that blood of Jesus.

When I see that blood, I, the Lord, will pass over you, and no plague shall be upon you to destroy you when I smite the land of Egypt.

And this day shall be unto you for a memorial. You shall keep it as a feast unto the Lord throughout all your generations. You shall keep it as a feast by ordinance forever, for all time. (Exod. 12:13b-14)

Christians keep the Passover today every time they take communion. Jesus fulfilled the Passover for us, taking us from the

Old Covenant into the New Covenant when He picked up the unleavened bread and said, "Take and eat. This is My body which is broken for you" (1 Cor. 11:24). Then He picked up the cup of Elijah and said, "This is the blood of the New Covenant, My blood, which is shed for you for the remission of sin (1 Cor. 11:25). It is shed for you and for all those who come after you and believe. My blood is on the lintel and on the doorpost protecting you, that from this point on, you might have everlasting life."

We read in Exodus that the Passover is to be kept forever, and we see Jesus echoing these very same words when He says, "As often as you do this, you do it in remembrance of Me" (1 Cor. 11:25). Jesus didn't give us a doctrine that said we should take communion once a month, once a week, or once a year. The early Christians took communion every day, and remembered Him each time they did it. In Israel today, the Christians, the completed Jews, and the Christian Arabs meet daily to take communion in remembrance of the Lord. Through partaking of this sacrament, they are bound and knit together to go out and minister in the Lord's name. In taking into themselves His body and His blood, they receive power from on high to do the job He has called them to do.

> Seven days shall you eat unleavened bread; even the first day, you shall put away all leaven out of your houses. (Exod. 12:15a)

From this, the rabbis decided that we have to have three separate sets of dishes—one for meat, one for dairy products, and one for Passover. If a dish has contained leaven at any time, it can never be used for Passover again, because the dish might have absorbed some of the leaven.

The Lord was saying to His people, "You shall go through the house, find anything that is leaven and put it outside the house. Get rid of it, burn it, destroy it somehow. Whatever you destroy, I'll replace and multiply for you after the Passover is over. You are to do all this in remembrance of your redemption."

God is saying the same thing to us. He's telling us to get the leaven out of our lives, to purify ourselves of everything that corrupts or adulterates our purity. He wants us all cleaned out and empty of self so He can fill us with His Spirit, His righteousness, and His holiness. But not everybody is obedient to celebrate the Passover wholeheartedly.

Some of our wealthy Jewish people, whose business involves leavened merchandise—liquor, for example—build a fence around the law of God. All leaven has to be put out of their possession for Passover, so the Talmud makes a special provision for getting around the law.

Let's say that we have a huge warehouse full of whiskey. It's leaven, it's got to be disposed of for the celebration of the Passover. We can rent the warehouse to a non-Jewish person for a seven-day period for a certain number of dollars which we will give to charity. After the eighth day, we can go back and pay the person to break the lease and so get back all our leaven. The Talmud says it's okay to do that, and that we actually did a good deed, by giving money to charity, but in our hearts, we know we've actually broken the commandment of the Lord.

> Whosoever eats leavened bread from the first day until the seventh day, that soul shall be cut off from Israel. (Exod. 12:15b)

Here God is not speaking about our being cut off from physical life, but He's speaking about our being cut off from eternal life, having our souls cut off from the Book of Life.

> And in the first day, you shall hold a holy convocation, and in the seventh day a holy convocation. No manner of work shall be done in them, save the preparation of that which every man must eat; that only may be done by you. (Exod. 12:16)

The first day and the seventh day of Passover are holy days. No manner of work may be done in them. No leaven is to be in the house. On days two through six, you may do whatever is necessary that you may eat, but no more.

> You shall observe the feast of unleavened bread, for in this selfsame day, I, the Lord of hosts, have brought you out of the land of Egypt. Therefore you shall observe this day throughout your generations by an ordinance forever.

In the first month, on the fourteenth day of the month at evening, you shall eat unleavened bread, and continue until the twenty-first day of the month at evening. Seven days there shall no leaven be found in your houses, for whosoever eats that which is leavened, that soul shall be cut off from the congregation of Israel, whether he be a sojourner, or one that is born in the land. You shall eat nothing leavened; in all your habitations shall you eat unleavened bread during the week of Passover. (Exod. 12:17-20)

Today, we still announce, as we start to celebrate the Passover, "Let all those who wish come and join with us in this Passover." The invitation is given by the people of Israel to any stranger or sojourner in their midst to come in and share in the salvation of the Lord. If they come in from the outside and partake of the Passover, they shall be saved.

This is the same invitation we give in our Christian churches when we invite people to come forward and accept Jesus Christ as their personal Savior. The wording is a little bit different, but the thought and intention are the same.

After Moses had received all these instructions from the Lord,
Then Moses called for all the elders of Israel and said unto them, Draw out, and take for yourselves lambs according to your families, and kill the Passover lamb. And you shall take a bunch of hyssop, dip it in the blood that is in the basin, and strike the lintel and the two sideposts with the blood that is in the basin; and none of you shall go out of the door of his house until the morning. For the Lord Himself will pass through to smite the Egyptians, and when He sees the blood upon the lintel, and on the two sideposts, the Lord will pass over the door, and will not suffer the destroyer to come into your houses to smite you. And you shall observe this thing for an ordinance unto you and to your sons forever.

And it shall come to pass that when you come to the land which the Lord Himself will give you, according as He has promised, that you shall keep this service. And when your children shall say unto you, What do you mean by this festival, and what do you mean by this service? then you shall say, It is a sacrifice of the Lord's Passover, for He passed over the houses of Israel in Egypt when He smote the Egyptians, but He delivered our houses. (Exod. 12:21-27a)

The sacrifice of the Lord's Passover in Egypt was a picture of the coming sacrifice of Jesus, the true Lamb of God, who would come into the world and be sacrificed for us. He would be the Deliverer of all men who would receive Him.

And the minute the people of Israel heard these words, they bowed their heads and worshiped the Lord. And the children of Israel went and as the Lord had commanded Moses and Aaron, so did they. (Exod. 12:27b-28)

At this point, the children of Israel were ready to believe and obey God. It had been almost a full year since Moses had come upon the scene, saying that the God of Abraham, Isaac, and Jacob had sent him. They had seen the devastation of the nine preceding plagues and didn't want to take any chances about this one falling on them. They were really persuaded that they had better obey God—or else.

So it came to pass at midnight that the Lord smote all the firstborn in the land of Egypt, from the firstborn of Pharaoh that sat on his throne unto the firstborn of the captive that was in the dungeon, and all the firstborn of the cattle. And Pharaoh rose up in the night, he, and all his servants, and all the Egyptians, and there was a great cry in Egypt, for there was not a house where there was not one dead.

And Pharaoh called for Moses and Aaron by night, and said, Rise up, and get yourselves forth from among my people, both you and the children of Israel, and go and serve the Lord as you have said. Take both your flocks and your herds, as you have said, and be gone. And ask your God to bless me, also, as you leave. (Exod. 12:29-32)

It happened exactly as the Lord told Moses it would happen. He had said that Pharaoh would kick them out of Egypt. Moses wouldn't have to ask him if they could go, Pharaoh would insist that they depart. This time, he said they could take their flocks and their herds, their women and their children, along with them. Furthermore, he asked Moses to pray for him, to entreat the Lord God that no further plague would be brought upon them.

> And the Egyptians were urgent upon the people to depart, that they might send them out of the land in haste, for they said, We are all dead men. (Exod. 12:33)

The Egyptians were urgent to get rid of the Israelites because all their firstborn were dying—the firstborn of the people, and of the flocks, and of the herds. The plague was spreading everywhere, and the Egyptians were afraid for their lives. Suddenly, when it was too late to save their firstborn, they had a good healthy regard and respectful fear of the Lord. They were urging the Israelites to hurry up and get out.

> And the people took their dough before it was leavened, their kneadingtroughs being bound up in their clothes upon their shoulders. And the children of Israel did according to the word of Moses, and they asked of the Egyptians jewels of silver, jewels of gold, and raiment.
>
> And the Lord gave the people favor in the sight of the Egyptians, so that they let them have what they asked. And they despoiled the Egyptians as the Lord said they would. (Exod. 12:34-36)

Mrs. Epstein, Mrs. Goldberg, and their friends all went to the houses of the Egyptians and said, "Give me your gold and your silver already," and they gave it to them. Later, some of that gold was used to make the golden calf, the abomination unto the Lord. And the rest of it was used in the building of the tabernacle in the wilderness. The gold alone would have been worth between fifteen and twenty million dollars today, an indication of what the Lord gave the people of Israel when He permitted them to despoil the Egyptians.

> So now the children of Israel journeyed from Rameses to Succoth, about six hundred thousand men on foot besides women and children. (Exod. 12:37)

Later, a count was taken, a census, indicating that there were 603,550 men twenty years of age and older in the Exodus from

Egypt. Any men under the age of twenty were counted as children. This means that between three to four and a half million people in all left Egypt during the Exodus. All of them had descended from seventy people in four hundred years of slavery. The Lord had said, "You shall be fruitful and multiply. I will multiply you." And He had surely done it.

> A mixed multitude went up with them, and flocks, and herds, and very much cattle. (Exod. 12:38)

Would this mixed multitude of foreigners and Egyptians remain loyal to the living God, or would they turn against the Lord? Would they cause the people of Israel to sin?

As a former Jewish rabbi, I have the temptation to say, "Yes, it was the mixed multitude that caused Israel to sin in the Exodus," but that's not the way it really happened. The mixed multitude were the staunchest believers. They were the ones who truly believed in the Lord, because they knew what it was like to be unsaved, and now they knew what it was like to be saved. But the people of Israel were coasting along on their knowledge that they were the chosen people, God's favorite, and they didn't have to do anything to deserve His favor.

"You have chosen us above all people, God," they were thinking, "so now we can do anything we want to and get away with it."

That's the attitude of many of the people of Israel and many Christians today. They live as if they're thinking, "We can do anything we want to Jesus Christ and get away with it. After all, He died for us, didn't He? We can always repent next week, or the week after that. We've got plenty of time to have our fling, and then we can repent. We've got a long time to live."

But suppose we die tonight without repentance? Suppose we die tonight holding a grudge, or a resentment, or a hatred? Suppose we die tonight not right with the Lord? Then where would we be?

> And they baked unleavened cakes of the dough which they brought forth out of Egypt, for it was not leavened; because they were thrust out of Egypt at a moment's notice, and they could not tarry, neither had they prepared for themselves any

victual.

> Now the time the children of Israel dwelt in Egypt was four
> hundred and thirty years. (Exod. 12:39-40)

The Lord had said the Israelites would be in the bondage of
slavery for four hundred years. What's the extra thirty years? Did
God make a mistake? No, He never makes mistakes. What had
happened was that the Israelites had enjoyed peace and prosperity
in Egypt under the reign of Joseph. But the minute Joseph died, the
Egyptians drove back the Hyksos Pharaohs who were Semitics and
cordial to the people of Israel because they were of the same race.
When they were driven back to the land of Canaan, the original
ruling body of Pharaohs took over, the Pharaohs who didn't know
Joseph, who had no love for the Semitic people. All this happened
exactly four hundred years to the day from the time the Lord
redeemed His people from slavery, just as He said He would. God
had kept His word exactly.

> So it came to pass, even the selfsame day, that all the hosts of
> the Lord went out from the land of Egypt. It was a night of
> watching and waiting unto the Lord for bringing them out
> from the land of Egypt. (Exod. 12:41-42a)

Today, Christians the world over are watching and waiting for
the Lord in the same way. God is telling us to look up, for our
redemption draweth nigh. Every sign is pointing to the fact that we
are in the last days. Jesus is on His way back. The King is coming
very soon. All signs are pointing to His imminent return.*

> This same night of watching unto the Lord is to be observed
> by all the children of Israel throughout all their generations.
> (Exod. 12:42b)

The children of Israel were to remember their redemption, their
deliverance, their salvation, for all generations. It is as if we were
there, and not our ancestors, but we ourselves were redeemed by
the Lord with a mighty outstretched hand. And, in fact, the Lord
Himself redeemed me on that night. Praise God that He did,
because then He brought me to the fullness of Jesus Christ, and I
saw the true redemption, the true Redeemer, the true Lamb of God.

And the Lord said unto Moses and unto Aaron, This is the

ordinance of the Passover. There shall no alien eat of it. (Exod. 12:43)

The word *alien* in this verse is a different word in the Hebrew from the word sojourner or stranger (v. 19). The word *alien* here describes one who deliberately alienates himself from partaking of this Passover festival of the Lord.

As Christians, we are commanded not to be alienated from Him when we partake of the Lord's supper. Saint Paul, in his first letter to the Corinthians, writes about how we must come to this sacrament:

> For I received from the Lord Himself that which I passed on to you—it was given to me personally; that the Lord Jesus on the night when He was treacherously delivered up *and* while His betrayal was in progress took bread, and when He had given thanks, He broke [it], and said, *Take, eat.* This is My body which is broken for you. Do this to call Me [affectionately] to remembrance. Similarly when supper was ended, He took the cup also, saying, This cup is the new covenant [ratified and established] in My blood. Do this, as often as you drink [it], to call Me [affectionately] to remembrance. For every time you eat this bread and drink this cup, you are representing *and* signifying *and* proclaiming the fact of the Lord's death until He comes [again]. So then whoever eats the bread or drinks the cup of the Lord in a way that is unworthy [of Him] will be guilty of (profaning and sinning against) the body and blood of the Lord. Let a man [thoroughly] examine himself, and [only] when he has done so should he eat of the bread and drink of the cup. For any one who eats and drinks without discriminating *and* recognizing with due appreciation that [it is Christ's] body, eats and drinks a sentence—a verdict of judgment—upon himself. That [careless and unworthy participation] is the reason many of you are weak and sickly, and quite enough of you are fallen into the sleep of death. (1 Cor. 11:23-30 TAB)

From his explanation, we understand that many of us today are sick and dying because we do not reverently appreciate the fact that it is the Lord's body and His blood of which we partake. When we are in that condition, we are like the aliens written about here in Exodus. We need to understand and know that we are partaking of the Lord's body and blood when we take communion. It is not a symbol, it's reality. God says, ''Don't alienate yourself from the sacrifice which I gave for you when I laid down My life.''

But every man's servant that is bought for money, when you have circumcised him, then he shall eat thereof. (Exod. 12:44)

In the Old Covenant, when a servant was bought with money and was circumcised, he was brought into a covenant relationship with God. The Lord had said, ''The circumcision is My sign and seal that I have a covenant relationship with this person. When anyone is brought into the covenant, then he may partake of the Passover.'' When we enter into the new covenant relationship with God by accepting Jesus as our personal Savior, then we can partake of the Lord's supper.

A sojourner and a hired servant shall not eat thereof. In one house it shall be eaten. You shall not carry forth ought of the flesh abroad out of the house, neither shall you break a bone thereof. (Exod. 12:45-46)

On the cross of Calvary, there was not one bone broken in the body of Jesus Christ. The Scripture was fulfilled, the requirement was met because Jesus was the Passover Lamb.

All the congregation of Israel shall keep it. And when a stranger sojourning with thee wishes to keep the Passover of the Lord, let all of his males be circumcised. And then let them come near and keep it, and he shall be as one that is born in the land of Israel and of the blood of Israel. But no uncircumcised person shall eat thereof. (Exod. 12:47-48)

Here God is speaking to us about circumcision of the heart. If you profess with your lips and believe with your heart that Jesus Christ is Lord, that He was crucified, dead, and buried, that He arose again, and that you and I go into Christian baptism and rise with Him into a new resurrected life, then Jesus has circumcised our hearts. When that has happened to us, Jesus invites us to come

71

near and keep His communion and His Passover. But one who cannot discern and appreciate what this sacrifice means should not partake of it.

> There shall be one law for him that is homeborn, and for the stranger that sojourns among you. (Exod. 12:49)

We are not to distinguish between those who have been born among us and the strangers among us who have accepted the Lord. We are not to elevate ourselves above them. The Lord says, "You're all equal in My sight the minute you accept Me. I don't have any grades of citizenship in My kingdom."

> Thus did all the children of Israel, as the Lord commanded Moses and Aaron, so did they. And it came to pass the very selfsame day, that the Lord did bring the children of Israel out of the land of Egypt by their hosts. (Exod. 12:50-51)

The Lord had kept His promise. He had brought His children out of the land of Egypt, out of the bondage of slavery, just as He had said He would. Hallelujah!

---

* See the author's *Next Visitor to Planet Earth*.

10

The Great Escape
(EXODUS 13—14)

The Lord spoke unto Moses, saying, Sanctify unto Me all the firstborn, whosoever openeth the womb among the children of Israel, both of man and of beast. It is Mine. (Exod. 13:1-2)

The first commandment given to Israel as a nation was that they were to observe the Passover for all generations. The second commandment was that from that day forth, the firstborn of the people of Israel and of their animals were to be dedicated unto the Lord in an act of sanctification.

"Just as I have given you the annual celebration of the Passover, which will remind you from this time forth of the great redemption which took place in your lives, so the sanctification of every male firstborn will keep the memory of the great salvation and redemption fresh and alive in every home blessed with a firstborn son."

Among Orthodox Jews, there is a ceremony called "redeeming the son" which is performed on the thirty-first day of the child's birth. And the firstborn of all the people of Israel keep the fourteenth day of Nisan or Abib as a fast, remembering the miracle wrought for them and their ancestors. If it had not been for God's grace, and His love, and His mercy, they would have died also.

73

And Moses said unto the people, Remember this day, in which you came out of Egypt, out of the house of bondage. For by strength of hand, the Lord brought you out from this place. There shall no leavened bread be eaten. This day you go forth in the month Abib. (Exod. 13:3-4)

The Lord Jesus Christ says to you and me as believers, "Do you remember the day when I took you out of bondage, out of slavery? Do you remember the day when you had your born-again experience? I want you to remember that day. I don't want you to forget it as long as you live."

And it shall be that when the Lord shall bring you into the land of the Canaanites, the Hittites, the Amorites, the Hivites, the Jebusites, which He swore unto your fathers to give you, a land flowing with milk and honey, that you shall keep this service in this month.

Seven days shall you eat unleavened bread and the seventh day shall be a feast unto the Lord. Unleavened bread shall be eaten through the seven days. There shall no leavened bread be seen with you, neither shall there be leaven in all your borders. (Exod. 13:5-7)

God, knowing that the rationalization of mankind would later try to build a fence around His law, charged them saying, "No leaven shall be found in any of your borders. It is to be destroyed completely. Border to border, you are to be clean throughout."

In the New Testament, the Lord, speaking by His Holy Spirit through Saint Paul, said, "There are three things we have to fight constantly—the world, the flesh, and the devil." Jesus says you can be *in* the world without being *of* it. You can be the true people of Israel. You can go forth and show the love of God in your life. You can be a living witness to somebody else. You can do all this by dying to yourself daily, by dying to your flesh. The enemy you have to fight, the devil himself, is a liar, a cheater, an accuser. He will try to rob you of all the blessings God has given you. But we are under the blood of Jesus Christ. We are under the blood of the perfect Lamb of heaven. And the devil cannot reach us. The Lord gave us His promise that the destroyer cannot come in unto us if we

74

stay under the blood of the Lamb.

You shall tell your son in that day, This is done because of what the Lord did for me when I came forth out of Egypt. And it shall be a sign to you, upon your hand, and for a memorial between your eyes, that the Scripture of the Lord may be in your mouth, for with a strong hand has the Lord brought you out of Egypt. (Exod. 13:8-9)

Here's another commandment, having to do with phylacteries. The phylacteries are little boxes made out of leather to be worn on the left arm and the forehead during the week, but not on the sabbath. The boxes contain verses of Scripture. The one worn upon the arm carries the Scripture Exodus 13:1-10 and 11-16. The one upon the forehead carries the Scripture Deuteronomy 6:1-9 and 11:13-21.

These four Scriptures were chosen because they relate the acceptance of the kingdom of heaven, the unity of God, and the Exodus from Egypt.

The Scripture for the left arm is next to the heart, which embraces the kingdom of heaven. And the Scripture on the forehead, near the mind, is telling the good news of the great redemption from Egypt. And we're to tell our sons, "This is because of that which the Lord did for *us* when *we* came forth out of Egypt. *We* took part in that great redemption from the bondage and slavery of sin."

You therefore shall keep this ordinance in its season from year to year. And it shall be when the Lord shall bring you into the land of the Canaanites, as He swore to you and your fathers, and He shall give it to you, that you shall set apart unto the Lord all that first openeth the womb, and all the firstlings that are males which you have coming from your beasts shall be the Lord's. Every firstling of an ass you shall redeem by substituting for it a lamb. And if you will not redeem it, the Lord says, then you shall break its neck, and all the firstborn of man among your sons you shall redeem. (Exod. 13:10-13)

An ass is an unclean animal. That which was unclean, the Israelites had to redeem with that which was clean. This is another picture of our redemption by Jesus Christ.   I am the jackass. And God loved me enough that He redeemed me with His Son, the Lamb of God, the Good Shepherd who lays down His life for the sheep. Jesus took my place on the cross. I belong there, but He went there for me.

When the Lord says, "If you will not redeem it, you shall break its neck," He is telling us that if we do not receive our redemption by the sacrifice of Jesus Christ, our neck is going to get broken, we are going to be cut off and destroyed. Jesus is saying, "There's no way to the Father except through Me, by My body, My blood, My sacrifice."

> Now, it shall be that when your son asks of you in time to come, saying, What is this? you shall say to him, By strength of hand the Lord brought us out from Egypt, from the house of bondage. And it came to pass, that when Pharaoh would hardly let us go, that the Lord slew all the firstborn in the land of Egypt, both all the firstborn of man, and the firstborn of beast. Therefore, I sacrifice unto the Lord all that openeth the womb, being males, but all the firstborn of my sons I redeem. (Exod. 13:14-15)

The redeemed firstborn of the family is to live a life unto the Lord. He is to be a picture of Christ for the rest of the family, a perfect example for them to follow. If the eldest son sins, it is the tendency of the other brothers to follow his example of wrong living. It is his responsibility to live an upright life so he won't cause his brothers to stumble.

> And it shall be for a sign upon your hand, and for frontlets between your eyes, for by strength of hand the Lord brought us forth out of Egypt.
>
> And it came to pass, when Pharaoh had let the people go, that God led them not by the way of the land of the Philistines, although the land of the Philistines was near, for God said, Lest peradventure the people now repent when they see war, and they return to Egypt. (Exod. 13:16-17)

God did not bring the Israelites by the shortest way into the promised land, because they would have had to fight the Philistines and perhaps they would have become discouraged and said, "Let's go back to Egypt."

But God led the people around about by the way of the wilderness by the Red Sea. And the children of Israel went up armed out of the land of Egypt. (Exod. 13:18)

The Israelites did not go up out of Egypt unarmed. There were over six hundred thousand men who were armed, able-bodied, equipped for war. This shows us where their faith and trust were —not in God's deliverance but in their own might.

And Moses took the bones of Joseph with him, for Joseph had strictly sworn the children of Israel, saying, Surely God will be with you, and you must carry my bones away from here when you leave Egypt. (Exod. 13:19)

Joseph had believed the word of the Lord, that in due time, after the four hundred years of bondage, the Lord would deliver His people. He had charged his brothers, saying, "Do not leave my bones in Egypt. *When* you leave—not *if* you leave—take my bones with you." And Moses was obedient to the oath that the children of Israel took (Gen. 50:25), and he carried the bones of Joseph with him.

And they took their journey from Succoth, and encamped at Etham, in the edge of the wilderness.

And the Lord went before them by day in a pillar of cloud to lead them along the way. And by night, He went before them in a pillar of fire to give them light, that they might go by day and night. And the pillar of cloud by day, and the pillar of fire by night departed not from before the people. (Exod. 13:20-22)

Jesus Christ Himself was the pillar of cloud by day, and the light of His Holy Spirit, the *shekinah* glory of the Lord, gave them light by night and led them in the way.

Notice that the Israelites did not *wander* in the wilderness for forty years; they were *led* in the wilderness for forty years until the last of the rebels died. The pillar of cloud and the pillar of fire stayed with them.

And when the pillar of cloud descended and it stayed, they did not move, because they knew the Lord was saying, "Stay." When He moved, they moved. There was no other way to go. He would never leave them nor forsake them until He had accomplished all that He purposed to do in their lives. And the same promise holds true for us today. He says, "I'll never leave you nor forsake you. Abide in Me, and I will abide in you. Don't think you're going to escape from Me until I have finished the work I have begun in you."

> And the Lord spoke unto Moses, by the Logos, by Jesus Christ Himself, saying, Speak unto the children of Israel, that they turn back and encamp before Pihahiroth, between Migdol and the sea, before Baal-zephon. Over against it shall you encamp by the sea. (Exod. 14:1-2)

No sooner had the Israelites begun their march than the Lord checked it. What was going on? They began to say in their hearts, "Hey! What is this? We've just escaped after four hundred years, and now He's telling us to turn back? He's going to let all those miracles go to waste? What kind of general is our God, telling us to turn back where we came from? It doesn't make sense!"

What if Pharaoh decided to pursue them? His horses and chariots could very easily overtake a multitude of three to four and a half million people going at a very slow pace.

And that was exactly what was about to happen. But the Lord had His reasons. God said,

> For Pharaoh will say of the children of Israel, They are entangled in the land. The desert has shut them in. They're not acquainted with it.
>
> I will harden Pharaoh's heart that he will follow after them, and I will get Me honor and glory upon Pharaoh and all his host, and the Egyptians will know that I am the Lord. And the people of Israel did so. (Exod. 14:3-4)

Even after the death of their firstborn, the Egyptians didn't hold fast to their belief that it was the Lord who had brought the plagues upon them. They had not yet learned in their hearts that He is God of the entire universe, so He would have to teach them yet one more time.

And it was told the king of Egypt that the people were fled. (Exod. 14:5a)

Pharaoh himself had kicked them out, but they hadn't said goodbye. He still had it in his mind that they were going to return one of these days, after going into the wilderness a three days' journey to sacrifice unto the Lord.

All the time, Pharaoh's magicians and sorcerers were telling him that the Israelites were never going to return, that they were gone for good. That bothered him, because if there were no slaves in Egypt, who would build cities for him?

And the heart of Pharaoh and his servants was changed toward the people and they said, What is this thing that we have done, that we have let Israel go from serving us?

He made ready his chariots, and he took his army with him, and he took six hundred chosen chariots and all the other chariots of Egypt, and captains over them.

And the Lord hardened the heart of Pharaoh, king of Egypt, and he pursued after the children of Israel, for the children of Israel went out with a high hand. (Exod. 14:5b-8)

That they went out "with a high hand" means that they went out confidently, boldly, and fearlessly.

And the Egyptians pursued after them, all the horses and chariots of Pharaoh, his horsemen, his army. They overtook them encamped by the sea beside Pihahiroth in front of Baal-zephon. (Exod. 14:9)

This is a landmark today, a tower in Migdol. The children of Israel were encamped exactly where the Lord told them to be when they were overtaken by the Egyptian army.

And when Pharaoh drew very close, the children of Israel lifted up their eyes and beheld the Egyptians marching after them, and they were sore afraid and cried out unto the Lord. (Exod. 14:10)

There were only six hundred chosen chariots and a few other chariots following them, against three to four and a half million people, and yet the Israelites were afraid. Their cry to the Lord was not a cry for help, it was a loud complaining to Him. And after they had complained to the Lord for a while, they turned to Moses and chewed him out.

> And they said to Moses, What's the matter, Moses? Is it because there were not enough graves in Egypt that you have brought us out here to die in this stinking wilderness? Wherefore have you dealt thus with us, to bring us out from Egypt? (Exod. 14:11)

They were giving Moses all the blame now. "How come you dragged us out of Egypt when we had it so good there?" they shouted at him.

> Did we not tell you while we were still there in captivity, Leave us alone that we may serve the Egyptians? For it would have been far better for us to serve the Egyptians than to die in this wilderness. (Exod. 14:12)

When they stopped griping long enough to catch their breath, the Holy Spirit descended upon Moses with the message from the Lord to the people of Israel. And Moses said unto the people,

> Fear ye not, stand still, and see the salvation of the Lord, which He will work for you today, for the Egyptians you have seen today, you shall never see again. The Lord will fight for you, and you shall hold and have your peace. (Exod. 14:13-14)

That's God's message to us today, no matter what test we are facing: "Stand still and see the salvation of the Lord. I, the Lord, will fight for you. It's not your battle, it's My battle. It's not your burden, it's My burden. It's not your circumstance, it's My circumstance. And the enemy who is among you today is not yours, but Mine.

"Give your burdens to Me, and I'll carry them for you. I've already done it on the cross of Calvary, so why should you be burdened? Bring your burden to Me, and I'll lift it from you completely and give you rest. And the enemy that you see today, you will never see again if you trust in Me, the Lord."

> And the Lord said to Moses, How come you're crying to Me? (Exod. 14:15a)

The minute the people of Israel complained to Moses, he knew

80

who had all the answers. He knew who was still in charge. But the Lord had given Moses the power and authority to act in His name. He wanted Moses to use the authority He had given to him. ''I have given you the gift of power and authority,'' He reminded Moses. ''Use it. Don't cry unto Me.'' And God said to Moses,

Tell the people of Israel to go forward. (Exod. 14:15b)

But how could they go forward? They were smack up against the Red Sea. They didn't have any canoes or sailboats. First they were told to turn back. Now they were facing the Red Sea, and the Lord said, ''Tell the people of Israel to move forward.''

It was preposterous. The men and teenagers might be able to get somewhere by swimming, but they had women and children with them. And there were lots of little kids still in diapers. Some of them were eating their Pablum, but God said, ''Tell the people to go forward.'' And that wasn't all He told them. There was more to His instructions than just that. ''After they move forward,'' God said,

Lift up your rod by faith and stretch out your hand over the sea, and divide it, and the children of Israel shall go through the midst of the sea on dry ground. (Exod. 14:16)

God was going to work an amazing miracle through the obedience of His servant Moses, but first, the people would have to take a step of faith. It is the same way with us today. If we want a miracle from God, we have to take a step of faith to show Him we are ready to receive what He has for us.

If we want to be healed of a physical affliction, we've got to step forward and draw nigh unto the Lord. He says, ''You draw nigh unto Me, and I'll draw nigh unto you. You come to Me, and I'll come to you. You take the first step of faith, believing Me for who I am, trusting Me for My promises, and I'll never disappoint you.''

The people of Israel didn't have time to make excuses or to argue, because Pharaoh's chariots were closing in on them. They had to move out into the deep water, whether they could swim or not. They had to move by faith, trusting that God would move when Moses lifted up his rod. They had to believe the waters would be divided so they could walk through on dry land. The alternative

81

was to get run over by the Egyptian horses and chariots.

Several years ago, a woman sent an article to the *Reader's Digest* reporting that science had just found that it was the shallow Reed Sea and not the deep Red Sea that the people of Israel crossed. Her argument was that crossing the Reed Sea wouldn't take any miracle at all, since it was only three and a half to four feet deep.

But my Bible says "Red Sea" very distinctly. And later a Spirit-filled Christian woman sent a letter to the *Reader's Digest*, saying, "Praise God if it was the Reed Sea. Can you imagine all those horses and chariots of Pharaoh drowning in three and a half feet of water?" Praise the Lord that He always has a witness to testify to the truth for Him!

> And the Lord said, And I, behold, I will harden the hearts of the Egyptians, and they shall go in after them, and I will get Me honor upon Pharaoh, upon all his host, his chariots, and his horsemen. And the Egyptians shall know that I am the Lord, when I have gotten Me honor and glory over Pharaoh, his chariots, and his horsemen. And the Angel of the Lord who went before the camp of Israel removed from before them and went behind them. (Exod. 14:17-19a)

The Angel of the Lord, the Redeeming Angel, Jesus Christ Himself, was leading them in the pillar of cloud. They had been following the Angel of the Lord. But now He removed Himself from in front of them and put Himself behind them to put a separation between the camp of the saved and the camp of the unsaved.

> And the pillar of cloud removed from before them and stood behind them, coming between the camp of Egypt and the camp of Israel. It was a cloud and darkness in the camp of Egypt, yet He gave light by night to the Israelites. And the one camp did not come near the other camp the whole night.

> And Moses stretched out his hand over the sea, and the Lord caused the sea to go back by a strong east wind all that night, and made the sea dry land, and the waters were divided. And the children of Israel went into the midst of the

sea upon the dry ground, and the waters were a wall to them
on their right hand, and on their left. (Exod. 14:19b-22)

If the waters had not been made as a wall of divine protection on
their right hand and on their left hand, the Egyptians could have
attacked them on either side. But with the walls of water, the only
way to attack them was to go in behind them, following them into
the midst of the sea. But the Lord was behind the Israelites as a rear
guard, taking care of the enemy all by Himself.

The Egyptians pursued. They went in after them into the
midst of the sea, even all Pharaoh's horses, his chariots, and
his horsemen. And it came to pass in the morning watch, that
the Lord looked down upon the host of the Egyptians through
the pillar of fire (through His Holy Spirit), and through the
pillar of cloud (through Jesus Christ), and He discomfited the
host of the Egyptians. (Exod. 14:23-24)

The Lord threw the Egyptians into utter confusion. The clouds
brought forth water, the skies sent out a sound. The arrows of the
Lord flew abroad at the Egyptians. Thunder and a ferocious
whirlwind hit the Egyptian army. A hurricane raging with tornado
force struck mercilessly at the Egyptians, amidst a darkness lit only
by the blinding glare of lightning as the Lord looked upon them
from black skies. The earth trembled and shook. "But You did
lead Your people like a flock by the hand of Moses and Aaron,"
David wrote (Ps. 77:20).

And the Lord took off the wheels of the chariots of the
Egyptians, making them drive heavily. (Exod. 14:25a)

The Egyptians were further hindered in their pursuit because the
lightning struck their chariot wheels and made them fall off. The
Egyptians were falling down and killing one another in confusion
as the terror of the Lord fell upon them.

No person of the children of Israel laid a hand upon the
Egyptians, only the Lord, that He might be glorified, that the
whole world would know for all eternity that He is the only one
worthy to receive honor, praise, and glory. He, the Lord Jesus
Christ. Hallelujah!

And the Egyptians said, Let us flee from the face of Israel, for the Lord fights for them against the Egyptians. (Exod. 14:25b)

And the Lord is still fighting for Israel against the Egyptians and against all the rest of the world that oppresses them. God has already fulfilled His promise that He spoke by the Holy Spirit through the prophet Isaiah eight hundred years before Jesus Christ:

Who has heard such a thing? Who has seen such a thing? Shall a land be born in one day? Or shall a nation be brought forth in a moment? For as soon as Zion was in labor she brought forth her children. (Isa. 66:8)

God had promised that there was coming a day when He would restore His people, Israel, to the land that He promised their forefathers. He fulfilled the promise of Isaiah 66:8 on May 15, 1948, when Israel came into existence as an independent nation.

God is always faithful to His word. We may break our covenant, but He never breaks His.

Then the Lord said unto Moses, Stretch out your hand over the sea that the waters may come back again upon the Egyptians, upon their chariots and horsemen. And Moses stretched forth his hand over the sea, and the sea returned to its strength when the morning appeared. And the Egyptians fled against it. And the Lord overthrew the Egyptians in the midst of the sea. And the waters returned and covered the chariots, the horsemen, even all the hosts of Pharaoh that went in after them. There remained not so much as one of them. (Exod. 14:26-28)

Every one of the Egyptians who went into the Red Sea was destroyed by the Lord, even the mighty Pharaoh (Ps. 136:15). The Lord's word came to pass exactly as He told it to Moses. The enemy that was before him that day, he would never see alive again. In the same way, every Christian has complete victory in Jesus Christ over all the circumstances in his life. We may not see the victory at this moment, but it is ours just the same because Jesus has assured us of victory. "I have overcome the world," He said, and He overcame it for us. All we have to do is to lift up our hands and start praising Him for the victory over the very circumstance in which we find ourselves. We can praise Him for the trial we are going through right now; we can praise Him for the lack we have right now. And when we are obedient to praise Him, we see that He keeps His word to supply all of our needs according to His riches in glory.

Jesus says to us, over and over again, "I have come into this world to give you life, and to give it to you more abundantly—spiritually, physically, mentally, and financially. It's all yours. Just reach up and touch the hem of My garment and you've got it. All it takes is a little faith, about the size of a grain of mustard seed. Those who have the faith of a tiny child will enter into My kingdom."

The victory of the Lord over the Egyptians was a total victory. They were all destroyed in the Red Sea.

But the children of Israel walked upon dry land in the midst of the sea. And the waters were unto them a wall on their right hand and on their left. Thus the Lord saved Israel that day out of the hand of the Egyptians. And Israel saw the Egyptians dead upon the seashore. And Israel saw the great work which the Lord did upon the Egyptians, and the people feared the Lord, and they believed in the Lord, and even in His servant, Moses. (Exod. 14:29-31)

When the Lord saved Israel, it was not a victory in which they could take pride for anything they had done. He had done it all. Unlike other nations that have thrown off the yoke of slavery, neither Israel nor its leader, Moses, could claim any merit or glory for the victory. The victory was given by the Lord and granted by the Lord.

11

Food and Water in the Wilderness
(EXODUS 15—17:7)

The fifteenth chapter of Exodus begins with a song of praise and thanksgiving which is notable for its poetic fire, its vivid imagery, and its quick movement. It gives remarkable expression to the mingled horror, triumph, and gratitude that the host of Israel had lived through during the fateful hours when they were in sight of Pharaoh's pursuing hosts. The sabbath on which this song is sung in the synagogue is called a sabbath of praise.

Even today, however, the Hebrew people observe the Passover in a state of semi-mourning because of a Hebrew oral tradition handed down from the time of Moses. The story goes like this:

It seems that the heavenly hosts were praising and thanking God with great joy for the deliverance of the Israelites from Egypt. And the Lord turned around to the angels and asked, "Why are you praising Me so joyfully?" They answered, "Because You've just delivered Your children Israel." And the Lord rebuked the heavenly host, saying, "Are not the Egyptians My children also? I am sorry that they did not come to salvation. I am sorry that they did not hear My word and that they had to be destroyed."

This picture of God our Father tells us that He loves each and every one of us. He's no respecter of persons. We are all His

87

children. And He is sorry when He has to spank one of us.

Nevertheless, Moses composed the song, and the people of Israel joined him in praising God. There was musical accompaniment with male and female choruses for the world's oldest song of national triumph, a hymn of thanksgiving and praise unto the Lord.

> Then Moses and the children of Israel sang this song unto the Lord, saying, I will sing unto the Lord, for He is highly exalted. The horse and his rider He has thrown into the sea. (Exod. 15:1)

In this verse, four Hebrew words show us the complete ruin of the military power of Egypt. The mainstay of its strength—horses, chariots, and riders—was utterly destroyed by divine might.

Then Moses sang,

> The Lord is my strength and my song, and He is become my salvation. This Jesus is my God, and I will glorify Him, my father's God also, and I will exalt Him. (Exod. 15:2)

To me, the most beautiful word in Hebrew is *salvation,* because that is the name of Jesus. Moses saw Jesus. He knew Him. Moses would exalt Him, he would lift Him up, and Jesus later promised, "If I be lifted up, I will draw all mankind unto Me."

> The Lord is a man of war. The Lord is His name. Pharaoh's chariots and his host has He cast into the sea, and his chosen captains are sunk in the Red Sea. The deeps cover them. They went down into the depths like a stone. Your right hand, O Lord, is glorious in power. Your right hand, O Lord, dashed in pieces the enemy. In the greatness of Your excellency, You overthrew them that rose up against You. You did send forth Your wrath, and it consumed them as stubble. (Exod. 15:3-7)

When Pharaoh and the Egyptians rose up against the Israelites, they lifted themselves up against God. Pharaoh put himself in a higher position than the Lord when he said, "Who is this God of the Israelites? I don't acknowledge Him. I'm the supreme power in the world." Any man who so exalts himself has to be brought low, and Pharaoh was brought low, all right.

Moses continued to sing of the victory of the Lord:

With the blast of Your nostrils the waters were piled up as a wall on the left and a wall on the right. The floods stood upright as a heap, and the deeps were congealed in the heart of the sea. The enemy said, I will pursue, I will overtake, I will divide the spoil. My lust shall be satisfied upon them. I will draw my sword, and my hand shall destroy them. But You did blow with Your wind. The sea covered them. They sank as lead in the mighty waters.

Who is like unto thee, O Lord, among the mighty? Who is like unto thee, glorious in holiness, fearful in praises, doing wonders? (Exod. 15:8-11)

Glorious in holiness means "exalted in the majesty of the holiness which is the distinguishing attribute of our God." He is a just and a holy God. *Fearful in praises* means "revered in praises." All the earth revered Him in a song of praise and thanksgiving for His acts were praiseworthy. As all people come to see what Jesus has done through all the history of mankind, they will be awed by all the miracles for which His people praise Him.

You stretched out Your right hand, and the earth swallowed them up. You in Your love have led the people that You have redeemed, that You have purchased. (Exod. 15:12-13a)

God had redeemed them by a type of Christ, by the picture of the true Lamb of God who would come into the world in the future. He had just redeemed them by the blood of the lamb that they sacrificed, the lamb whose blood they put on the lintel and the sideposts of each door. They were obedient to the Lord, and so He had redeemed them.

You have guided them in Your strength to Your holy habitation. All the peoples of the earth have heard; they tremble. Pangs of terror have taken hold on the Philistines. Then were the chiefs of Edom afraid; the mighty men of Moab, trembling takes hold upon them. All the inhabitants of Canaan are melted away.

Fear and dread shall fall upon them. By the greatness of Thine arm they shall be as still as a stone, O Lord, till Thy people pass over which Thou hast purchased.

You will bring them in, You will plant them in the mountain of Your inheritance, the place, O Lord, which You have made for Yourself to dwell in, the sanctuary, O Lord, which Your hands have established. The Lord shall reign for ever and ever. (Exod. 15:13b-18)

God is still sitting upon His throne. Nothing can happen in this world without His divine permission, because nobody has any power over the Lord Jesus Christ. He is victorious, and He is triumphant.

For the horses of Pharaoh went in with his chariots, with his horsemen into the sea, and the Lord brought back the waters of the sea upon them, but the children of Israel walked on dry land in the midst of the sea.

Then Miriam the prophetess, the sister of Aaron, took a timbrel in her hand, and all the women went out after her with timbrels and with dances. And Miriam sang unto them, saying, Sing ye to the Lord, for He is highly exalted; the horse and his rider has He thrown into the sea. (Exod. 15:19-21)

Miriam is the first prophetess mentioned in the Bible, and she led the women in singing and dancing in the Spirit, praising God.

Then Moses led Israel onward from the Red Sea, and they went out into the wilderness of Shur. And they went three days (thirty-three miles) into the wilderness, and they found no water. When they came to Marah, they could not drink of the waters of Marah, for they were bitter; therefore was the name of it called Marah, which means bitter.

And the people murmured against Moses, screaming, What shall we drink? (Exod. 15:22-24)

The people were mad at Moses again, and they were loud in their complaints against him. "How come you brought us out here to die of thirst?" they yelled at him. "Why didn't you leave us back where we told you to leave us?"

They had just gone through the Red Sea and seen their enemies thoroughly defeated. They had just sung a glorious hymn of praise and thanksgiving, but when they came upon bitter water, they dug out their old grievances against Moses.

Do you think that perhaps the Lord might give you and me some bitter water to drink once in a while, just to see what we will do? Will we praise Him and thank Him for that bitter water? Or will we murmur and complain against Him?

When the people murmured against Moses, he cried unto the Lord again. It was getting to be a habit with him.

So he cried unto the Lord, and the Lord showed him a tree, and he cast it into the waters, and the waters were made sweet. (Exod. 15:25a)

That tree is a picture of the Branch, Jesus Christ. Just as the tree was cast into the bitter water, making it sweet, so Jesus heals and redeems all that touches Him. When we invite His presence by praising and thanking Him for what is bitter to us, He sweetens it for us.

And there He, the Lord, made for them a statute and an ordinance, and there He proved them. And He said, If you will diligently listen to the voice of the Lord your God, and will do that which is right in His eyes, and you will listen to and obey His commandments, and keep all of His statutes, I will put none of the diseases upon you, which I have put on the Egyptians; for I am the Lord Thy God that healeth thee. (Exod. 15:25b-26)

We can claim this promise of healing in every area of our lives. All we have to do is to be obedient unto the Lord.

And they came to Elim, where there were twelve springs of water, and seventy palm trees. And they camped there by the waters. (Exod. 15:27)

The twelve springs of water represented the twelve tribes of Israel and the twelve disciples of Jesus Christ. The seventy palm trees represented the seventy followers Jesus sent out.

And they took their journey from Elim, and all the congregation of Israel came unto the wilderness of Sin, which is between Elim and Sinai, on the fifteenth day of the second month after their departure out of the land of Egypt. And the whole congregation of the children of Israel murmured against Moses and against Aaron in wilderness. And the children of Israel said unto them, Would to God that we had died by the hand of the Lord in the land of Egypt when we sat by the fleshpots and ate bread to the full, for you have brought us forth into this stinking wilderness to kill this whole assembly with hunger. (Exod. 16:1-3)

Corned beef and pastrami and lox and bagels are good, but we need to remember that man does not live by bread alone, but by every word that proceeds out of the mouth of God.

When the Israelites left Egypt, they left with great herds of cattle and flocks. The only reason they could be crying with hunger now would be that they had picked up the abomination of the Egyptians. Instead of using some of their flocks and herds for food, they were worshiping them!

Then said the Lord unto Moses, Behold, I will cause to rain bread from heaven for you, and the people shall go out and gather a day's portion every day, that I may prove them, whether they will walk in My Scripture, in My law, or not. (Exod. 16:4)

The Lord said, "I will send bread from heaven for *you,* Moses, because you are My prophet, you are My priest.

Moses and Aaron were among His priests, and Samuel was among those who called upon His name; they called upon the Lord, and He answered them. He spoke to them in the pillar of cloud; they kept His testimonies, and the statute that He gave them. (Ps. 89: 6-7 TAB)

And the people may share in that bread, but they are to gather only enough for one day at a time and not try to save anything for tomorrow." The Lord would see whether or not they would be obedient to Him this time.

It shall come to pass that on the sixth day they shall prepare to bring in twice as much as they gather daily. (Exod. 16:5)

God was going to supply a double portion of the bread from heaven on the sixth day because the following day was to be kept as a sabbath, a day of desistance unto the Lord, a day of ceasing from all labor.

And Moses and Aaron said unto all the children of Israel, At evening you shall know that the Lord has brought you out from the land of Egypt. And in the morning, you shall see the glory of the Lord, for He has heard your murmuring, your griping, your complaining against the Lord. For what are we that you murmur against us? (Exod. 16:6-7)

Moses' attitude was that he was absolutely nothing except an instrument of the Lord. There was no point in anyone's griping against him.

And Moses said, When the Lord shall give you in the evening flesh to eat, and in the morning bread to the full, because the Lord has heard your murmurings which you murmur against Him, what are we? Your murmurings are not against us, but they are against the Lord.

And Moses said unto Aaron, Say unto all the congregation of the children of Israel, Come near before the Lord, for He has heard your murmurings. And it came to pass, as Aaron spoke unto the whole congregation of the children of Israel, that they looked toward the wilderness, and behold, the glory of the Lord appeared in the cloud. (Exod. 16:8-10)

In the cloud which was with them, the Israelites actually saw the *shekinah* glory of God, the radiance of the Lord Himself.

And the Lord spake unto Moses, saying, I have heard the murmurings of the children of Israel. Speak unto them, saying, At dusk you shall eat flesh, and in the morning you shall be filled with bread; and you shall know that I am the Lord your God. (Exod. 16:11-12)

"I'm going to give you exactly what you're asking for," God was saying. "I'm going to give you enough rope to hang yourself."

And it came to pass, at evening, that the quails came up and covered the camp; and in the morning, there was a layer of dew around the camp. And when the layer of dew was gone up, behold, upon the face of the wilderness, there lay a fine scalelike thing, as fine as the hoarfrost on the ground. And when the children of Israel saw it, they said to one another, Manna (meaning What is it?), for they knew not what it was.

And Moses said unto them, This is the bread which the Lord has given you to eat. This is the thing which the Lord has commanded, Gather of it every man according to his eating, an omer for every man. According to the number of your persons shall you take it, every man for them that are in his tent. And the children of Israel did so, and some gathered more, and some gathered less. And when they had measured it out with an omer, he that gathered much had nothing left over, and he that gathered little had no lack of anything. They gathered every man according to his eating. (Exod. 16:13-18)

Notice the miracle here. The Lord supplied the exact amount of every need. If a man gathered too little, it multiplied to go all the way. If he gathered too much, it turned into just enough.

And Moses said unto them, Let no man leave of it until the morning. (Exod. 16:19)

This is an important lesson for us. Our faith and trust have to be completely in the Lord. If we trust in ourselves by putting something aside for a day when maybe we think God won't supply our needs, we will be disappointed. But when we trust in His provision, we are never disappointed or put to shame.

Nothwithstanding, they did not listen to Moses, but some of them saved it until the next morning. It bred worms, and it rotted, and Moses was very angry with them. And they gathered it morning by morning, every man according to his eating, for when the sun waxed hot, it melted.

And it came to pass that on the sixth day they gathered twice as much bread, two omers for each person, and all the rulers of the congregation came and told Moses. And he said unto them, This is that which the Lord has spoken. Tomorrow is a solemn rest, a holy sabbath unto the Lord. Bake that which you will bake today, and boil that which you will boil today. All that remains over, lay it up for you to be kept until the morning. (Exod. 16:20-23)

Now another miracle would take place. During the week, when the Lord told them not to save any of it until the next morning, the leftovers brought forth worms and maggots. The manna rotted.

But the extra manna gathered on the sixth day, according to God's commandment, was still fresh and sweet on the sabbath.

Hebrew oral tradition tells us that the manna tasted like whatever you wanted it to be in your mouth, whatever you were hungry for. The manna could be baked, boiled, broiled, or eaten raw. You could do anything you wanted with it. Manna was the only ingredient you needed for a feast with a great variety of flavorful dishes. It was a total miracle—manna from heaven.

The *Midrash Rabbah* on Exodus (p. 303), commenting on Psalm 145:16, says:

'Thou openest Thy hand, and satisfiest every living thing with favour.' It does not say 'every living thing with *food,*' but with *'favour,'* that is, He grants to each one his request. In the millennium, too, God will grant the request of each individual. Should you wonder at this, then see what He has done for Israel in this world, when He brought down for them the manna, in which all kinds of flavours lodged, so that each Israelite could taste therein anything he particularly liked, for it is written, *These forty years the Lord thy God hath been with thee; thou hast lacked nothing* (Deut. 2, 7). What is the meaning of *'thou hast lacked nothing'* (dabar). When a man desired anything special to eat, he had only to say 'I wish I had a fat capon to eat', and the morsel of manna in his mouth immediately acquired the taste of fat capon. They had only to say the word (dabar) and the Lord performed their will. R. Abba said: They were even spared the utterance of their wish, for God fulfilled the thought still in their heart and they tasted their heart's desire. A proof that it was so? For Ezekiel says, *My bread also which I gave thee, fine flour, and oil, and honey, wherewith I fed thee* (XVI,19.) One verse tells us, BEHOLD, I WILL CAUSE TO RAIN DOWN BREAD FROM HEAVEN FOR YOU, and another verse says, *And the taste of it was like* wafers made with honey (Ex. XVI, 31), and yet another, *And the taste of it was as the taste of a* cake baked with oil (Num. XI, 8). How do you reconcile these three verses?—The young tasted therein the taste of bread, the old the taste of honey, and

95

the babies the taste of oil.

Later, Jesus would come and say, "Your forefathers ate manna in the wilderness and died. But he who eats of Me, Jesus, the One who is sent by the Lord, he will never die. I am the Bread of Life from everlasting to everlasting."

And they laid it up until the morning as Moses commanded, and it did not rot, neither was there any worm found within it. And Moses said, Eat that today, for today is a sabbath unto the Lord. Today you will not find it in the field. Six days you shall gather it, but on the seventh day, which is the sabbath, there shall be none. (Exod. 16:24-26)

There would be no need for more manna on the seventh day, because the Lord had already supplied their needs in advance. But what happened?

It came to pass on the seventh day that there went out some of the people to gather the manna and they found none. And the Lord said to Moses, How long do you refuse to keep My commandments and My law? See, the Lord has given you the sabbath, therefore He gives you on the sixth day bread for two days. Let every man stay in his place. Let no man go out of his place on the seventh day. So the people rested on the seventh day. And the house of Israel called the bread manna. It was like coriander seed, white; and it tasted like wafers made with honey. (Exod. 16:27-31)

The Israelites ate manna for forty years. In it, the Lord supplied every single thing that they needed in their system. It was a balanced diet, containing every vitamin, every protein, everything necessary for human health. Perfect nutrition, resulting in perfect health, came from a little wafer that tasted like it was made from honey.

The other miracle of the manna was the fact that it was sent by the Lord as a picture of the Trinity: first came down a layer of dew, then the manna, then another layer of dew for protection, giving us a picture of the Father, the Son, and the Holy Spirit.

And Moses said, This is the thing which the Lord has commanded: Let an omer full of manna be kept throughout your generations, that they may see the bread wherewith I fed you in the wilderness, when I brought you forth from the land of Egypt.

And Moses said unto Aaron, Take a jar, and put an omer full of manna therein, and lay it up before the Lord, to be kept throughout your generations. As the Lord commanded Moses, so Aaron laid it up before the Testimony to be kept.

And the children of Israel did eat the manna forty years, until they came to a land inhabited. And they did eat the manna until they came unto the borders of the land of Canaan. Now an omer is the tenth part of an ephah. (Exod. 16:32-36)

The jar of manna was later kept in the ark of the covenant. And it did not go bad. There were no worms. It did not rot. It stayed in the ark of the covenant with the rod of Aaron, with the broken tables of the Ten Commandments, and with the new tables until Nebuchadnezzar's destruction of the temple in Jerusalem in the year 586 B.C. After that, the manna disappeared.

The Book of Revelation tells us that the ark is up in heaven. But the people of Israel are still looking for the ark of the covenant down here on earth because they don't realize that our ark of the true covenant of God has come in Jesus Christ.

And all the congregation of the children of Israel journeyed from the wilderness of Sin, by stages, according to the commandment of the Lord, and encamped in Rephidim. But there was no water for the people to drink. Therefore, the people spoke with Moses and said, Give us water that we may drink. And Moses said, Why are you striving with me? Why are you fighting with me? And why do you continually keep on trying the patience of the Lord? (Exod. 17:1-2)

"When you come against me," Moses said, "you come against the Lord. When you come against the Lord, you are coming against the One who is supreme, the One who has promised to take care of you. You don't have to argue with Him, asking for water. If you ask in love, He will give you water."

And the people there continued to thirst for water. And the people murmured against Moses and said, Why have you brought us up out of Egypt, to kill us and our cattle with thirst? And Moses cried unto the Lord, saying, What shall I do with this people? They're almost ready to stone me.

And the Lord said unto Moses, Pass on before the people, and as you pass on before the people, take with you the elders of Israel and your rod, wherewith you smote the river. Take that in your hand, and go. And behold, I, the Lord, will stand before you upon the rock in Horeb. You shall smite the rock, and there shall come water out of it, that the people may drink. And Moses did so in the sight of the elders of Israel. (Exod. 17:3-6)

Every elder, every prince of every tribe was there. And they all saw the miracle.

And the name of the place was called Massah (proof) and Meribah (contention) because of the striving of the children of Israel, and because they tried the patience of the Lord, saying, Is the Lord among us or not? (Exod. 17:7)

After all the miracles they had seen, they were still unfaithful and blind enough to ask, "Is the Lord among us or not?"

Massah means that they wanted proof, and *Meribah* means that they murmured against the Lord. They were going to continue to murmur and scream to the Lord until they were persuaded that He was really among them.

But the minute they put the Lord to the test, the minute they tried to prove Him, He kept His promise. He gave them water. He will always give us living water when we ask Him.

12

Moses' Helpers—in Battle and in Court

(EXODUS 17:8—19:2)

Then came Amalek, and fought with Israel in Rephidim. And Moses said unto Joshua, Choose us out men, and go out, and fight with Amalek. Tomorrow I will stand on the top of the hill with the rod of God in my hand. (Exod. 17:8-9)

The Amalekites were descendants of Esau, the brother of Jacob. They were a tribe of predators who had their home in the desert of Israel. But a nomadic tribe is quite capable of raiding an enemy some distance from home. During the battle, Moses would stand on top of the hill, interceding with God, while the youthful Joshua would be the general in charge of the army.

So Joshua did as Moses had said to him and fought with Amalek, and Moses, and Aaron, and Hur went up to the top of the hill. And it came to pass that when Moses held up his hand, Israel prevailed, but when he let down his hand, Amalek prevailed. (Exod. 17:10-11)

As long as our hands are lifted up in praise, in worship, and in thanksgiving, no matter what the circumstances, the Lord and His people prevail. But the minute we put our hands down and stop praising God, the enemy overcomes us. In all things we have to praise God and give thanks to Jesus Christ.

But Moses' hands were heavy, and they kept getting heavier. And the other men took a stone and put it under him, and he sat thereon. And Aaron and Hur held up his hands, one on one side and one on the other side. And his hands were steady until the going down of the sun. (Exod. 17:12)

Just as Aaron and Hur held up the hands of Moses, you and I are to constantly hold up the hands of our pastors in prayer. Pastors get tired. Their hands get heavy.

And Joshua discomfited Amalek and his people with the edge of the sword. And the Lord said unto Moses, Write this for a memorial in the book. Rehearse it in the ears of Joshua, that I will utterly blot out the remembrance of Amalek from under heaven. (Exod. 17:13-14)

In every generation, the Lord would come against Amalek, because the descendants of Amalek were always coming against God's people, the people of Israel. Haman, in the time of Esther, was a descendant of Amalek. He got blotted out. Agag was a descendant of Amalek. In obedience unto the Lord, Samuel killed him. In the time of Jesus, Herod killed over two thousand innocent babies, trying to destroy the Christ child. He was a descendant of Amalek, and he, too, was blotted out. Haman, Agag and Herod found out that no man can come against God's people and live. But as long as God's people turn to the Lord in repentance, in prayer, and in supplication, the Lord will hear them. He will save, He will heal, He will deliver.

So Moses built an altar unto the Lord, and he called the name of it Jehovah-nissi, which means in the Hebrew, Jehovah the Lord is my banner. (Exod. 17:15)

The Lord's banner over me is love, and when that banner is over me, I am divinely protected by the grace of Jesus Christ, the mercy of the Lord. Jehovah is also my witness, to stand between me and all my enemies.

And Moses said, Because theirs is a hand against the throne of the Lord, the Lord will have war with Amalek from generation to generation. (Exod. 17:16)

In the Book of Revelation, Amalek is Babylon. Today, the

physical Babylon is gone, but the spiritual Babylon is still with us, Amalek, the spiritual harlot. And in this generation, the Lord continues to have war with Amalek, just as He said He would.

Now Jethro, the priest of Midian, Moses' father-in-law, heard of all that God had done for Moses and for Israel His people, and how the Lord had brought them up out of Egypt, out of bondage, out of slavery. And Jethro, Moses' father-in-law, took Zipporah, Moses' wife, after Moses had sent her back to her father, and he took her two sons, of whom the name of one was Gershom, for Moses said, I have been a stranger in a strange land. And the name of the other one was Eliezer, for the God of my father, said Moses, was my help, and He delivered me from the sword of Pharaoh. And Jethro, Moses' father-in-law, came with Moses' sons and his wife unto Moses into the wilderness where he was encamped at the mount of God. (Exod. 18:1-5)

A year and a half had elapsed from the time Zipporah took the kids and went home to daddy, and now daddy was bringing them back.

And Jethro said in a message to Moses, I your father-in-law am coming unto you, and your wife, and her two sons with her.

Moses went out to meet his father-in-law, and he bowed down and kissed him. They asked each other of their welfare and they came into the tent. Moses told his father-in-law all that the Lord had done unto Pharaoh and the Egyptians for Israel's sake, and all the travail that had come upon them by the way, and how the Lord had delivered them. And Jethro rejoiced for all the goodness which the Lord had done to Israel, in that He had delivered them out of the hand of the Egyptians.

And Jethro said, Blessed be the Lord who has delivered you out of the hand of the Egyptians, out of the hand of Pharaoh, who has delivered the people from under the hand of the Egyptians. Now I know that the Lord is greater than all gods, yes, in the very thing in which they took pride He showed Himself infinitely superior to all their gods. (Exod. 18:6-11)

Moses was a very good witness for the Lord. He told his father-in-law all that took place in the year when the Lord brought plague after plague upon Egypt. In witnessing to his father-in-law, Moses won him to the Lord. Jethro realized, from Moses' account of all that had happened, that God is greater than all other gods, that there's only one Lord, only one God, only one King in the universe. Jethro forsook his idolatry, became a proselyte to Judaism, and accepted the living God as his Deliverer, his Redeemer, his Healer, and his Savior.

So Jethro, Moses' father-in-law, took a burnt offering and sacrifices for God. And Aaron came, and all the elders of Israel, to eat bread with Moses' father-in-law before God. (Exod. 18:12)

Jethro brought a sin offering, a guilt offering, and a peace offering to God, acknowledging before the elders and before God that he was a sinner, that he was guilty. And the elders led him in a sinner's prayer. He asked God for the forgiveness of his sin, and God was faithful and just to forgive him of his sins. As Jethro offered the burnt offering to the Lord, the heavenly Holy Spirit came down and consumed it. Jethro knew he was a forgiven sinner, accepted by the Lord. After he had brought a peace offering, he walked out rejoicing, knowing that God had made peace with him, and that he had made peace with God.

God's acceptance of an offering by sending down fire from heaven happened in Solomon's experience also:

When Solomon had finished praying, the fire came down from Heaven and consumed the burnt offering and the sacrifices, and the glory of the Lord filled the house. The priests could not enter the house of the Lord, because the glory of the Lord had filled the Lord's house. (2 Chron. 7:1-2)

A footnote in the Amplified Bible has this to say about Solomon's experience:

Young Solomon seems, and doubtless is, utterly sincere as he offers this prayer of which God shows His approval by His miraculous demonstration of His presence, in the next verse It raises the ever-present question, How could Solomon have begun his career like this, and have written his unquestionably divinely inspired books, and yet have fallen eventually into utter defiance of God's will? Not as the result of one false step, as with David, but as the habit of his life for the remainder of his days! Not broken with unspeakable sorrow for his awful sin, as was his penitent father (Ps. 51), but without ever apparently repenting or confessing his awful defiance of God and His explicit commands and warnings, given to Solomon personally (2 Chron. 7:17-22). Possibly in this closing sentence of Solomon's prayer, we detect the fallacy in the young king's thinking. He seems to be saying in substance, "O Lord God, *I am Your responsibility* now; it will be for *You to see that my face does not turn* away from You; and not for my sake, but [since my name is identified with this temple as well as Yours, You must keep my face turned toward You] for Your own sake!" God lost no unnecessary time in attempting to set the young man straight as to whose is the responsibility for sin—in his case specifically (7:12, 17-22). But there is no evidence that Solomon applied it to himself, though he preached a bit to others, he seems to have *considered himself exempt* from obeying God's commands—an attitude which has brought disaster upon every person who has ever taken it, however great, or wise, or rich, or otherwise sufficient.

Then Jethro and the elders broke bread together before God. It was unleavened bread, a symbol of the coming communion of Jesus Christ.

And it came to pass on the next day that Moses sat to judge the people. And the people stood about Moses from the morning until the evening.

And when Moses' father-in-law saw all that he did to the people, he said, What is this thing that you do to the people? Why do you sit by yourself alone, and all the people stand about you from morning until evening?

And Moses said to his father-in-law, Because the people come unto me to inquire of God. And when they have a dispute, it comes unto me, and I judge between a man and his neighbor, and I make known to them the statutes of God and His laws.

And Moses' father-in-law said unto him, The thing that you do is not good. You will surely wear out both yourself and this people that is with you, for the thing is too heavy for you. You are not able to perform it for yourself alone. (Exod. 18:13-18)

Jethro knew that Moses could not possibly bear the pastorate alone with four and a half million people to take care of. If he didn't delegate some authority, Moses would surely wear himself out. Not only that, but the people would get sick and tired of standing in line waiting for their appointment to see him.

Jethro thought he saw a way to handle the situation. He said to Moses,

Listen now unto my voice, and I will give you counsel, and as I give you counsel, the Lord God will be with you. You shall represent the people before God, and you shall bring their causes to God. And you shall teach them the statutes and the laws, and you shall show them the way wherein they must walk, and the work they must do.

Moreover, you shall provide out of all the people able men, such as fear God, men of truth, who hate unjust gain, and you shall place them over thousands, hundreds, fifties, and tens, to be their rulers. Let them judge the people at all seasons. Every great matter they shall bring to you, but every small matter they shall judge themselves, so they shall make it easier for you, and they will bear the burden with you. If you shall do this thing, and God commands you so to do, then you will be able to endure the strain, and all this people also shall go to their places in peace.

So Moses listened to the voice of his father-in-law, and did all that he had told him. And Moses chose able men out of all Israel. He made them heads over the people, rulers of thousands, rulers of hundreds, rulers of fifties, rulers of tens. So they judged the people at all seasons. The hard cases they brought to Moses, but every small matter they judged themselves.

And Moses let his father-in-law depart, and he went his way into his own land. (Exod. 18:19-27)

Following his father-in-law's sound advice, Moses let elders be chosen by the Spirit of the Lord to help him judge the people. It was a good idea, and it worked out, just as Jethro believed it would.

In the third month after the children of Israel had gone forth out of Egypt, that very same day they came into the wilderness of Sinai. And when they had departed from Rephidim, and had come into the wilderness of Sinai, they encamped in the wilderness before the mount. (Exod. 19:1-2)

13

God Speaks to His People

(EXODUS 19:3—20:12)

And Moses went up unto God, and the Lord called down to him out of the mountains, saying, You shall say to the house of Jacob, and tell the children of Israel, You have seen what I did unto the Egyptians and how I bore you on eagles' wings and brought you unto Myself. (Exod. 19:3-4)

The house of Jacob were those who were still moving in arrogance and defiance, still cheating, lying and stealing. The children of Israel were those who had been born again. Moses had two groups with him, those who believed, and those who did not believe. And just as God brought the Israelites to Himself, so Jesus does the very same thing for us. He went to the cross that He might bear us on eagles' wings to Himself. It is by His shed blood that we are enabled to come to Him. And this is what God told Moses to tell the people:

Now therefore, if you will hearken unto My voice, in deed, in truth, and keep My covenant, then you shall be My own treasure from among all the peoples, for all the earth is Mine. And you shall be unto Me a kingdom of priests, and a holy nation. These are the words which you shall speak unto the children of Israel. (Exod. 19:5-6)

Every Israelite was to be a priest unto the living God, a witness for Him, made holy because He is holy.

> And Moses came and called for the elders of the people. He set before them all these words which the Lord commanded him. And all the people answered together, and said, All that the Lord has spoken we will do. And Moses reported these words of the people unto the Lord. And the Lord said unto Moses, Behold, I come unto you in a thick cloud, that the people may hear when I speak to you, and they may also believe you forever. And Moses told the words of the people unto the Lord. (Exod. 19:7-9)

God was making sure that the people would know that Moses wasn't making things up in his own head, but that the Lord had spoken unto him. And Hebrew oral tradition says that when Israel heard the voice of the Lord speaking to Moses out of the cloud, that every generation—past, present, and future—heard the voice of God at the same time. Nobody could have any excuse for saying, "I don't know that God spoke to me." They would know it because they had heard His voice for themselves.

> And the Lord said unto Moses, Go unto the people, and sanctify them today and tomorrow, and let them wash their garments. And let them be ready for the third day, for on the third day, the Lord will come down in the sight of all the people upon Mount Sinai. (Exod. 19:10-11)

God wanted the people to sanctify themselves, to get rid of all the garbage and filth of heathenism and idolatry. He wanted them to be cleansed for the miracle that would take place on the third day when the Lord would come down in their sight. We are reminded that the Lord Jesus Himself was resurrected on the third day, and we want to be ready for Him when He comes again.

> And you shall set bounds for the people round about, saying, Take heed to yourselves, that you go not up in the mount, or touch the border of it. Whosoever touches the mount shall be surely put to death. No hand shall touch him, but he shall surely be stoned or shot through. Whether it be a man or a beast, it shall not live. When the ram's horn sounds long, they

shall come up to the mount.

> And Moses went down from the mount unto the people, and he sanctified the people, and they washed their garments. And he said unto the people, Be ready against the third day, and come not near a woman. (Exod. 19:12-15)

The men of Israel were not to touch their wives for the three days of their preparation for meeting God. Their minds were to be staid on Him and not on their wives, that they might be thoroughly sanctified.

> And it came to pass on the third day when it was morning, there was thundering, lightning, and a thick cloud upon the mount, and the voice of a horn exceedingly loud. And all the people that were in the camp trembled. And Moses brought forth the people out of the camp to meet God. And the people stood at the furthermost part of the mount. (Exod. 19:16-17)

That must have been some introduction. Three to four and a half million people of Israel, and Moses standing there, saying, "People, I want you to meet your living God." And the Lord saying, "How do you do. I'm glad to know you."

> Mount Sinai was wrapped in smoke because the Lord descended on it in fire, and the smoke thereof ascended as the smoke of a furnace, and the whole mount quaked greatly. (Exod. 19:18)

The mountain became like a volcano, and smoke billowed from the top of it. It must have looked like the pictures you've seen of an atomic bomb blast. The Lord had set off a chain reaction of a few atoms to let them know that He is the Lord.

> And when the voice of the horn had waxed louder and louder, Moses spoke and God answered him by a voice. And the Lord came down upon Mount Sinai, to the top of the mount, and the Lord called Moses to the top of the mount, and Moses went up.
>
> And the Lord said unto Moses, Go down and charge the people, lest they break through unto the Lord to gaze, and many of them perish. (Exod. 19:19-21)

If the people of Israel broke through to gaze at the Lord, they would die, because they would not be breaking through in an attitude of worship, but just to satisfy their idle curiosity. It would be a blasphemous act instead of an act of reverent worship.

> Let the priests also, that come near to the Lord, sanctify themselves, lest the Lord break forth against them. (Exod. 19:22)

To sanctify themselves, the priests had to be washed, outwardly and inwardly. They had to be in a state of complete repentance. God is a holy God, and unholiness cannot come in contact with holiness without perishing. When the high priest entered into the holy of holies on the Day of Atonement, if he was not right with the Lord, he would die instantly. Since nobody could enter the holy of holies to take him out, he had a rope tied around his ankle when he entered in. That way, he could be dragged out, if necessary.

> And Moses said to the Lord, The people cannot come up to Mount Sinai, for You did charge us, saying, Set bounds about the mount and sanctify it.
>
> And the Lord said unto him, Go, get yourself down, and you shall come up, you and Aaron with you. But let not the priests and the people break through to come up unto the Lord, lest He, the Lord, break forth upon them. So Moses went down unto the people, and he told them. (Exod. 19:23-25)

Then the people waited for the great pronouncement, which would be the Ten Commandments.

In the Hebrew, the Ten Commandments are called the Ten Living Words. (Speaking of Moses, Luke wrote: "This was the man who at the assembly in the desert intervened between the angel who spoke to him on Mount Sinai and our fathers; he received *living Words* [italics mine] to be given to us" [Acts 7:38 Moffatt].) They're also known as the Decalogue, and they are supreme among the precepts of the Scriptures, both for their far-reaching importance and also on account of the awe-inspiring manner in which they were revealed to the whole nation of Israel.

Thunder, lightning, the sound of rams' horns, and flames of fire enveloping the smoking mountain of Sinai heralded the coming of

110

the majestic voice of God to pronounce the words which from that day to this have been the guide of conduct for much of mankind. In these United States of America, for example, we have three billion laws to uphold the Ten Living Words God gave us at Mount Sinai.

The revelation of the Ten Commandments was a remarkable event in the history of humanity. It was the birth hour of the religion of the Spirit where mankind would move in the Spirit of God and not in the flesh. That birth was destined in time to illumine the souls and order the lives of all men, not just the people of Israel. The Decalogue is a sublime summary of human duties binding upon all of mankind, a summary unequaled for its simplicity and solemn comprehensiveness. The commandments are a divine epitome of the fundamentals of Israel's creed and life and of Christianity's creed and life.

These commandments are written on the walls of synagogues and churches all over the world. They will never cease, and their empire will never cease. Their prophetic cry is truth, and the word of our God shall stand forever.

The first five commandments or statutes show us our proper relationship with God, a vertical relationship. They show us how to get along with God our Father, God the Son, and God the Holy Spirit. The last five commandments deal with horizontal relationships, how men are to get along with one another. Putting the vertical and the horizontal together, we come up with a cross on which we are to die to self in order that His will might win out.

God spoke all these words, saying, I am the Lord thy God, who brought thee up out of the land of Egypt, out of the house of bondage. (Exod. 20:1-2)

As far as the Hebrew people are concerned, "I am the Lord thy God" is the first commandment. Jesus said, "Before Abraham was, I AM." (John 8:58). Other Scriptures assure us that He existed before anything else and that He actually made everything that is:

In the beginning was the Word, and the Word was with God, and the Word was God. The same was in the beginning with God. All things were made by him; and without him was not anything made that was made. (John 1:1-3)

God, who at sundry times and in divers manners spake in time past unto the fathers by the prophets, hath in these last days spoken unto us by his Son, whom he hath appointed heir of all things, by whom also he made the worlds. (Heb. 1:1-2)

Because the Lord says, "I AM," we are to believe in the existence of God. If He is not the great I AM, we are nothing; we are not even created yet.

God does not speak about Himself as an impersonal force, as an "it," and He does not speak about Himself as nature or world or reason. He is a person, and He is a personal God.

The God of Israel, the God of Jesus Christ, and the God of every true believer is the source not only of power, but of all life. He gives us our consciousness. He gives us personality. He gives us moral purpose and ethical action. He has made us in His image and in His likeness. We are made to take on the attributes and character of God Himself.

In the New Testament, these attributes are known as the fruit of the Spirit. God says we are to become like Him—long-suffering, kind, gracious, slow to anger, forgiving, and loving. We are not to hold a grudge, resentment, or hatred.

When the Lord says, "I am the Lord thy God," we know He is the God not merely of past generations, but of us. We're not speaking about a God who took our ancestors out of Egypt and that's all He did. He's the Lord *our* God, right now, and of every individual in every generation yet to come.

To the people of Israel in the wilderness, God did not say, "I am the God of Abraham, Isaac, and Jacob," but, "I am the God who delivered *you*. I am more than just Lord of lords and King of kings. I am a Deliverer, I am a Healer. I give life, and I sustain it. I supply every need. Not even a sparrow falls from the sky unless I ordain it. So why should you ever worry about anything as long as I am God Almighty?"

When God told the people of Israel that He is the Lord their God who brought them up out of Egypt, He did not talk about Himself as the Creator of heaven and earth, because they already knew that.

This time, He was giving them a new revelation of Himself, not only as the God of all creation but also of the destinies of men and women.

"I have given you a new revelation of Myself in this historic deed," God was saying. "I am the One who delivered you from every circumstance of slavery and bondage. You are free because I have made you free. And the greatest thing that can happen in your life is for Me to be your God."

This God has a moral claim on our lives as our Benefactor and our Redeemer. Because He bought us with a price, He has a claim on our gratitude and our obedience.* We bring our acceptable sacrifice to Him when we thank Him and praise Him for all He is and all He has done for us.

The reference to the redemption from Egypt by the Lord is of the deepest significance to all mankind. God is proclaimed as the God of freedom. In the light of this truth, history becomes one continuous revelation of the gradual growth of freedom and justice on earth through the one living God.

And we see Jesus coming into the world in fulfillment of what was promised to the people of Israel, perfect freedom from our sins, our transgressions, and our iniquities. And then He gives us the greatest freedom of all—the freedom from the temptation to sin. He steps between us and the sin and sets us free from that temptation.

The second commandment, as the Hebrews look at it, concerns the unity and the spirituality of God:

You shall have no other Gods before me. (Exod. 20:3)

This commandment affirms that there are no other gods besides God. The foundation of Jewish and Christian life is not merely that there is only one God, but that this one only and true God is *my* God. The sole ruler and guide in all that I do is Jesus Christ. There is nothing between me and my Lord. He is a living God, and there is one God, one Lord, one faith, one baptism.

Judaism speaks constantly about the unity of God. When we come to Jesus, we see that He is the Father, He is the Son, and He is the Holy Spirit, all in one, God in three persons.

113

One translation of this verse reads, "You shall have no other gods before My face." That means that nothing shall receive the worship due Him, neither angels nor saintly men and women are to receive adoration as divine beings. Jews and Christians alike are forbidden to pray to any being other than God Himself.

The same commandment also forbids belief in witchcraft, sorcery, or any form of superstition. Furthermore, he who believes in God will never put his trust in chance or in luck, because everything that happens is by divine appointment of the Lord, in His divine will.

> You shall not have a graven image, to worship it. (Exod. 20:4a)

This commandment forbids the worship of the one God in the wrong way. From the very beginning, God taught the people of Israel that He is a Spirit, and that we are to worship Him in Spirit and in truth. We are not to make any graven image and worship the object made by our hands. This commandment probably hampered the development of painting and sculpture among the people of Israel because they were afraid of breaking the commandment. It was of vital importance at the time to enable them to keep a pure concept of God, not tainted by the practice of the heathens in worshiping gods made with their own hands.

There's nothing wrong with painting a picture. We can even have a picture of Jesus, but we don't worship the picture. We can have a cross around our neck, but we don't worship the cross. We remember the One who went to the cross for us. If we turn to any kind of image and bow down to it, we are guilty of idolatry. God says, "You shall have no image of any sort."

I praise God that we have no actual pictures of what Jesus Christ looks like. The Lord deals with each of us as individuals in this, and He gives each of us a different picture in our minds of what Jesus looks like.

For many years, I taught that since Jesus was of the tribe of Judah, He had to have brown eyes and brown hair. And when I saw some artist's conception of Him with blue eyes and blond hair, I couldn't receive it. Then someone said to me, "Well, wasn't Jesus conceived by the Holy Ghost? And isn't the Holy Spirit symbolized by the color blue?'' I had to admit that the artist could be right.

> You are not to worship any likeness of anything in the heavens above, or anything in the earth beneath, or in the water under the earth. You shall not bow down yourself to them or serve them, for I, the Lord your God, am a jealous God. (Exod. 20:4b-5a)

The Egyptians worshiped cows, jackals, and the Nile River. They also worshiped the stars, the sun, and the moon. And some of us do the very same thing today when we open a newspaper and read our daily horoscope. When we do that, we are still worshiping the heavenly bodies, and that is an abomination to God. When you start relying on your horoscope for information, Satan gets a powerful hold on your life, and he starts moving you away from Jesus Christ. You start conforming to what the horoscope says, which is exactly what Satan wants. Satan's commandment would say, ''Worship anything you want to. Worship everything but God.''

When God tells us that He is a jealous God, He means that He can become righteously indignant. He is entitled to do that, but we are not. God has not given us that right. He is the only one who can be righteously indignant, because He is the only righteous one in the whole universe. Without Him, we are nothing. In His righteous indignation, God might say, ''You better believe I'm going to take the belt to you if you're not obedient, because I have a claim on your life. I bought it with My blood.''

God is entitled to be a jealous God, all right, because we belong to Him. Further, He says that He will visit

> The iniquities of the fathers upon the children unto the third and fourth generation of them that hate Me. But I will show mercy and steadfast love to a thousand generations of those who love Me and keep My commandments. (Exod. 20:5b-6)

If a parent is carrying a grudge, a resentment, and a hatred toward God, he naturally passes that on to His children. God allows us to pass on our own sins, including hatred of Him, to our children. But look at His promise here! In the third and fourth generation, He will divinely intervene and arrest that process. And then He will show mercy unto the thousandth generation of them that love Him and keep His commandments. Jesus says, "If you love Me, you will keep My commandments, and I will show mercy unto the thousandth generation." Because we love Jesus Christ and keep His commandments, therefore, a thousand generations from now, God will still be showing mercy to our descendants. It is an everlasting covenant.

God desires to be all in all to His children, and He claims an exclusive right to our love and obedience. He hates cruelty and unrighteousness. He loathes impurity and vice. Even as a mother is jealous of all evil influences that might come in contact with her children, God is jealous when instead of seeking after purity and righteousness, we give our heart allegiance to idolatry and unholiness.

Christians even today are forever getting involved in idolatry, paying so much attention to the things of the world that they neglect to pay attention to the things of God and to God Himself.

I remember back when I never went to the synagogue because I was too busy polishing my car. My car was my god, and I worshiped it. If anyone laid a hand on my car, I had a fit. I wasn't worshiping the Lord my God, I was worshiping my car.

Anything that comes between us and the Lord in any form is an unholy thing, an idolatrous thing. And God's righteous indignation against our idolatry is the very essence of His holiness.

The ancient peoples believed that the more gods they worshiped, the better off they were. They also believed that the richer the gods of a people were, the greater their power. These pagans made their gods look rich by covering their wood or stone with gold and silver, decorating it with jade and emeralds. But no matter how expensively decorated they were, the gods were still absolutely powerless.

In the midst of His righteous indignation over these heathen deities, God also showed His mercy and loving-kindness, however. He would tolerate the abomination of heathen idol worship, degrading as it was, and morally devastating as it was, if the heathen did not know any better. As long as a heathen was ignorant of the truth of God's Word, God still showed His love to him until some person came along and showed him the true love of the One God. After that, of course, the man would be held guilty if he clung to his idol worship.

The Scripture does not teach, here or elsewhere, that the sins of the guilty fathers shall be visited on the *innocent* children, but only on the guilty ones, the ones who hate Him. This was a big step up from what had prevailed in society before that time. There was a time when a father could be put to death for the sin of his son, or a son could be put to death for the sins of his ancestors, or a whole family could be wiped out for the sin of one person in it. But here, God is saying that from now on, each person will be responsible for only himself.

He says the same thing in another portion of Scripture:

The fathers shall not be put to death for the children, neither shall the children be put to death for the fathers; only for his own sin shall anyone be put to death. (Deut. 24:16)

Human experience plainly teaches the moral interdependence of parents and children. The bad example set by a father frequently corrupts those who come after him. His most dreadful bequest to his children is not a liability to punishment for what *he* has done, but a tendency toward the commitment of fresh offenses of a similar nature. When we study the lives of the nineteen kings of Israel at Samaria, we learn that one king after another was worse than his predecessor. The fathers had taught their sons to be worse sinners than they themselves had been. Every parent has the obligation to show the love of God to his children. That love is a powerful restraint against evil actions.

One translation of the Bible speaks of God remembering the sins of the fathers when He is about to punish the children. Here God is distinguishing between the moral responsibility for his own sins which falls exclusively upon a sinful parent, and the natural consequences of the predisposition to sin inherited by the descendants.

God tells us parents that we have an obligation to train up our children in the way they should go. If we don't fulfill our duty, and our children happen to sin, we're to blame. Because He is just and holy, God takes all these things into consideration. He tempers justice with mercy to the third and fourth generation, and then He divinely intervenes and arrests the process. Where sin abounded in three or four generations, grace now abounds unto the thousandth generation! For a thousand generations, His mercy and grace and love will be shown to those who love God and keep His commandments.

The love of God is the essence of all Judaism and Christianity, and from the love of God springs obedience to His will. We are not forced to be obedient, but we obey Him out of love for Him who first loved us. I praise God that He loved me first, and now I can love Him.

The third commandment given by God is the one against perjury and profane swearing:

> Thou shalt not take the name of the Lord thy God in vain, for the Lord will not hold him guiltless that takes His name in vain. (Exod. 20:7)

Many people think that if they swear and utter an irreverent exclamation, "Jesus Christ!" they have taken the Lord's name in vain. They have, but there's more to it than just that.

When we have professed before men that we are Christians, we have taken His name. If we have taken His name but we continue to live a pagan life, doing things which are not Christlike, we are guilty of having taken His name in vain. We have professed to be little Jesus Christs, and yet we're not walking in His way, the way of the truth and the life. When we're not doing what Jesus would do, but we're doing what is evil in the eyes of the Lord, we have taken His name in vain.

This third commandment also forbids us to dishonor God by invoking His name to swear to what is untrue or to join His name to anything that is unholy. In the Hebrew, *vain* means "falsehood, vanity, anything that is unreal or groundless." We are not to bring the Lord's name into anything that fits that definition, because His name is holy.

We are to swear to the truth in God's name only when we are required to do so in a court of law. At other times, the Scripture says, "Let your aye be aye, and your nay be nay." If you're a person of honor, the one to whom you are speaking will take you at your word. When you say yes, you mean yes. When you say no, you mean no.

This commandment also forbids using God's name in any sort of flippant oath. According to the rabbis, God's name is not to be uttered unnecessarily in common conversation. But the Lord Jesus Christ says, "You are to glorify Me and exalt Me and lift Me up." That being the case, we constantly use His name to praise Him and to ask for blessings on His people in the name of Jesus. There is power in the very name of Jesus. And when we are a people who praise Jesus, who worship Him, we are entitled to call upon Him by name.

The Lord says He will not hold a person guiltless, He will not leave a person unpunished, who swears to a lie. Perjury is an unpardonable offense in the courts of law. It has to be, because dishonesty can destroy human society. During the Talmudic period, the rabbis accompanied their teaching on this commandment with a very solemn warning to anyone about to take an oath in a court of law.

In various ages, and even today, some saintly men have avoided swearing altogether. The Essenes, a Jewish sect in the days of Christ, held that he who cannot be believed without swearing is already condemned. Let your yes be yes and your no be no, say the sages and rabbis of the Talmud.

In the fourth commandment, God says,

Remember the sabbath day, to keep it holy. Six days shall you labor and do all of your work, but the seventh day is a sabbath unto the Lord your God. In it, you shall not do any manner of work, you, nor your son, nor your daughter, nor your manservant, nor your maidservant, nor your cattle, nor the stranger that is within your gates. For in six days the Lord made heaven and earth, the sea, and all that is in them. And

119

He desisted from all further activity on the seventh day, and therefore, the Lord blessed the sabbath day, and He hallowed it. (Exod. 20:8-11)

When Jesus comes in the fullness of His Second Coming and in the glory of His flesh, He will say, "I am your sabbath rest, and you are to rest in Me." Until then, we will have a sabbath day.

In the fourteenth chapter of Romans, the Holy Spirit spoke through Saint Paul, saying that if your faith is weak and you happen to be hung up on a particular day to worship, that's all right. That's kosher. If you want to worship the Lord on Saturday, the seventh day of the week, that's fine. If your faith happens to be a little stronger, and you want to worship the Lord on Sunday, the first day of the week, just as the disciples did, that's okay too. If you want to make your day of desistance, your sabbath rest, on Monday, and your faith is built to the point where you know that Jesus is the Author and the Finisher of it, then you can make Monday your special day kept holy for the Lord. Any day is fine, but it is better for us not to get hung up on any particular day. Above all, we are not to look down our noses at someone else just because he keeps a different day for his sabbath.

As Christ fulfilled the law, He freed us from having to keep any particular day as the sabbath. If we have to work every day of the week except Thursday, we can dedicate that day unto the Lord as our special day of worship, our day of desistance, our day of praise and thanksgiving to Him. The word *sabbath* in the Hebrew means, simply, "desistance." The sabbath day, the day of desistance, begins with sundown on Friday evening and ends with sundown on Saturday. The Lord is saying, "I will supply all your needs during the six work days of the week so that you can take one day of rest and desist from the activity of generating money."

The institution of the sabbath was known to the people of Israel long before their experience with the manna in the wilderness. The sabbath was a treasured and sacred institution inherited from the days of the patriarchs, from what God had revealed to Abraham, Isaac, and Jacob, because God Himself made the world in six days and then He rested on the seventh day.

When the Lord says that we are to *remember* the sabbath day, He's saying that we are to keep it in mind during the rest of the week and to prepare ourselves for its sanctifying influence on our lives. According to the Talmudic rabbis, the Holy Spirit, the *shekinah* glory of God's presence, is much more glorious for you on the particular day that you dedicate unto the Lord as your sabbath than on any other day of the week. They said that God gives you a double anointing of His Holy Spirit on the day of your worship, praise, and thanksgiving.

The Hebrew prayer, prayed as the sabbath comes in, is a song of praise and thanksgiving to God for the day of desistance. After the prayer is a song of worship, and then the ceremony of the lighting of the sabbath lamp and the sabbath candle. The special prayer ushering in the sabbath cannot be said by the man of the house. It is said by the woman.

Hebrew oral tradition says that Abraham suffered greatly when Sarah died because there was not a woman in the tent to light the sabbath lamp and pray the sabbath prayer. Then, when Isaac brought Rebekah into Sarah's tent, she lit the sabbath lamp, prayed the sabbath prayer, and the Holy Spirit returned to bless Abraham and Isaac again.†

The sabbath prayer is the only one that a Hebrew woman is allowed to bring to the Lord. It goes like this:

Blessed art thou, O Lord our God, King of the universe, who has sanctified us and made us holy by His commandments and commanded me to light this sabbath lamp, and to call forth Your Holy Spirit.

God says that we are to keep our day of desistance unprofaned by workday purposes. In addition to being a day of rest from labor, the sabbath is to be a holy day, set apart for the building up of the spiritual element in man, for the edification of the spirit of man and the body of believers. The sabbath is not given to be a day for ballgames or other recreation.

Worship and religious instruction are an essential part of a sabbath kept holy unto the Lord. As we study the Holy Scriptures on our day of desistance, we get deeper and deeper into the Word, who is Jesus Christ. And the Holy Spirit begins to reveal to us what God wants us to know. We've all had the experience of reading a verse of Scripture that we've read many times before—maybe we even know it by heart—and all of a sudden, we understand something in it that we've never seen before. That's the Holy Spirit in action. And the Holy Spirit in action on our day of desistance has proved to be the greatest educator of Israel and of Christianity. The highest education of all is received in the school of the Holy Spirit.

If the rabbis are right, and there is a double portion of the Holy Spirit present on our day of desistance, I surely want to stay in His Word so I can get the full benefit of His extra presence. It's like God giving it to us wholesale, and I'm always in favor of that.

This commandment shows us that work on six days of the week is as essential to man's welfare as rest is to him on the seventh day. No man, however rich, is freed from the obligation of doing work. When Jesus tells us, "Occupy until I come," He's telling us plainly that we are to go out and work, to do what He has shown us, and to follow in His footsteps wherever He leads us. Idleness invariably leads to evil thoughts and to evil deeds. If we are idle, the enemy comes in and starts attacking the mind. The first thing we know, we're putting our evil thoughts into action.

The sabbath was something quite new to the heathen. It never existed in any nation until the people of Israel started observing it. The sabbath was a reminder that God is a God of freedom, even freedom from labor once a week. And if it is noble to labor, it is even nobler to pause to praise God, to rest in God, and to seek God on one day of the week.

Isaiah spoke of the sabbath as a delight. It is to be a voluntary, congenial, happy, and cheerful day. Besides being a day for worship and thanksgiving unto God, it's a day filled with love, joy, and the peace that passes understanding. The sabbath plants in the home of every believer a little corner of heaven. Each father is a priest, and each mother who lights the sabbath candle is an angel of light.

The fifth commandment tells us:

Honor your father and your mother, that your days may be

long upon the land which the Lord thy God gives to you. (Exod. 20:12)

Why did God put this commandment on His side of the tables of statutes? Logically, it seems to belong among the ordinances showing us how to conduct our relationships with other people. But God put the honoring of parents with the commandments dealing with our relationship with Him because He knew that if we did not honor our earthly parents, we could not possibly honor our heavenly Father. If we cannot show respect, reverence, awe, and fear of our mother and father, the persons who stand before us as representatives of God Himself, we cannot possibly love and honor God.

This is the only commandment that carries a promise with it, a promise of long life. And the obligation to honor our parents does not end when they leave this earthly life. It is an obligation which extends beyond the grave. We are to revere the memory of our departed parents in our actions forever, reflecting honor on them by the way we conduct ourselves.

Disobedience toward parents can be justified only in extremely rare cases where godless parents attempt to guide their children into lives of crime. In Jewish and Christian law, children have the right to disobey their parents only when to obey them would be to break God's law or the law of the land.

Proper respect toward parents may sometimes involve immeasurable hardship. Yet the duty remains. Jesus said that one of the signs of the end times would be the disobedience and dishonor of children to parents. And He wasn't speaking only of teenagers. He was speaking also of people in middle age who take their old parents and stick them in some old folks' home because they can't be bothered with them any longer. That's disobedience to parents, too. And the Lord said that when we saw these signs coming to pass, we should look up because we could know that our Redemption was drawing nigh. And it is true that we should look up, because the King is coming very soon. The next visitor to planet earth will be Jesus Christ Himself.‡

The honoring of your parents will be rewarded with happiness and blessing. Loving homes are infinitely more important to the well-being of a people than its schools, its economic life, or its political structure. Proper respect to parents is actually the ground of national permanence and prosperity. If we revere, love, and honor our parents, our nation will stand.

If, on the other hand, a nation thinks of its parents and its past with contempt, it may well contemplate its future with despair. It will perish with moral suicide.

Parents are to bring their children up in the nurture and admonition of the Lord. The Lord gives parents the promise that if they will train up their children in the way they should go, when they are old, they will not depart from it. In other words, if our parents bring us up right, we will turn out right. The words in the Hebrew mean that if our parents will literally pull us up by the roots of our hair to bring us to a full knowledge of God, even if we do depart from right living for a brief season, God will always bring us back to the right way. It's a guarantee.

Praise God for His promise that He will always bring us back. We can count on that promise because all of His promises are Yea and Amen in Jesus, and Jesus never fails.

---

* See the author's *Phenomenon of Obedience*.

† See the authors' *Jesus in Genesis*.

‡ For a full discussion of the signs of the end times, see the author's *Next Visitor to Planet Earth*.

14

The People Get Tired of Listening to God
(EXODUS 20:13-21)

After the first five commandments dealing with our proper
relationship to God, we come to five commandments dealing more
with our relationship to other people. The correct translation of the
first of these is,

Thou shalt not murder. (Exod. 20:13)

This commandment requires a respect for the sanctity of human
life. We are made in the image and likeness of Jesus Christ. God
made man in His exact reflection. If the first man, Adam, had
looked in a mirror, he would not have seen a man as we know a
man. He would have seen an exact reflection of Jesus Christ, in all
His radiance.

The words in the Hebrew reveal that we were made also in the
character of God. Adam had all of the fruit of the Spirit which are
the attributes of Jesus Christ.

The infinite worth of human life is based on the fact that man is
created in the image and in the likeness of God. God alone gives
life, and He alone may take it away. The intentional killing of any
human being, apart from capital punishment legally imposed by a
judicial tribunal or in war for the defense of national and human
rights, is absolutely forbidden in this commandment.

When war is declared by the leaders of a country, the sixth commandment gives us no right to say we are conscientious objectors. The commandment does not mean, "Thou shalt not kill." It means, "Thou shalt not willfully and intentionally murder another human being." Sometimes, God commands His people to go to war for themselves and their nation. According to His Word, our president is a divinely constituted authority. If our president says we are to go to war, we are to go. If we reject his authority, Romans 13 says we are rejecting the authority of God Himself.

In the day in which this commandment was given, the life of a child was as nothing among the heathen people. If a child became ill, they would expose him to the elements to let him die more quickly. "Why bother with the sick child?" was their thinking. "We can always get another one." But to the believer in the One true God, the life of a child was as sacred as that of an adult, because that child was made in the image of God. When Jesus walked the earth as a man, He said, "Suffer the little children to come unto Me. Deny them not, for of such is the kingdom of heaven."

In ancient Greece, unwanted children were abandoned on a lonely mountain to perish. But child murder has been long looked upon with horror by Christians and Jews. When the Romans went into Jerusalem and took the people of Israel captive, they sneered at the Israelites who said it was a crime to kill a child.

Hebrew law makes a careful distinction between homicide and willful murder. In the case of manslaughter, God provided for cities of refuge, places to which the accidental slayer of a man could escape to safety. The Lord said, "I am the Judge. I am the One who executes vengeance." If a person was pursued, the avenger of blood who was chasing him was not permitted to kill him within a twenty-mile radius of a city of refuge.

The manslayer would have to stay in the city of refuge, separated from his family, until the high priest died. After that, he could go back to his family. Before he could claim refuge, he had to present himself before the elders, and they would examine him to find out if he had ever held a grudge, a resentment, or a hatred against the person whom he had killed. If he had harbored such a feeling, the killing was to be regarded as willful murder even if the circumstances surrounding the death seemed to point to an accidental homicide.

Jewish and Christian ethics enlarge the notion of murder to include the doing of any thing by which the health and well-being of a fellowman is undermined. This concept acknowledges that in addition to the sin of commission of murder, there are also sins of omission leading to the same thing. A sin of omission would include the failure to save a man from destruction when it was possible.

Jesus described such a sin of omission when He told the story of the man lying by the side of the road, seriously injured because some robbers had beaten him up. The priest and the Levite who passed the man by would have been guilty of murder if the good Samaritan had not come along and saved the man's life. Love was flowing from the life of the good Samaritan exactly as Christ said it should flow from all of us.

The seventh commandment is,

Thou shalt not commit adultery. (Exod. 20:14)

When Jesus came along, He said, "I permitted Moses to give the people of Israel a bill of divorcement, because their hearts were very hard. They were a stiff-necked and arrogant people. But now that I have come into the world in the flesh, I say there is only one ground for divorce, and that is adultery."

Before Jesus came, there was no need to permit divorce for the cause of adultery, because adulterers were stoned to death and the surviving spouse would not need a divorce in order to remarry.

The commandment against infidelity in marriage warned both husband and wife alike that they were not to profane the covenant of marriage. Marriage is a three-way covenant among you, your wife, and the Lord Jesus Christ. When you get married, you get married in the name of the Lord.

The minute you call on the name of the Lord and ask Him to be a witness to your marriage, it becomes a three-way covenant. If you profane the marriage, if you break the covenant, you have come

127

against the Lord your God. He's the One you have cheated.

The sin of adultery covers far more than just physical adultery in a sexual relationship. It includes immoral speech, immodest conduct, and association with persons who scoff at the purity of Jesus, the purity of womanhood, and the sanctity of the home.

The eighth commandment deals with the sanctity of property:

Thou shalt not steal. (Exod. 20:15)

I remember the time when I used to sell my soul for a dime. I would pass by the newspaper rack outside the drugstore and pick up a newspaper without leaving a dime for it. I'd rationalize and say, ''What's a little dime between friends? After all, the guy who puts these papers here is my buddy. He'd be glad to let me have one for free.'' I didn't realize then that for ten cents I was selling my soul, I was cutting myself off from the Lord.

The enemy will try to buy you as cheap as he can get you. He reads your past performance record, and then he puts temptation in the way, knowing what obstacles can cause your downfall. But we can stand against Satan if we stand in the power of Jesus. If we call upon the name of Jesus, the enemy has to flee from us. When we start thanking and praising God, the enemy runs away. He cannot stand the praises of God-fearing people because God dwells in them. He inhabits the praises of His people. And where God is, the devil cannot stay. He is a defeated foe.

Property represents the fruit of industry and intelligence, both of which are gifts from God. Any aggression against the property of our neighbor, therefore, is an assault on a gift from God. When we steal another man's property, we're coming against God Himself.

This commandment has a wider application than merely forbidding outright robbery. It forbids every illegal acquisition of property by cheating, embezzlement, forgery, or by otherwise legal transactions in which a person takes advantage of the ignorance or embarrassment of another for the purpose of gain.

The ninth commandment states,

Thou shalt not bear false witness against thy neighbor. (Exod. 20:16)

The three preceding commandments are concerned with wrongs

inflicted against our neighbor by actual deed. This commandment is concerned with wrong inflicted by word of mouth.

In the Book of James in the New Testament, we are reminded that the very same mouth that sings praises unto the Lord is sometimes used to curse other people. Maybe you say, "Praise the Lord!" with one breath, and with the next one say, "Blankety-blankety-blank-blank!" when somebody cuts across the freeway and gets in front of your car. We're cussing the guy instead of praying for him. This is one form of injury inflicted by word of mouth.

The prohibition against bearing false witness embraces all forms of gossip and slander. When Jesus Christ came into the world, He said if we gossip about somebody behind their back, we've killed them already. The seeds of destruction have been planted. If we cannot say something to somebody's face, we shouldn't say it at all.

We are not to criticize or judge another person's faith. Let Jesus be who He is. He will deal with all people. We can't play His part.

When I am witnessing to Jews, I am often asked the question, "Where was God when six and a half million of our people were dying in the gas chambers?" And the only answer the Lord has ever given me for this question is, "Seven million Christians went with them, including four million Lutherans and two million Catholics. If the seven million Christians and the six and a half million Jews had not died, Israel would not have come into being, because the world would not have done anything about the State of Israel."

The world had been sitting on the Israel situation since the Balfour Declaration of 1917. Modern Israel was purchased with the blood of the Jewish and Christian martyrs who died for their faith. It was really the same faith. The six and a half million Jews were still waiting for their Messiah, and the seven million Christians knew that their Messiah had already come.

Some modern theologians look at this commandment and say that it only prohibits an Israelite from slandering a fellow Israelite. They allege that "neighbor," in the commandment to love your neighbor as yourself, means only their fellow Israelite. But God says that everyone is neighbor to everyone else.

When the Lord was getting ready to lead the children of Israel up out of Egypt, he told them to despoil the Egyptians. "Let every man ask of his *neighbor* jewels of silver, jewels of gold, and raiment," He said. God Himself was calling the Egyptians neighbors to the Israelites. And God is still saying to the people of Israel, "The Egyptian is your neighbor, the Babylonian is your neighbor, the Arab next door that you can't stand is your neighbor. You're to love all them as you love yourself."

In this commandment, as in all the moral precepts in the Scriptures, the Hebrew word *neighbor* is equivalent to "your fellowman." We are to love our fellowman as we love ourselves. We are to treat our fellowman the way we want to be treated.

I used to look in the mirror and see the most perfect being in the world, excusing myself for everything, rationalizing about all my wrongdoing, considering myself perfect. And then one day, the Lord spoke to me from the other side of that mirror, saying, "That's the way I want you to live. That guy—you—that lives next door to you, you are to love in the way you love yourself. As you rationalize and make excuses for yourself, you are to rationalize and make excuses for him. When he breaks your sprinkler head, love him in spite of it. When he breaks the aerial on your car, love him in spite of it, just as you love yourself."

It was a great lesson that I had to learn, and I'm still learning it.

Now we come to the tenth and last of the great commandments, the prohibition against coveting:

> You shall not covet your neighbor's house, your neighbor's wife, or his manservant, or his maidservant, or his ox, or his donkey, or anything that is your neighbor's. (Exod. 20:17)

The word *covet* means to long for the possession of anything that we cannot get in an honest and legal manner. And this commandment goes to the root of all evil action. If we can live by it, we can abide by the other nine.

The unholy instinct that is the impulse of the predator, the desire for unlawful gain, is at the root of nearly every sin against our neighbor and our fellowman. The man who does not cover himself with the Lord will covet his neighbor's goods. He can't help himself. He will bear false witness, he will rob, he will murder, and he will commit adultery with the neighbor's wife. The tenth commandment demands self-control. Every man and every woman has it in his or her power to let his or her desires master him or to master those desires. Without self-control, there can be no worthy human life.

The rabbis writing in the Talmud said that the one who is strong is the one whose passions do not control him; he controls his passions.

When the Ten Commandments had been given,

The people perceived the thundering, the lightning, the voice of the horn, the mountain smoking, and when the people saw it, they trembled and stood afar off. And they said unto Moses, You speak with us, and we will hear, but let not God speak to us, lest we die. (Exod. 20:18-19)

The people had heard the Ten Commandments, but now they refused to hear any further revelations from God. Man constantly tries to avoid hearing the voice of God, but he cannot escape. Wherever he goes, the Lord says, "Behold, I am with you. I will never leave you or forsake you. Wherever you go, you're going to take yourself and Me along. There's no point in trying to run away. It's impossible."

And Moses said unto the people, Fear not, for God is come to prove you, and that His fear may be before your faces, that you sin not. (Exod. 20:20)

In Hebrew, to fear the Lord is to see the Lord. If you fear the Lord and see Him, you will stand in awe of Him, you will revere Him, you will respect Him, but most of all, you will love Him. Everything you do will be motivated by your love of God. You wouldn't offend Him for anything.

Nevertheless, Moses moved the people twelve miles from Mount Sinai.

And the people stood afar off, but Moses drew near unto the thick darkness where God was. (Exod. 20:21)

As Moses drew near to God, God drew near to him, and God began to tell him many more things that would be of great benefit to him in leading the Israelites.

15

Meanwhile, Back on the Mountain . . .

(EXODUS 20:22—22:15)

And the Lord said unto Moses, Thus you shall say to the children of Israel, You yourselves have seen that I have talked with you from heaven. You shall not make gods to share with Me My glory and your worship; gods of silver or gods of gold you shall not make for yourselves. (Exod. 20:22-23)

The people were standing afar off, about twelve miles away, when Moses went into the thick cloud where the Lord spoke to him in His *shekinah* glory. And God told Moses to remind the Israelites that they themselves had been eyewitnesses to His glory. They themselves had actually heard Him from heaven. And once again God spoke a warning against making idols to worship. He said,

An altar of earth you shall make unto Me. (Exod. 20:24a)

Here, God was demonstrating the simplicity of what He required. He didn't need a big palace, a big temple or a fancy sanctuary, just a simple altar of earth.

And there you shall sacrifice your burnt offerings, and your peace offerings, your sheep, and your oxen. In every place where I cause My name to be mentioned, I will come unto you, and I will bless you. (Exod. 20:24b)

Wherever He causes the name of Jesus to be mentioned, that's

133

where the Lord is. Wherever we gather in the name of the Lord, whether it's in a building, in an open field, or up on a mountaintop, we are the church, we are the body of Jesus Christ.

> Now, if you will make Me an altar of stone, you shall not build it of hewn stone, for if you lift your tool upon it, you have profaned it. (Exod. 20:25)

The Lord says we are not to make Him a fancy altar, but just use the natural stones that he has provided for us.

> Neither shall you go up by steps to My altar, that your nakedness be not exposed upon it. (Exod. 20:26)

God said that His altar was to be made without steps, because His priests would be dressed in short tunics, and He didn't want them to expose themselves when they bowed down to worship Him.

An old Jewish legend says that as the Lord was creating the universe, one of the angels was carrying all the stone for the earth. Just as he was flying over Jerusalem, his sack broke, and all the rocks landed in Israel. God provided plenty of natural stone for the Israelites to use in building altars to worship Him.

> Now these are the ordinances which you [Moses] shall set before them [the Israelites]: If you buy a Hebrew servant, six years shall he serve you, and the seventh year, he shall go out free for nothing. (Exod. 21:1-2)

The Lord was starting to give Moses the laws and ordinances for governing the people of Israel. The Israelites were to keep the statutes, but more than that, they were to reflect them to the heathen who lived around them, so that they would see that God is a living God, that He can take the worst of all people and make of them a people dedicated to Him, who would love Him and be obedient to Him.

Unfortunately, the people of Israel decided that they were chosen to be a privileged people instead of understanding that they were chosen for missionary service. Consequently, they failed in their mission. And because the natural Israel failed so miserably, God had to bring forth a spiritual Israel through Jesus Christ. And the spiritual Israel is going to go out and fulfill the great commission to go into all the world to be witnesses for Him and to make disciples of all nations. Physical Israel failed; it couldn't live up to the ordinances. But spiritual Israel came forth to do the job.

In the first of the ordinances, the people were told something about the nature of their relationship to hired servants. A man might buy a slave by paying off the slave's creditors, but the man so purchased would have to serve his master for only six years. In the seventh year, the master would be required to let the servant go free.

> If he came to you by himself, he shall go out by himself, but if he came married, then his wife shall go out with him. If his master has given him a wife, and she has borne him sons and daughters, the wife and her children shall be her master's, and he shall go out by himself. But if the servant shall plainly say, I love my master, I love my wife, I love my children, and I will not go out free, then his master shall bring him unto God. He shall bring him to the door, or to the doorpost, and his master shall bore his ear through with an awl, and he shall serve him forever. (Exod. 21:3-6)

When Jesus came into the world, God in the flesh, He said something very strange: "You're to leave your father, your mother, your daughter, your son, your husband, your wife, and you are to follow Me. You are to forsake everything and everybody and follow Me."

Although the slave has an earthly master, his true master is the Lord his God. And when the Lord says to him, "It's now the seventh year, Abie. It's time for you to go home, free. But you have to leave your wife and children behind," what will Abie do? Will he trust God with his wife and his children, leaving them behind and knowing that the Lord, by His love, His grace, and His mercy will bring them to him in His own good time? Or will he go to his earthly master and say, "I will stay on with you and serve you the rest of my life because I'm not trusting God"?

If he does the latter, his earthly master is to take him to the door and pierce a hole in his ear with an awl to signify that the man has listened to an earthly master instead of to his heavenly God. If the man could have received faith to stand fast, he would have seen the salvation of the Lord. The Lord would surely have given him his wife and his children. But since he was not willing to stand, he would be a slave for the rest of his life.

> Now if a man shall sell his daughter to be a maidservant, she shall not go out as the menservants do. If she does not please her master, who has not espoused her to himself, then he shall let her be redeemed. To sell her to a foreign people he shall have no power, seeing he hath dealt deceitfully with her. (Exod. 21:7-8)

In the Hebrew, a maidservant means a secondary wife. This was a day of polygamy. The people of Israel knew better, but they practiced polygamy anyway.* And at the time, it was no disgrace to be a concubine. There was nothing degrading about it. Furthermore, the offspring of a concubine had the same rights in matters of inheritance as the children of the first wife.

If a maidservant was designated to be the secondary wife of the master of the house but he found her displeasing for any reason, he had to allow her father or other male relatives to buy her back. He could not sell her to a foreign people. The abominable practice against which this ordinance was directed—that of selling maidservants into foreign slavery—is still practiced in some parts of the Middle East today.

In the Talmud, the rabbis explain that in the case of a maidservant who does not please her master, both the master and the father of the girl have obligations toward her. The master has acted deceitfully in that he has not consummated the marriage, and the father had a natural obligation from the beginning, on account of selling her. The Lord further specified, for the protection of the girl,

> If he espouses her to his son, he shall deal with her after the manner of daughters. (Exod. 21:9)

In other words, if the maidservant is going to be his daughter-in-law, the master must treat her as he does his own daughters. The bondswoman is to be regarded as a freeborn girl who has just gotten married. There is to be no distinction, because she is free in the Lord. The particular rights that are due her are set forth in the verses that follow:

If he takes unto himself another wife, her food, her raiment, her conjugal rights are not diminished. (Exod. 21:10)

Even if the maidservant's master, her husband, is not enchanted with her any more, and takes to himself another wife, the Lord says he's got to keep on fulfilling his duties and obligations toward her. He can't withhold anything.

Now if he does not do these things, then she shall go out for nothing, without money. (Exod. 21:11)

If he fails to honor all his obligations toward her, she is free to go back home to her father, no matter how much money the master might have invested in her. If he does not do right by her, he can no longer claim her as his property.

Now we go to regulations concerning other areas of interpersonal relationships:

He that smites a man so that he dies, he shall surely be put to death. But if a man lie not in wait, but God causes it to come to him (the death happens by accident), then I will appoint you a place where he may flee. (Exod. 21:12-13)

Murderers were to be put to death, but in the case of involuntary manslaughter, God would provide a place where the killer could go for sanctuary. We have already discussed the matter of cities of refuge in connection with the commandment that says, "Thou shalt not murder."

The English people had a sanctuary law for years. A man who had committed a crime could go into a church and claim sanctuary there. The law itself could not touch him as long as he remained in the house of God. These sanctuary laws remained in existence until just about ten years ago when they were abolished.

In Israel, if a man went in to the altar of God and held on to the horns of the altar, no man could touch him, because God was giving him divine protection. The man knew that he was a sinner, but he was asking for forgiveness of his sin. And the Lord was granting it.

David made the mistake of condoning the killing of a man who was in the sanctuary of the Lord, and the Lord said, ''Because you have done this, death will not depart from your house, even though I promised you that from you would come a king who would live forever and a kingdom which would last forever.'' Jesus the Messiah would be called the son of David, but death would not depart from David's house, because he had murdered, not just Uriah, but he had condoned the murder of a man who was in the sanctuary, holding on to the altar of the Lord.

> Now if a man comes presumptuously upon his neighbor, to slay him with guile (premeditated murder), you shall take him from My altar that he may die. And he that smites his father and he that smites his mother shall surely be put to death. (Exod. 21:14-15)

A father and a mother stand in the place of God to their children. If a child struck his parent, he was to be put to death. Striking a parent was the same as striking the Lord. And you strike the Lord only one time.

> And he that steals a man and sells him or is found with him in his possession, shall surely be put to death. (Exod. 21:16)

This statute is talking about the crime of kidnapping. It took us until the Lindbergh case to come back to this law which provides the death penalty for kidnapping.

> He that curseth his father or his mother shall surely be put to death. (Exod. 21:17)

Again, this is a strong penalty, because cursing a parent is the same as cursing the Lord.

> And if a man quarrel and one smites the other with a stone, or with his fist, and he does not die, but he is in bed, if he rises up again and walks upon his staff, then he that struck him shall be cleared. Only he shall pay for the loss of his time, and he shall cause him to be thoroughly healed. (Exod. 21:18-19)

The guilty party had to pay the expense of the doctor and the dentist as well as reimbursing his victim for his loss of time on the job.

> If a man smites his servant, his bondsman, or his bondswoman with a rod, and he dies under his hand, he shall

surely be punished. (Exod. 21:20)

There would be punishment but usually no death penalty in such cases, because, according to the rabbis, the bondsman would not be an Israelite, therefore he was not really a human being. He was only money. There was no fixed punishment for this offense, but each case had to be judged on its own merits. If the master struck his servant with a rod, not intending to injure him severely, but just to punish him or to call forth obedience from a rebellious slave, the punishment would be relatively light. But if it came out that the master was a brutal man who was cruelly beating his slave, then he was to be beheaded.

The reason for such a severe penalty in this case was that the Israelites were supposed to show the heathen the same love of God that God had showed toward them. The Israelite was to be a reflection of God's love to the heathen who did not yet know the Lord. If the Israelite was willfully showing him brutality and cruelty instead, he was sinning against God Himself, and such a man deserved capital punishment.

Now, notwithstanding, if this servant continues a day or two, the master will not be punished, for he has merely injured his own property.

And if men fight together, and they hurt a woman who is pregnant, so that her fruit departs (her child dies), and yet no other harm follows, he shall surely be fined, according as the woman's husband shall lay upon him. And he shall pay as the judges determine. (Exod. 21:21-22)

When two men have a fight and there's a woman standing nearby who is accidentally struck, causing her to lose her unborn child, the woman's husband is entitled to collect a fine for the loss of the child.

And if any harm follows, then you shall give life for life, eye for eye, tooth for tooth, hand for hand, foot for foot, burning for burning, wound for wound, stripe for stripe. (Exod. 21:23-25)

This was the old way of doing things. But when Jesus came, He said, "If someone strikes you, turn the other cheek." It was an entirely new way of looking at things.

So if a man smites the eye of his bondsman, or the eye of his bondswoman and he destroys it, he shall let him go free for his eye's sake. And if he smites out his bondsman's tooth, or his bondswoman's tooth, he shall let him go free for the tooth's sake.

Now if an ox gore a man or a woman, that they die, the ox shall surely be stoned and its flesh shall not be eaten, but the owner of the ox shall be found not guilty. But if the ox were wont to gore in the past, and warning has been given to its owner and he has not kept it in, but it has killed a man or a woman, the ox shall be stoned to death and its owner shall also be put to death. (Exod. 21:26-29)

In some parts of the United States today we have laws concerning what are termed "attractive nuisances." If we have a swimming pool with a little fence around it and a child climbs over that little fence and drowns in the pool, we are guilty under the law. We're required to make every effort to keep children safe on our property.

If we have a dog, and we know he bites, it is our duty to keep him penned up where he can't get to anyone to injure them. We have many laws in the United States today that have evolved out of God's laws for the people of Israel.

If a ransom is put on a man's life, then he shall give for the redemption of his life whatever is put upon him. If the man's ox has gored another's son or daughter, according to this judgment shall it be done unto him. If the ox gores a bondsman or a bondswoman, he shall give unto their master thirty shekels of silver, and the ox shall be stoned. If a man leaves an open pit, or digs a pit and does not cover it, and an ox or an ass falls in, the owner of the pit shall make it good, and give money to the animal's owner, but the dead beast shall be his. (Exod. 21:30-34)

Later, the rabbis said that if an ox fell into a pit on the sabbath day, a man could set aside the sabbath law and climb in to rescue the ox. But when Jesus healed a man on the sabbath, the Pharisees rose up in arms and wanted to do Him in. No wonder Jesus was so critical of them. They were putting the value of an animal above the worth of a human being made in the express image of God.

Now, if one man's ox hurts another's, so that it dies, then they shall sell the live ox, and divide the price of it, and the dead ox also they shall divide between them. If it's known that the ox has gored in times past, and the owner has not kept it in, he shall surely pay ox for ox, and the dead beast shall be his own.

If a man steals an ox or a sheep, and he kills it or sells it, he shall pay five oxen for one and four sheep for a sheep. (Exod. 21:35-22:1)

Why was the price of an ox more than the price of a sheep? God has a good sense of humor, and an ox is about five times stronger than a sheep. You can really put an ox to work, but you can't do much with a sheep.

If a thief is found breaking in and is smitten so that he dies, there shall be no bloodguiltiness for him. (Exod. 22:2)

If you caught a thief breaking into your home and killed him, you were not guilty of murder or even of manslaughter. If a thief entered your house in the middle of the night and you didn't attack him first, he would probably attack you; therefore the person who happened to deliver a fatal blow to the thief breaking into his house at night would not be guilty of murder.

But if the sun be risen upon him, there shall be bloodguiltiness for him. (Exod. 22:3a)

Why the distinction? If a man breaks into your house in the daytime, you can see him and defend yourself without killing him. Slaying a thief after daybreak is murder, because it is not absolutely necessary for you to take his life. Perhaps you can even talk him out of robbing you. It may be that you will be able to talk to him about the Lord and so save his soul as well as his life and your property.

If you catch a thief in your house but don't kill him,

He shall make restitution; but if he has nothing, then he shall be sold for his theft. (Exod. 22:3b)

The rabbis' addition to this particular law was that if the value of the stolen animal was less than the price of a slave, the thief could not be sold. If the thief was sold, he could be sold only for the price of the stolen article and not for the fourfold or fivefold fine that was imposed in Exodus 22:1

> If the theft be found in his hand alive, whether it be an ox, an ass, or a sheep, he shall pay double. (Exod. 22:4)

The Lord says he's going to have to pay twice. He must return the stolen animal and give the owner another animal of equal value as a fine. This rule was extended to all stolen articles. If you got caught with a loaf of bread, you had to return two loaves of bread. If you got caught with thirteen tapes, you had to give back twenty-six tapes.

> If a man causes a field or a vineyard to be eaten, and lets his beast loose, and it feeds in another man's field; of the best of his own field, and of the best of his own vineyard, shall he make restitution. (Exod. 22:5)

This law applies to the man who *causes* a field or a vineyard to be eaten by his cattle. In other words, he willfully sends his cattle to graze in a field that doesn't belong to him. If they wander there without any negligence on his part, he is not liable. But if he *willfully* sends them in, he *is* liable.

When the damage is estimated, the best of the injured man's field is to be taken as the basis for calculating the value of the whole. Even if the animals grazed in the worst part of the field, the man's neighbor must repay him from the best of *his* field.

The man who willfully sends his cattle to graze in another man's field is breaking one of the Ten Commandments—do not steal—by sending his cattle to steal from another man's field. But if he repents, asks the Lord to forgive his sin, and obeys this command to make restitution by giving the best of his produce to his neighbor, the Lord will honor his faith and obedience by forgiving his sin and even blessing him.

> If a fire breaks out and it catches in thorns, so that the shocks of corn, or the standing corn, or the field, be consumed, he that kindled the fire shall surely make restitution. (Exod. 22:6)

If you start a fire in your field and the wind carries the sparks into a neighbor's field, causing a fire to break out there, you must make restitution. You should have thought about that wind before you started the fire!

> If a man delivers unto his neighbor money or stuff to keep, and it is stolen out of the man's house; if the thief is found, he shall pay double. If the thief is not found, then the master of the house shall come near unto God to see whether he has not put his hand unto his neighbor's goods. (Exod. 22:7-8)

Suppose you go to your neighbor and say, "I'm going to Mexico, and I want you to do me a favor and take charge of my valuables." He agrees to do you the favor, but when you return from your trip, he tells you, "There's been a theft. Somebody broke into my house, and your valuables have disappeared. The thief cannot be found."

Your valuables have been stolen and the thief can't be found. What then? Remember, there was no such thing as a homeowner's policy in those days.

If your neighbor declares before God—that is, with the Lord as his witness—that he has not embezzled or stolen what you entrusted to him, then he is free from all obligation. All he has to do is to say, "In the name of God, I have not touched my neighbor's goods." If he perjures himself in saying this, his punishment will come from God. God is both judge and jury and will send His judgment upon the person who takes His name in vain.

> For every manner of trespass [willful, deliberate sin], whether for ox, for ass, for sheep, for raiment, for any manner of lost thing, of which one says, This is it, the cause of both parties shall come before God; he whom God shall condemn shall pay double unto his neighbor. (Exod. 22:9)

"Every manner of trespass" includes sin, transgression, and iniquity. When Jesus went to the cross, He covered us on all bases. Surely He has borne our *sin*—our rebellious nature, handed down to us from Adam. We are natural-born rebels; we inherited a sinful nature. But the *second* Adam, Jesus Christ, came into the world to restore eternal life to you and me by His sacrifice on the cross.

143

Transgression includes trespass. A wedding ring on a beautiful blonde says, "Do not trespass"; yet we go ahead and trespass. Or we trespass by sending our cattle into another man's field. Those trespasses are transgression—and Jesus covered us on that point too.

Iniquity includes the sin of omission. If we see our brother sinning and say nothing to him, we become accessories after the fact. That's iniquity.

Praise God that Jesus delivered and freed us from sin, transgression, and iniquity!

In a matter of deliberate trespass, the Israelites actually had the faith to believe that God would pronounce judgment right then and there. They didn't have to wait for eternity. Both parties appeared before God, and the man whom God declared to be guilty had to pay his neighbor double for whatever he had stolen.

> If a man delivers unto his neighbor an ass, or an ox, or a sheep, or any beast to keep and it dies, or it is hurt, or it is driven away, no man seeing it, an oath of the Lord shall be between them both, to see whether he has not put his hand unto his neighbor's goods; and the owner thereof shall accept it, and he shall not make restitution. (Exod. 22:10-11)

If there is any doubt as to the trustee's honesty, the name of God is again brought into the act. If the trustee says, "No, in God's name, I have not touched your goods," the owner of the lost animal cannot require him to make restitution. A man's word is his bond.

> But if it is stolen from the trustee, he shall make restitution unto the owner thereof. (Exod. 22:12)

It seems strange that the trustee does not have to make restitution in case of accidental loss or death, but he does have to pay for an animal that was carried away by a band of marauders whom he was powerless to stop. The reason is that in the case of theft, it is assumed that the trustee was *paid* to take care of the animals and exercised insufficient care; therefore he has to make restitution.

> If it be torn in pieces, let him bring it for a witness, and he shall not make good that which is torn. (Exod. 22:13)

If the trustee can produce the torn flesh of the animal entrusted to him as evidence that it was not stolen but was killed by a wild beast, he is not held responsible. *However,*

> If a man borrows ought of his neighbor and it is hurt or it dies, the owner thereof not being with it, he shall surely make restitution. But if the owner thereof is with it, he shall not make it good. If it be a hireling, he loses his hire. (Exod. 22:14-15)

If you *ask* your neighbor to lend you something, you are then responsible for seeing that no harm comes to it. If you fail in that responsibility, you have to make restitution unless the owner is present at the time the damage is done.

We see that in the time of Moses, many finely detailed statutes and ordinances were necessary to enable men to live at peace with one another. This was all looking toward the day when the Prince of Peace would come and fulfill all the law. He would be able to sum up the law into two commandments:

> Thou shalt love the Lord thy God with all thy heart, and with all thy soul, and with all thy mind. . . . And thou shalt love thy neighbor as thyself. (Matt. 22:37, 39)

But until He came and sent His Holy Spirit to live in man, there was no way a man could fulfill the law by living in the spirit of love. Until He came, all the details of the law would have to continue to be spelled out.

---

* See comments on Genesis 2:24 in the author's *Jesus in Genesis*.

145

16

More Rules and Regulations

(EXODUS 22:16—23:19)

As God continued to give Moses rules for dealing with the sins of mankind, He said,

> If a man entices a virgin that is not betrothed and he lies with her, he shall surely pay a dowry for her to be his wife. (Exod. 22:16)

From Deuteronomy 22:28, we learn that this law applies whether a girl is seduced or raped. It does not, however, apply to a virgin who is betrothed—espoused, or engaged to be married. Seduction of an espoused virgin is a crime on a par with adultery, and the punishment is death by stoning. If the offense takes place within the city, both parties are put to death; if it happens in the field, the man alone suffers capital punishment. The reasoning is that in the city a girl's screams will be heard if rape is being committed. In the country, there might be no one to hear her scream; therefore she is given the benefit of the doubt as to whether she was raped or was a consenting party. The man, however, is stoned, whether his crime is rape or seduction.

Why is the punishment for seduction of a virgin so much more severe if she happens to be engaged? Among Orthodox Jews, the great ceremony is the engagement—the espousal, the betrothal.

The marriage contract is signed at that time, and the marriage is just a consummation of the engagement. If the couple decide to break their engagement, they have to go through a regular divorce proceeding.

The Hebrew language has two words for virgin: *almah,* an espoused virgin, and *bethula,* a virgin who is not espoused, or betrothed. Isaiah 7:14 states that a virgin *(almah)* will conceive and bear a son, and will call His name Immanuel. In this prophecy the Lord specifies very clearly that the mother of the Messiah will be a virgin who is betrothed.

Because Mary was espoused to Joseph when she was found to be with child, he had it in his power to "put her away." He could have had her taken out and stoned to death for committing adultery. Being a good man, however, he decided to put her away by divorcing her quietly. Then the angel appeared to him and told him that Mary was still a virgin and he should not be afraid to take her as his wife.

The law given in Exodus 22:16, however, deals only with the seduction of a *bethula,* a virgin who is not engaged, and the punishment seems relatively mild. In such cases the man is obliged to marry the girl, with no possibility of a subsequent divorce; he's stuck with her from that day forth. In addition, he has to pay fifty shekels of silver as a dowry. Without this additional penalty, the seducer might demand to marry the girl "for free," thinking that under the circumstances the father would be anxious to see his daughter safely married. Originally, this dowry was paid to the father. In later times, it was received by the bride herself, so that she might enter with proper dignity into her new home.

> If her father utterly refuses to give her unto him, he shall pay money according to the dowry of virgins. (Exod. 22:17)

According to the rabbis, the same law applies if the girl herself "utterly refuses" to marry the man. Whether the refusal comes from the girl or from her father, the man must pay fifty shekels of silver before he is free to go his way.

Verse 18 deals with witchcraft, a subject that is treated in the New Testament as well as the Old:

You shall not suffer a sorceress to live. (Exod. 22:18)

This law against witchcraft is directed against the spirit of the enemy—against Satan himself. Although the rabbis did not believe there was any reality in witchcraft, they condemned it because it was a denial of the unity of God. The Hebrews constantly speak about the unity of God: Satan is constantly attacking this unity. To allow a sorceress (witch) or a warlock to live negates the unity of God and is an abominable form of idolatry.

When the seventy rabbis went down into Egypt to translate the Hebrew Scriptures into Greek, the word for sorceress, or sorcerer, was translated *poisoner*—one who poisons. Ancient witchcraft was steeped in crime and immorality. It poisoned the populace by hideous practices and superstitions. These explain why God sandwiched this command between the laws dealing with sexual license and the condemnations of unnatural vice and idolatry.

Two things about the wording of this command are unusual. One is the use of the feminine noun *sorceress* rather than the masculine *sorcerer*. The first person on earth to be enticed by Satan was Eve. Because Eve behaved "like a man" in confessing her guilt to God, He did not condemn her for her action. Adam, however, refused to take the blame for his disobedience. He passed the buck from himself to his wife and back to God—and man has been passing the buck ever since! Adam said to God, "You gave me that woman and she gave me the fruit. It's Your fault that I ate it; I'm not responsible." Therefore God cursed the ground for Adam's sake. Perhaps Eve's direct involvement with Satan explains why witchcraft is practiced predominantly by women. We hear far more about witches than about warlocks.

The other unexpected choice of words in this command is "shall not suffer to live." It is fashionable, but unfair, to trace all the horrors connected with the persecution of witches in medieval and colonial times to this verse. Even though witchcraft is a sinister danger, the Lord does not here command that witches be put to death, but says, "You shall not suffer them to live." The prohibition is against patronizing a witch and thus enabling her to support herself by her nefarious profession. This law applies to the sorcerer as well. There is no justification in the Bible for what took place in Salem, Massachusetts, during the seventeenth century when witches were burned at the stake.

Today we can deal with witchcraft and other occult practices in the name of Jesus, who defeated Satan upon the cross. All we need do is to take the authority that He gave us. Teenagers from our area have exercised this authority to shut down places where sexual immorality and perversion, witchcraft and sorcery were being practiced. Groups of them have gone by such places and, in the name of Jesus, have bound Satan and taken authority over the house where these satanic practices were going on. Pleading the shed blood of Christ, they asked God to shut the place down. Within a week or two, the place was closed.

The Lord gave you and me that same authority. He said, "You can do greater things than I have done. On the cross, I gave you My power of attorney. Any time you sign my name to a blank check, I will back you up—if you have the faith to *believe* I will. When you march in front of a place that is involved in sorcery and witchcraft, believe I'm standing with you—and if you want that place closed up, it shall be done."

Whoever lies with a beast shall surely be put to death. (Exod. 22:19)

Sexual perversion is the sin that caused God to send a flood to destroy all living creatures except those with Noah in the ark. Homosexuality was prevalent in the days before the flood, and men were even lying with animals. Seeing these practices, the Lord said, "I will destroy all flesh. I am sorry that I made man in My image and in My likeness. I have given him My character so that he may act in My character, but he has gone astray. My Spirit shall no longer strive with him. I will limit his days to 120 years; I will give him 120 years to repent."

We see nobody in the time of Noah repenting—nobody going before the Lord and saying, "We will not commit homosexual acts. We will not have sexual intercourse with animals." Therefore the Lord destroyed that generation with a flood.*

He who sacrifices to any god but the Lord—he who sacrifices to an idol—shall be utterly destroyed. (Exod. 22:20)

In the Hebrew, the word for *god* is plural *(gods),* and it means idols. And when the Lord says "utterly destroyed" in the Hebrew, He's speaking not just of physical destruction or death, but of spiritual destruction as well. The man who sacrifices to an idol is eternally damned. He has blasphemed God's Holy Spirit.

A stranger you shall not wrong or oppress, for you yourselves were strangers in the land of Egypt. (Exod. 22:21)

Stranger in the Hebrew means "resident alien." God says, "When you were in slavery in Egypt, you were not shown any love, grace, or mercy except by Me, the Lord your God. Now you are to let My love come through you to any alien who is among you—any stranger who does not know God. He may never see God except through you. The only Bible he will ever read is *you*—your life, your witness. Therefore you are not to oppress him or take advantage of him."

Although God made the law of hospitality very clear and emphasized it by repeating it in Exodus 23:9, this command was often deliberately and willfully ignored by the people of Israel, or was changed to suit their convenience whenever the opportunity arose. Our rabbis interpreted this law to apply only to the stranger who is Jewish. "It's okay," they said, "to take advantage of a resident alien of another race."

That God did not so limit this command is clearly shown in the Talmud, which was written from the beginning of the destruction of the Temple. It specifies that the stranger (resident alien) was not required to adopt the Jewish faith, even if he worshiped the sun god or practiced some other form of idolatry.

"You shall not wrong," according to the rabbis, means that the stranger must not be ignored and that nothing must be done in any way, even by a word, to injure him or to hurt his feelings. The stranger should have the same treatment enjoyed by one's own brethren.

This law shielding the alien from wrong is of vital significance in the history of religion. Only with it does true worship begin

151

through faith. The alien is to be protected, not because he is a member of one's family, one's clan, or one's religious community, but because he is a human being. In this law concerning the alien, the concept of humanity was born—the concept of love and grace and mercy.

The next commandment is given over and over again throughout the Bible:

> You shall not afflict any widow or fatherless child. If you afflict them in any way and if they at all cry unto Me, says the Lord, I will surely hear their cry. My wrath shall wax hot and I will kill you with the sword and your wives shall be widows and your children shall be fatherless. (Exod. 22:22-24)

The person who takes advantage of a widow or an orphan is coming directly against God, because the Lord Himself is the head of such a defenseless person. A widow has no covering on earth; her head has gone home to be with the Lord Jesus Christ, who is now her Head. If you take advantage of a widow or an orphan, you are putting Christ on the cross once again.

The punishment for afflicting widows and orphans may sound harsh to you, but to me it sounds like a just and holy God—a God who can bring grace and judgment at the same time. The words of Jesus show us the same kind of God. In Matthew 5:40 He says, "If a man steals a jacket, run after him and give him your coat—and praise God that you are not the guy who had to steal the jacket. You can thank Me that you had a jacket to be stolen. But for My grace, you would be in the position of the thief."

> If you lend money to any of My people, even to the poor that are with you, you shall not be to him as a creditor, neither shall you lay upon him interest. (Exod. 22:25)

For 276 years the rabbis argued over the interpretation of "My people." Who *are* God's people? The Rothschilds and other Jewish financiers interpreted "My people" to mean only the people of Israel, and they threw out the commandment given in verse 21 about not oppressing strangers. The early Christians, however, rightly interpreted "God's people" to mean all people on the earth, and they never went into the banking business. All of humanity is God's people, and He wants to save each and every one of them.

When the Lord says, "You shall not be to him as a creditor," He means that, if you have sufficient means to lend money to a person in need, you are to *give* it to him. The Lord promises that if you give money to a needy person, He (the Lord) will return it to you tenfold, twentyfold. You're not to be as a creditor to the one who borrowed the money—not to hound him to return it. That's a pretty specific command. If, in spite of it, you insist on the return of your money, you must not charge interest.

> If you ever take your neighbor's garment in pledge, you shall restore it to him before the sun goes down. For that is his only covering. It is his garment for his skin. In what shall he sleep? And it shall come to pass that when he cries unto Me I will hear; for I am a gracious God. (Exod. 22:26-27)

If your neighbor borrows money from you and you take his garment as pledge, you'd better make sure you return it to him before the sun goes down. If the Lord feels him shivering in the cold, somebody is going to have to answer for it! "Give it back to him and trust Me," says the Lord.

> You shall not revile God, nor curse a ruler of your people. (Exod. 22:28)

Romans 13 is wrapped up here in this one commandment. No matter what people you belong to, what country you live in, your ruler—king, president, governor, mayor—wasn't placed in authority by accident. The *Lord* put him in that position. When you go to a physician or a dentist, he is a divinely ordained authority, just as ministers of the Gospel are divinely ordained. When you come against a divinely ordained authority, you're coming against God. This principle is given in both the Old and the New Testaments. You must not curse a ruler of your people, because all authority stems from the Lord Jesus Christ.

> You shall not delay to offer from the fullness of your harvest and from the outflow of your presses. (Exod. 22:29a)

The Lord says you are to bring your tithes *without delay* into the storehouse, into the house of the Lord (Mal. 3:10).

"Well, Lord, I'm kind of short just now. I'll do it next week, next month, six months from now."

The last message given by the Lord to the people of Israel through the prophet Malachi concerned their failure to tithe: "You are cursed with a curse. And you're going to come to Me and say, 'Lord, why are we cursed already yet?' And I will reply, 'Because you have robbed Me.' And then you're going to ask Me another Jewish question: 'How could we rob God?' And I'm going to tell you that you have robbed Me in your tithes and in your offerings." And then He says,

> Bring your tithes and your offerings into the storehouse, that there may be meat in My house so that others can come in and be blessed. And see if I won't open the windows of heaven unto you and bless you beyond your wildest imagination. Then I will come against the devourer—that which devours your income—and rebuke him so that your blessing will go to the fullest extent. (Mal. 3:10-11)

Your car will get better mileage; your tires will last longer; your transmission won't fall out; your kids won't get sick. That's the promise that God gave you and me through Malachi.

While I was speaking in Pittsburgh one spring, a woman came running up to me after my sermon and said, "Pastor Esses, when you were here two years ago, I told you I was in the real-estate business and that I wanted to make thirty thousand dollars a year. I asked you what I had to do to make this much money. You told me I'd have to step out on faith and pay the Lord a tithe on thirty thousand dollars—three thousand dollars a year."

I said, "Yes, I remember telling you that."

She went on, "Well, I want to tell *you* something. For the last two years I've given the Lord three thousand dollars a year, and I've been making so much money that I wish the Lord would cut it back a little bit."

Praise God for His faithfulness, and do not delay to bring your tithes to God in faith and obedience, for He promises you an overflowing blessing in return.

The firstborn of your sons you shall give unto me. (Exod.

22:29b)

Here God repeats the commandment which He first gave Moses at the time of the Exodus from Egypt (Exod. 13:2). The Lord says that the firstborn *belongs* to Him. He is no respecter of persons, and when He passed judgment on all the firstborn of Egypt, He also passed judgment on the firstborn of Israel. From that time on, the firstborn of Israel are to be dedicated unto the Lord—given to the Lord in a total dedication.

Likewise shall you do with your oxen and with your sheep. Seven days it shall remain with its dam, its mother; on the eighth day you shall give it unto Me. And you shall be holy unto Me. Therefore, you shall not eat any flesh that is torn of beasts in the field; you shall cast it to the dogs. (Exod. 22:30-31)

God wants the first of all we possess: the first fruits, the firstborn son, and the firstborn animal. If the animal is an unclean animal—say, a jackass—we substitute for the unclean animal a clean animal, usually a lamb.

The jackass is a picture of you and me. For this jackass (myself), God substituted His own Lamb, Jesus Christ, who died in my place. Before I knew Him, He loved me and went to the cross for me. Because He was the firstborn of the dead, I became the firstborn of the living. I was unclean, but He made me clean. I praise God that He loved me before I loved Him!

You shall not utter a false report. (Exod. 23:1a)

This command forbids originating a rumor—any report that is groundless or untrue. You get on the telephone: "Hello, Sadie, did you hear what happened? Make sure you don't tell anybody!" So what does Sadie do? She calls up Becky, and the false report you've uttered soon spreads throughout the community.

The Talmud explains this commandment as a warning not to spread slander or even to *listen* to it; you're to stop it right there. The rabbis say that three people are killed in slandering: the person who is slandered, the slanderer, and the person who passes on the slander.

The Talmud also applies the words of this text to false evidence

155

given in a trial—perjury. The witness must not make a statement of
which he is not absolutely certain. If he's not certain, he will say,
"I don't know; I'm not sure."

Put not your hand with the wicked to be an unrighteous
witness. You shall not follow a multitude to do evil. (Exod.
23:1b-2a)

Do you remember the lynching parties we used to see in cowboy
movies? They were multitudes doing evil.

Here the Lord is saying the very same thing He says in the New
Testament. The Jesus of the Old Testament and the Jesus of the
New Testament are one. "Judge not, lest you be judged" (Matt.
7:1). Don't criticize, or you may be subjected to the same harsh
criticism when *you* goof.

Mary Magdalene—Mary of the city of Magdala—was caught in
adultery and brought out to Jesus. A great multitude of the men of
Israel followed, ready to stone her to death. Jesus bent over and
started writing in the sand: Moe, Izzie, Jack, Abie. All these men
were standing there with rocks in their hands, ready to begin the
execution. Jesus looked up and said, "Okay. The one without sin
may cast the first stone." And Moe, Izzie, Jack, and Abie dropped
their stones and ran back home to mama. Jesus knew what they
were.

Then Jesus picked Mary up off the ground and said, "Where are
your accusers? I don't see them." They had all gone back home to
mama because they knew they were guilty. But the important
message Jesus gave Mary was, "I forgive you; go, and sin no
more" (John 8:11). He forgave her right then and there. And
because she was truly a repentant sinner—as all of us are—she was
the first one to see Him after His Resurrection.

Neither shall you bear witness in a cause, turning aside after a
multitude to pervert justice. Neither shall you favor a poor
man in his cause. (Exod. 23:2b-3)

If you're sitting as a judge or on a jury, don't favor a man just
because he's poor. And don't favor him because he's rich either.
Just listen to the case and obey the Spirit's ruling. The Lord says,
"I'll take care of it. I am Lord."

> If you meet your enemy's ox or his ass going astray, you shall surely bring it back to him again. (Exod. 23:4)

The natural reaction, if you saw your enemy's ox or jackass going astray, would be to stand there and say, "Praise the Lord! He's losing his animals." But the Lord Jesus Christ says, "Go out of your way. Get that animal and bring it back to your enemy. And see if I don't bless you because you have shown love. That's what I'm all about. I'm love; I'm gracious; I'm merciful."

> If you see the ass of him that hates you lying under his burden, you shall forbear to pass by him. You shall surely help him with it. (Exod. 23:5)

If you see the animal belonging to your enemy loaded down with a heavy burden, the Lord tells you that you are to help that animal. In so doing you bring to life the words of Jesus: "If you do this unto the least of any one of these, you have done it unto Me (Matt. 25:40). If you help even an animal, you have done it unto Me." Whether the owner of the animal is a friend or an enemy, you are to help that poor overburdened beast.

> You shall not wrest judgment of the poor in his cause. Keep yourself far from a false matter; and slay not the innocent and the righteous: for I will never justify the wicked. (Exod. 23:6-7)

By "the wicked," the Lord means those who remain unrepentant, those who will not change their ways; the Lord says He will never justify such people. The word *justified* means *just as if I'd* never committed a sin. Jesus, by going to the cross and taking with Him our sin, our transgression, and our iniquity, justified you and me—made us *just as if* we had never sinned. But if we remain in our way, in our stubbornness, in our rebellion, the Lord will never justify us. The Lord says that rebellion is as the sin of witchcraft, and stubbornness is as the sin of idolatry (1 Sam. 15:23).

The Lord says, "If you're going to remain rebellious and stubborn, you're not with Me. I'll spit you out of My mouth. Because you're not for Me, you're against Me. And if you're lukewarm—neither hot nor cold—I'll still spit you out of my mouth. You have to take a stand. You have to know whom you have believed, whom you have trusted, to whom you have committed your life until that day which is coming.''

The person who remains in an unrepentant state will never be justified. But if he comes to the Lord and says, ''Lord, forgive me of my sins,'' the Lord will forgive him and will wash him whiter than snow. It's as simple as that.

> And you shall take no gift, for a gift blinds them that have sight and perverts the words of the righteous. (Exod. 23:8)

Let's say you're serving as a judge or a juror, or you're in a position of authority, and somebody comes and offers you a gift. The Lord says you're not to take that gift; because it's going to blind your eyes. You're going to feel obligated to the person who gave it to you, and you won't be *able* to make a righteous decision.

> A stranger you shall not oppress, for you know the heart of a stranger because you yourselves were strangers in the land of Egypt. (Exod. 23:9)

''You know what a stranger feels like, because you were strangers for four hundred years,'' God reminded them. This same commandment was given in Exodus 22:21.

> Six years you shall sow your lands and gather in the increase thereof; but in the seventh year you shall let it rest and lie fallow, that the poor of your people may eat; and what they leave the beasts of the field shall eat. In like manner you shall deal with your vineyard, and with your oliveyard. (Exod. 23:10-11)

There's the promise of the Lord. He says, ''You can work for six years; then I want you to take a year's vacation.'' Isn't that beautiful?

One day Jesus and His disciples got in a little rowboat on the Sea of Galilee and He told them, ''We're going to the other side'' (to the Golan Heights of Syria). Then He fell asleep. In the middle of the lake a terrific storm arose, and the waves were about to swamp the boat. The disciples called for Jesus: ''Master, wake up! We're going to drown!'' And He replied, ''What kind of Jewish nuts are you anyway? I *told* you that we're going to the other side. Where's your faith?''

So here the Lord says, ''If you'll trust Me, if you'll believe Me, you will have an increase in the sixth year to take care of the seventh year and the eighth year. By your *faith* it will be done.''

Six days you shall do your work, but on the seventh day you shall rest, so that your ox and your ass may have rest, and the son of your handmaid and the stranger may be refreshed. And in all things that I have said unto you, take heed. And make no mention of the name of other gods, neither let it be heard out of your mouth. (Exod. 23:12-13)

The Lord forbade the people of Israel even to mention the names of the idols worshiped by their neighbors; yet we see the Israelites taking their children and sacrificing them to the fire gods, Chemosh and Molech (2 Kings 17:31; Acts 7:43). They picked up the idolatry and the abomination of the Canaanites, so that they could sleep with the male or female prostitutes in the temples of Baal and Ashtaroth. And the Lord said, ''What I thought to do unto them I will do unto you, because they are far more righteous than you are. I did not give them My laws, My Scriptures, and My commandments; but I *have* given you My instructions. All you have to do is open up the package and find out how to get along with Me and with one another; but you have refused to open the package.''

Three times in the year you shall keep a feast unto Me. The feast of unleavened bread you shall keep. (Exod. 23:14-15a)

The feast of unleavened bread is the Passover. We keep the Passover today every time we take communion, because Jesus is *our* Passover. At the Last Supper, He kept the Passover for us.

As I commanded you, you shall eat unleavened bread for seven days at the appointed time in the month of Abib, for in it you came out of Egypt. None shall appear before me empty. (Exod. 23:15b)

As you go up to the Lord's table for the Lord's Supper, don't come to Him empty. Bring Him your praise, your thanksgiving, your worship. Say to Him, ''Thank You, Lord, for saving me, for redeeming me, for bringing me out of bondage and out of

slavery.''
And the feast of harvest, the first fruits of your labors, which you have sown in the field; and the feast of the ingathering, at the end of the year, when you gather in your labors out of the field. So three times in the year all your males shall appear before the Lord God. (Exod. 23:16-17)
The three major Jewish festivals named in verses 14-16 are known today as Passover, Pentecost, and the Feast of Tabernacles. Pentecost comes fifty days after Passover, because it commemorates the giving of the Ten Commandments, exactly fifty days from the time the people of Israel left Egypt on the day after the first Passover. It was during the festival of Pentecost, when Jews from all parts of the world were gathered in Jerusalem, that God fulfilled the great promise given in Joel 2:28: "In the latter days I shall pour out My spirit upon all flesh."
What a transformation Pentecost made in Peter, the chicken who denied Jesus! "Lord, I'll die for you any time" he had boasted when there was no immediate danger. But when the chips were down and someone came up to him and said, "Pete, you speak like a Galilean," he denied everything.
"What? Who—me?"
"We saw you with Jesus."
"I never heard of Him."
Twice more, Peter denied his Lord (John 18:17-27). But after the Resurrection Jesus said, "Wait in Jerusalem until you receive power from on high" (Luke 24:49). Peter waited, along with a hundred and nineteen other disciples, and at Pentecost, Peter the Chicken became Peter the Lionhearted. He stood there in front of that crowd of Jews and preached a sermon beginning with Abraham and ending with Jesus Christ.
Then the Jews asked him, "What is it that we have to do?" (Acts 2:37). And the Holy Spirit fell upon all of them, and three thousand people came to the Lord Jesus Christ that very day.
On Pentecost the Lord gave us both the Ten Commandments and His Holy Spirit. He passed us from the letter of the law to the Spirit of the law. Where the Spirit of the Lord is, there is liberty. Praise

God that He's always faithful to keep His promise!

> You shall not offer the blood of My sacrifice with leavened bread. (Exod. 23:18a)

In this commandment, God is speaking specifically about Jesus Christ. The Lord's sacrifice is Jesus Himself. Jesus will go to the cross without leaven—that is, without spot or blemish. He will be absolutely perfect.

> Neither shall the fat of My feast remain all night until the morning. (Exod. 23:18b)

As the Passover Lamb, Jesus was taken down from the cross before sunset.

Another picture of Jesus' crucifixion is found in the story of Abraham and Isaac. When the Lord commanded Abraham to sacrifice Isaac, the son for whom he and Sarah had waited so long, He told him to travel three days' journey to Mount Moriah, and make the sacrifice there. Isaac was thirty years of age at that time—the age of Jesus when He began His ministry. In obedience to the Lord, Isaac was willing to carry wood on his back for the sacrifice and to lie down on the altar to be sacrificed to God. But he asked his father one question: "Where is the burnt offering for the sacrifice?" The Holy Spirit descended upon Abraham, and he answered, "The Lord Himself will provide the sacrifice" (Gen. 22:8).*

Two thousand years later, the Lord Himself did provide the Sacrifice on Mount Moriah, just a few hundred yards away from the place where Abraham's altar stood. There your Jesus and my Jesus went to the cross for you and me. I praise God that He keeps His word!

> The choicest first fruits of your land you shall bring into the house of the Lord your God. You shall not boil a kid in its mother's milk. (Exod. 23:19)

In an area where water is scarce, as it is in many parts of Israel, it is a frequent practice to cook a baby animal, such as a goat, in milk from its own mother. The Lord said, "This practice is cruel. All the beasts of the field are food to you. You can roast meat, broil it, bake it, or cook it any way you choose, except by boiling a baby animal in its mother's milk.''

From this verse of Scripture our rabbis derived all the Jewish dietary laws in the Talmud. When we eat meat, we have to wait six hours for it to pass through the digestive system before we can eat any dairy products. We have to have three different sets of dishes: one for milk and all dairy products, one for meat, and one for Passover. The dishes used for the Passover feast cannot be contaminated by food eaten during the rest of the year.

---

* See the author's *Jesus in Genesis*.

17

Promises of God

(EXODUS 23:20—24)

The greatest promise found in the Bible was given to the people of Israel through Moses:

I send My Angel before you, to keep you on the way and to bring you into the place which I have prepared for you. (Exod. 23:20)

"The way" is the way of truth and of righteousness. And the Angel of the Lord is Jesus Christ Himself, who keeps us in the way, in the life, in the resurrection, in the truth. The truth will set us free, and Jesus will bring us into that place He has prepared for us. He told His disciples, "I go on before you to prepare a mansion for you. And I will send you My Holy Spirit, the Comforter, who will show you everything that I have spoken to you about" (John 14:2,26).

Take heed of Him and harken to His voice. Be not rebellious against Him, for He will not pardon your trangression if you rebel against Him; for My name is in Him. (Exod. 23:21)

Through Moses, God charges the people of Israel to take heed of Jesus. "Don't ignore Him, for there's only one way your transgression will be forgiven: by Him. He and I are One. My name is in Him."

Moses, I believe, knew the true name of the Lord, and he called upon that name: *Yeshua* ("Jesus" in Hebrew).

But if you shall indeed listen and harken unto His voice and do all that I speak, then I will be an enemy unto your enemies and an adversary unto your adversaries. For My Angel—My Redeeming Angel, the Angel of the Lord, Jesus Christ Himself—shall go before you. *He* will bring you in unto the Amorites, the Hittites, the Perizzites, the Canaanites, the Hivites, and the Jebusites, and *I* will cut them off. (Exod. 23:22-23)

In this passage, God speaks of Himself first as God the Father and then as God the Son: "Listen to *His* voice and you will hear *Me* speaking. *He* will bring you into the territory of your enemies, and *I* will cut them off."

You shall not bow down to their gods, nor serve them, nor do after their doings: but you shall utterly overthrow them, and break in pieces their pillars. (Exod. 23:24)

The Lord is saying, "You shall not do anything else other than that which I have commanded you. I have gone before you, I am going before you now, and I will continue to go before you; but you have to be obedient to Me. Don't try to figure out what I have in My mind. My ways are not your ways; My thinking is not your thinking. Don't ask one another, 'What kind of cruel God do we have, who kills women and children and innocent babies?' Just be obedient. I have passed judgment upon these people, and I am the One who's driving them out."

The people in the land of Canaan were involved in the worship of Baal, Ashtoreth, and the fire gods. They sacrificed their babies to the fire gods, and some of their children were raised as temple prostitutes from three months of age. So the Lord says, "Drive them out from before you. Don't even permit any pillar that they have to stand."

You shall serve the Lord your God and He will bless your bread and your water and I will take sickness away from the midst of thee. (Exod. 23:25)

Romans 6:23 tells us where this sickness came from: "The

wages of sin is death.'' The Lord says, ''If you are obedient to Me, I will bless your bread and your water, and I'll even give you a bonus: I'll keep you from getting sick.'' That's one of the fifteen hundred promises in the Bible in regard to healing.

When we are sick, the Lord may be trying to give us a message: ''Hey, Michael, you haven't listened to Me lately. You've done something that is not kosher. Pay attention already. I'm talking to you.''

> None shall miscarry nor be barren in your land. The number of your days I will fulfill. (Exod. 23:26)

''Both your wives and your animals will be fruitful,'' God said. ''I will permit you to live your entire life span, instead of cutting your life short because of your disobedience.''

Everything hinges on obedience.* The Lord speaks constantly about the phenomenon of obedience, saying that obedience is even better than sacrifice (1 Sam. 15:22). The obedience that He wants from us is the sacrifice of our hearts. ''I want your praise, your thanksgiving; I want you to worship Me in spirit and in truth. I want your mind, your mouth, and your heart to speak the same message.'' Sometimes when we try to pray, the Lord says, ''I don't hear a word you're saying, because I can look into your heart and your mind, and I know exactly what's there. You might fool yourself, your wife, your husband, your relatives, but you're not fooling Me.''

> I will send my terror before you. I will discomfit all the people before whom you come. I will make all your enemies turn their backs unto you. And I will send the hornets before you, which shall drive out the Hivite, the Canaanite, and the Hittite from before you. I will not drive them out from before you in one year; lest the land become desolate, and the beast of the field multiply against you. (Exod. 23:27-29)

Here is another promise to the people of Israel that is dependent on obedience: ''I will cause your people to inherit even the farmlands of the enemy. I'll drive them out just a little at a time, so that you'll have time to reap the harvest they planted. You will just walk in and take over where they left off.'' How great is the love, the grace, the mercy of the Lord!

> But little by little I will drive them out from before you, until you are increased—until I increase you and you become a mighty nation—and you inherit the land. I will set your border from the Red Sea even unto the sea of the Philistines, and from the wilderness unto the river Euphrates. For I will deliver the inhabitants of the land into your hand; and you shall drive them out from before you. You shall make no covenant with them, nor with their gods. (Exod. 23:30-32)

The ninth chapter of Joshua tells how Joshua—a man who was otherwise perfectly obedient to God—was tricked by the Hivites into disobeying this specific commandment to make no covenant with the inhabitants of Canaan. The Hivites, one of the seven nations whom God said He would drive out from before Israel, knew that the inhabitants of Canaan were being driven out by the Lord Himself. So they came to the elders of Israel dressed in ragged garments, wearing beat-up shoes, and carrying polluted water and stale bread. They said to the elders. "We would like to make a covenant with you." The elders took the Hivites to Joshua, and when he saw their clothes and their food, he believed their story that they came from a distant land and were not Canaanites at all. "Make a covenant with us," they said, "and we'll be your slaves to draw your water and cut your wood." And because Joshua failed to look beneath the surface, he made a covenant with them. He was fooled just like Eve was.

When he learned his mistake, Joshua still had a choice. He could keep his covenant with man, or he could keep his covenant with God. Although God's commandment was the higher covenant, Joshua disobeyed that command and allowed the Hivites to stay among the people of Israel. He should have broken his covenant with man, because the Lord had said, "If you permit them to live, they will become a thorn in your side. You will pick up their abominations and you will become worse than they are. And that which I thought to do unto them, I will do unto you, because to you I have given much and from you I expect much."

It thrills me to read in the New Testament that salvation is to the

Promises of God

Jew first (Rom. 1:16). But then I get scared to death when I read the converse of that promise—that judgment also comes to the Jew first. The Lord says, "I've been speaking to you for thousands of years. I have given you much, and I expect much from you (Luke 12:48). It's time you grew out of the Pablum stage and got to the meat stage."

Here in Exodus the Lord designates the boundary lines of the Promised Land and says, "This land that I'm giving you as an inheritance is yours forever—*until* you do that which is evil in My eyes."

> They shall not dwell in your land lest they make you sin against Me: for if you serve their gods, they will surely be a snare and a trap unto you. (Exod. 23:33)

The Lord says, "I know the two weaknesses of Israel: sex and finance. If you permit these people to live among you, they will cause you to sin against Me in these two areas. You will serve their sex gods and goddesses, and you'll get trapped just as they are."

> And unto Moses, the Lord said, Come up unto the Lord, you and Aaron, Nadab, and Abihu, and seventy of the elders of Israel; and worship afar off. Moses alone shall come near unto the Lord: but the others shall not come near; neither shall the people come up with him.
>
> And Moses came and told the people all the words of the Lord, and all the ordinances, and all the people answered with one voice and said, All the words which the Lord has spoken we will do. (Exod. 24:1-3)

The Hebrew reads, "All that the Lord has spoken and all that He *will* speak we will do." When Jesus was on the cross, the Jews who passed by mocked Him by saying, "What's a big-shot Messiah, the Savior of the world, doing on a cross? If You're going to save us, save Yourself." Praise God for the prayer of Jesus: "Forgive them, Father, for they know not what they do or what they say. They never have known what I was talking to them about."

Jesus asked His Father to forgive the people who had screamed, "Crucify Him! Let His blood be upon us and upon all of our generations to come." Praise God that He heard that prayer and granted us forgiveness right then and there. Otherwise, there wouldn't be one messianic Jew on the face of the earth—because we took upon ourselves, unto all generations, the blood of Christ.

> And Moses wrote all the words of the Lord, and he rose up early in the morning and built an altar under the mount, and twelve pillars, according to the twelve tribes of Israel. And he sent the young men of the children of Israel, who offered burnt offerings, and sacrificed peace offerings of oxen unto the Lord. (Exod. 24:4-5).

Because there was sin in Israel, the sin offering had to be made before the burnt offering. Then the Holy Spirit came down and consumed the burnt offering. After this visible evidence of the Holy Spirit's presence assured the people of Israel that God had made peace with them and they had made peace with God, the peace offering was made.

Before the coming of Jesus, Moses was the true high priest of Israel (see Psalms 99:6; 106:23) because Aaron, the nominal high priest of Israel, was a sinner from the very beginning. Inspired by the Holy Spririt, Moses told the people of Israel, "The Lord will send you a prophet, one who is like unto me." This prophecy was fulfilled in Jesus Christ.

On the Mount of Transfiguration, it was Moses and Elijah whom the disciples saw with Jesus. The true priesthood passed from Moses to Jesus, and the mantle of the prophet Elijah fell on Him. In this way Jesus Christ became king, prophet, and priest in fulfillment of the Old Testament prophecies.

> And Moses took half of the blood and put it in basins; and half of the blood he dashed against the altar. And he took the book of the covenant, and he read in the hearing of the people. And they said, All that the Lord has spoken and all that He will speak, we will do and obey. (Exod. 24:6-7)

Here is the everlasting covenant that God made with Israel on Pentecost, fifty days after they left Egypt. To bind the people of Israel in this covenant, Moses read the Ten Commandments to them again and obtained their promise to obey all that the Lord had spoken and would speak. Then

Moses took the blood and sprinkled it on the people and said, Behold the blood of the covenant which the Lord has made with you in agreement with all these words. (Exod. 24:8)

The sprinkling of the blood was a picture of the coming of Jesus Christ and the shedding of His blood. The people of Israel were bound by the blood of the sacrifice as we're bound by the blood of Jesus Christ if we accept His sacrifice. Jesus said, "This is the new covenant in my blood which is shed for you for the remission of sin" (Luke 22:20). With His own blood He takes our sin, our transgression, and our iniquity from us.

The Lord has never broken the covenant that He made with the people of Israel at Pentecost. The people of Israel may have broken it, but God has never broken it. The Jews are still bound by the blood, because this was a picture of Jesus Christ. As soon as they accept Jesus Christ, they're saved.

Then went up Moses, Aaron, Nadab, and Abihu, and seventy of the elders of Israel. And they saw the God of Israel. (Exod. 24:9-10a)

Nadab and Abihu were Aaron's two eldest sons. Nadab would be next in line to become high priest after his father.

What these men actually experienced is beyond our comprehension. Through the Holy Spirit, they beheld the majesty of the God of Israel, a revelation of Jesus Christ sitting upon the throne of grace. And they had a vision:

And there was under His feet the like of a paved work of sapphire stone like the very heaven in clearness. (Exod. 24:10b)

The color of sapphire is white and blue: white for the purity of Jesus Christ and blue, the color of the Holy Spirit.

And upon the elders of the children of Israel He laid not His hand. And they beheld God and they did eat and drink. (Exod. 24:11)

The Lord let them have that vision without laying His hand on them. It was actually Jesus Christ that they saw, because the Scripture says that no man has ever seen God and lived.

Now the Lord said unto Moses, Come up unto Me into the

169

mount, and be there: and I will give you the tables of stone, and the law, and the commandments which I have written; that you may teach them. And Moses rose up, and Joshua, his minister: and Moses went up into the mount of God. And unto the elders he said, Stay here until we come back unto you; and behold, Aaron and Hur are with you: whoever has a cause, let him come near unto them. (Exod. 24:12-14)

Moses warned the elders not to go any farther, lest the Lord strike them dead. Unholiness cannot come in contact with holiness. And he left Aaron and Hur in charge of dealing with the elders' gripes and grievances.

And Moses went up unto the mount, and a cloud covered the whole mount. And the glory of the Lord—the *shekinah* glory of God, which is the Holy Spirit—abode upon Mount Sinai, and the cloud covered it six days: and the seventh day He called unto Moses out of the midst of the cloud. And the appearance of the glory of the Lord was like a devouring fire on the top of the mount in the eyes of the children of Israel. (Exod. 24:15-17)

When the Holy Spirit descended on the disciples at Pentecost, it was like tongues of flames coming down. Here the Holy Spirit was seen by the children of Israel as a devouring fire.

And Moses entered into the midst of the cloud. He went up into the mount, and Moses was in the mount forty days and forty nights. (Exod. 24:18)

Moses actually entered into the glory and remained there forty days and forty nights without eating or drinking. During that time he was communing with the Lord; the Lord spoke to him face-to-face. Moses actually beheld the Holy Spirit of God, and they had perfect communion together.

---

* See the author's *Phenomenon of Obedience*.

18

The Tabernacle and the Ark

(EXODUS 25—26:30)

And the Lord spoke unto Moses saying, Speak unto the children of Israel, that they take for Me an offering; of every man whose heart makes him willing, you shall take My offering. (Exod. 25:1-2)

The Lord said, "If a man is not willing to give an offering, don't take it; I don't want it."

And this is the offering which you shall take of them: gold, silver, and brass, and blue, purple, and scarlet. (Exod. 25:3-4a)

The only three metals allowed in the tabernacle were brass, silver, and gold, and the only three colors were blue, red, and purple. The blue and the brass correspond one to another. The brass represents sin, and the blue is the color of the Holy Spirit, who convicts us of sin. Through the conviction of the Holy Spirit, we come up to the level of silver, the symbol of redemption, which corresponds to the color red (the blood of Jesus Christ). Purple and gold symbolize the majesty of God the Father. Through the red blood of Jesus Christ, we are brought through the silver stage of redemption and, after being sanctified, come to the level of being gold and purple like God. Then the words of Jesus will come into effect: "I and the Father are one (John 10:30); and as I am in Him and He is in Me, so shall We be in you" (John 14:11, 20).

Further offerings were to include

Fine linen, and goats' hair, and rams' skins dyed red, and seal skins, and acacia wood. (Exod. 25:4b-5)

The children of Israel left Egypt with great wealth, having despoiled the Egyptians exactly as God said they should. Now the skins, linens, metals, and precious stones that they brought with them are to be used for building the tabernacle of God in the wilderness. The acacia wood was miraculously supplied by God. In this wilderness it has never been found again in quantities great enough to build a tabernacle of this size. That's one small miracle of God right there.

Oil for the light because you will be a light, spices for the anointing oil, sweet incense, onyx stones, and stones to be set in the ephod, and in the breastplate of the high priest. And let them make Me a sanctuary, that I may dwell among them. (Exod. 25:6-8)

In the Hebrew, the word translated "dwell" is *shekinah*. By His Holy Spirit, His *shekinah* glory, the Lord was going to be present among the people of Israel.

Now the Lord not only gives Moses the blueprint, the plan, of the tabernacle; He actually gives him the vision to *see* what the tabernacle will be like, what every garment and furnishing is to look like: the table of showbread, the golden altar, and the altar of burnt offering.

According to all that I show you, the pattern of the tabernacle, the pattern of all the furniture thereof, even so shall you make it. And they shall make an ark of acacia wood: two cubits* and a half shall be the length thereof, a cubit and a half the breadth thereof, and a cubit and a half the height thereof. You shall overlay it with pure gold; within and without you shall overlay it, and you shall make upon it a crown of gold round about. And you shall cast four rings of gold for it, and put them in the four corners thereof; and two rings shall be on the one side of it, and two rings on the other side of it. And you shall make staves of acacia wood, and overlay them with gold. You shall put the staves into the rings on the sides of the ark, wherewith you shall bear the ark. (Exod. 25:9-14)

The ark of the covenant was to be borne only on the shoulders of the priests, never on a cart.

The staves shall be in the rings of the ark. They shall not be taken from it. And you shall put into the ark the testimony which I shall give you. (Exod. 25:15-16)

The testimony is the Decalogue, the Ten Living Words, the testimony of God Himself.

The ark of the covenant remained with the people of Israel until the year 586 B.C., when Nebuchadnezzar destroyed Jerusalem and the temple.

The people of Israel are still looking for the ark of the covenant. But because we've read the end of the story, the Book of Revelation, we know that the ark of the covenant is up in heaven. The true Covenant is Jesus Christ, who came into the world and gave us the everlasting covenant in His blood, in His body. All we need to do is call upon the name of the Lord Jesus Christ, and we are saved.

You shall make the ark cover of pure gold; two cubits and a half shall be the length thereof, a cubit and a half the breadth thereof. You shall make two cherubim of gold, of beaten work you shall make them, at the two ends of the ark cover. And make one cherub at the one end, and one cherub at the other end. With the ark cover shall you make the cherubim on the two ends thereof. (Exod. 25:17-19)

The cherubim were not to be made separate from the ark cover but as parts of it, because this was the mercy seat of God. "When you come to My mercy seat," the Lord says, "I will speak to you from between the two cherubim. And when you come to My mercy seat, you'd better come with a reasonable and holy sacrifice." There's only one way we can approach the mercy seat and the throne of grace, and that is through the body and blood of Jesus Christ.

The cherubim shall spread out their wings on high, screening the ark cover with their wings, and with their faces one to another; toward the ark cover shall the faces of the cherubim be. (Exod. 25:20)

The cherubim were to be facing each other, and their wings were to be spread out so that the eye of man could not behold the mercy seat. If a man came into the holy of holies by accident and saw the mercy seat of God, he would be destroyed. So the cherubim, with their outstretched wings, hid the mercy seat until Christ was upon the cross. Then the veil of the temple was torn from top to bottom, so that man can enter the holy of holies and can come to the mercy seat protected by the blood of Jesus.

And you shall put the ark cover above and upon the ark; and in the ark you shall put the testimony that I shall give you. And there I will meet with you, and I will speak with you from above the ark cover, and from between the two cherubim which are upon the ark of the testimony I shall speak to you of all the things which I will give you in commandment unto the children of Israel. (Exod. 25:21-22)

Praise God that He will speak, and that there's a man to hear when He speaks!

And you shall make a table out of acacia wood: two cubits shall be the length thereof, a cubit the breadth thereof, and a cubit and a half the height thereof. And you shall overlay it with pure gold, and make thereunto it a crown of gold round about. And you shall make unto it a border of an handbreadth round about, and you shall make a golden crown to the border thereof round about. And you shall make for it four rings of gold, and put the rings in the four corners that are on the four feet thereof. Close by the border shall be the rings for places for the staves to bear the table. (Exod. 25:23-27)

The table described here is the table of showbread. In Hebrew, showbread is called "the bread of the presence." The presence of God is the Holy Spirit of God—so this was the bread of the Holy Spirit. It was kept in the tabernacle as an expression of thanksgiving and an acknowledgment that God was the giver of daily necessities for the children of Israel, just as He is for us

Christians. He says, "I will supply all of your needs according to My riches in glory (Phil. 4:19). All you need to do is trust Me for it—but do you have the faith to trust Me for it?" That's the crux of the matter, because faith and obedience go hand in hand.

Leviticus 24:5-9 tells us that the showbread consisted of twelve loaves of bread, made of wheat flour, the number of loaves corresponding to the number of the tribes of Israel. On the sabbath the loaves were placed on the table of showbread, arranged in two rows of six. They were left there until the following sabbath, and then they were removed and eaten by the priests. The bread of the presence was divinely protected by the Holy Spirit, so that it never became stale or dry. When it was removed and eaten on Friday evening, it was just as fresh and moist and wholesome as when it was placed there the previous week.

Only one person who was not a priest ever ate any of the showbread, and that was King David. From him was coming the great King, the Messiah of Israel and the Savior of the world. Jesus was never called the son of Abraham, Isaac, or Jacob, but the son of David. Therefore David was permitted to eat of the showbread.

> You shall make the staves of acacia wood and you shall overlay them with gold, that the table may be borne with them. And you shall make the dishes thereof, the pans thereof, the jars thereof, the bowls thereof, withal to pour out: of pure gold you shall make them. And you shall set upon the table showbread before me always. (Exod. 25:28-30)

The Lord didn't say the bread was to be put there just for that particular time; He said *always*. The bread of our presence today, our showbread, is Jesus. At the Last Supper, on the night of the Passover, He said, "Take and eat; this is My body which is broken for you." Your Jesus and my Jesus is the holy bread which is always present before the Lord.

Jesus made a strange statement about the people of Israel. He said, "Your forefathers ate manna—bread from heaven—in the wilderness, and they died. But he who eats of Me, the Bread of Life, shall never die. He'll never even hunger or thirst. Eat, and you shall be satisfied: you'll not want for anything."

175

And you shall make a candlestick of pure gold. (Exod. 25:31a)

Notice all the gold that's being used. If you belong to a church and the stewardship committee says, "We're going to erect a new sanctuary and we're going to spend $150,000," don't get shook up. That little tabernacle in the wilderness cost $15 million. The stewardship committee didn't worry about it, because the Lord said, "I'll take care of it. All you need to do is trust Me."

Of beaten work shall the candlestick be made: even its face and its shaft, its cups, its knobs, and its flowers shall be of one piece with it. And there shall be six branches going out of the sides thereof; three branches of the candlestick out of the one side thereof, and three branches of the candlestick out of the other side thereof. (Exod. 25:31b-32)

The menorah, or lampstand, has one central shaft representing Jesus Christ, the Light of the world. Three branches come out of each side of this shaft, so that the lampstand holds seven candles. These represent the seven manifold spirits of God, described in the Book of Revelation and in Isaiah 11:2 as the spirits which would rest upon Jesus Christ: the spirit of wisdom and understanding, the spirit of counsel and might, and the spirit of knowledge and of the fear of the Lord (Isa. 11:2). The three flowering branches represent the Father, the Son, and the Holy Spirit.

Three cups made like almond blossoms on one branch, each with a knob and a flower; and three cups made like almond blossoms on the other branch, each with a knob and a flower: so for the six branches going out of the candlestick. (Exod. 25:33)

God's number is three. He's always representing Himself and calling attention to Himself, saying, "I am the Father; I am the Son; and I am the Holy Spirit. If you have eyes to see, see; if you have ears to hear, hear; if you have a heart that understands, perceive and know and understand what I'm talking to you about."

And on the candlesticks shall be four cups made like almond blossoms, and the knobs thereof, and the flowers thereof. And a knob under two branches of one piece with it, and a knob under two branches of one piece with it, and a knob under two branches of one piece with it, for the six branches going out of the candlestick. Their knobs and their branches shall be of one piece with it, the whole of it one beaten work of pure gold. And you shall make the lamps thereof seven: they shall light the lamps thereof to give light over against it. And the tongs thereof, and the snuffdishes thereof, shall be of pure gold. Of a talent of pure gold shall it be made, with all these vessels. And see that you shall make them after their pattern, which is being shown to you in the mount. (Exod. 25:34-40)

The Lord not only describes the lampstand to Moses; He actually shows him what it is to look like. Moses is a witness to what God wants on earth, which is what is already in heaven. And everything is made out of gold: the snuffdishes, the lampstand, the mercy seat, the cherubim, the ark of the covenant, the table of showbread.

When the Lord lit that lampstand, it remained lit until the time of Christ. According to Josephus, the Jewish historian, the lamp in the temple went out when Jesus was born, because the Light of the world had come into the world. Josephus was a most accurate historian who lived in the time of Christ. The people of Israel still consider him a traitor, however, because he became a completed Jew in Jesus Christ. As he wrote about Jesus, he felt His love and accepted Him as his personal Savior.

Moreover you shall make the tabernacle with ten curtains of fine twined linen, of blue, purple, and scarlet. (Exod. 26:1a)

God says, "I want all of the Trinity represented in the tabernacle: the blue, the purple, and the scarlet."

With cherubim, the work of skillful workmen, shall you make them. The length of one curtain shall be twenty-eight cubits, and the breadth of one curtain four cubits: all the curtains shall have one measure. (Exod. 26:1b-2)

"I don't want them made separate, but I want them made as one measure." That was some drapery job!

Five curtains shall be coupled together one to another; the other five curtains shall be coupled one to another. And you shall make loops of blue upon the edge of one curtain that is

177

outmost in the first set; and likewise shall you make in the edge of the curtain that is outmost in the second set. (Exod. 26:3-4)

Everything in the tabernacle had to have some blue upon it, and all holy utensils had to be covered with blue when the tabernacle was moved. Blue is the color of the Holy Spirit, and the Lord wanted everything to be covered and protected by the Holy Spirit. The pillar of flame that led the people of Israel by night was blue. Any pure flame is actually blue, the color of the Holy Spirit. The Lord is saying, "I am divinely protecting you on each side by My Holy Spirit, even on the curtains. There shall be loops of blue on each side, on the left and on the right."

You shall have fifty loops that you shall make in the one curtain, fifty loops that you shall make in the edge of the curtain that is in the second set. The loops shall be opposite one to another. (Exod. 26:5)

Here the Lord brings in another significant number, *fifty*. The high priest could not start his ministry until he was thirty years of age, and at fifty years of age he had to retire. Jesus started His ministry at the age of thirty, exactly fulfilling the law for the priesthood. Also it was fifty days from Passover to the giving of the Ten Commandments, and fifty days from the Passover meal that Jesus observed with His disciples until God poured out His Holy Spirit on them. So the number fifty represents Pentecost and the giving of the commandments.

And you shall make fifty clasps of gold, and couple the curtains together with the clasps: and it shall be one tabernacle. And you shall make curtains of goat's hair for a tent over the tabernacle: eleven curtains shall you make them. (Exod. 26:7)

For years it puzzled me that the Lord specified eleven curtains rather than twelve—one for each of the tribes of Israel. Then I realized that the missing curtain represents Dan, the tribe of Judas Iscariot. Dan is not mentioned in the Book of Revelation as being one of the tribes that will be left as a witness for the Lord. There were to be eleven curtains to cover the tabernacle because eleven disciples would remain true to Jesus Christ, but the twelfth would betray the Lord.

At the Last Supper the Lord was gracious enough to call Judas to salvation four different times (John 13). If Judas had come back to the Lord and asked forgiveness, Jesus would have forgiven him. Instead, he went back to the legalism represented by the high priest. If we go back to the law, there's no forgiveness. It's impossible to live under the law. There is not one of us who has not sinned and fallen short of the glory of God (Rom. 3:23). But praise God! Jesus takes our sin from us before we have done it. And if we come to Him in repentance, He is faithful and just to forgive us of our sin (1 John 1:9).

Many of the numbers used in the Bible have symbolic significance. *Three* is the signature of the Trinity: God the Father, God the Son, and God the Holy Spirit. *Four* is the signature of nature and of creation itself. Four and three together make *seven*, the number which represents totality. God the Father, Son, and Holy Spirit is ever present in His creation and in nature. God is the ruler of all nature and all mankind and all the earth and all the universe. The book of creation, Genesis, opens with the number seven. In seven days, God brought everything into being. The entire Levitical system is built on sevens. There are seven days in the week, and seven colors in the rainbow.

Multiplying three times four gives us *twelve*—the number of tribes in Israel and the number of apostles. The number *ten* also appears in the Bible a number of times. The first letter in Hebrew in the name of God (YHWH) and Yeshua (Jesus) is *ten*. The Apostles waited in Jerusalem for ten days to receive the power from on high, the Baptism in the Holy Spirit. So we see that the number ten has great significance also.

> The length of one curtain shall be thirty cubits, and the breadth of one curtain four cubits: and the eleven curtains shall be all of one measure. And you shall couple five curtains by themselves, and six curtains by themselves, and shall double the sixth curtain in the forefront of the tabernacle. And you shall make fifty loops on the edge of the one curtain that is

outmost in the first set, fifty loops in the edge of the curtain which is outmost in the second set. And you shall make fifty clasps of brass, put the clasps into the loops, and couple the tent together, that it may be one. And the overhanging part that remains of the curtains of the tent, that half curtain that remains, shall hang over the back of the tabernacle. And a cubit on the one side, and a cubit on the other side of that which remains in the length of the curtains of the tent, it shall hang over the sides of the tabernacle on this side and on that side, to cover it. (Exod. 26:8-13)

The loops were probably made of woven goat's hair and the clasps of copper or bronze, because this outer curtain was not part of the actual tabernacle. Unlike the linen curtains, it was only a protection from rain, dust, and sun.

Note that there were eleven curtains of hair as against ten of linen. Two cubits of the eleventh curtain are accounted for in verse 9. The eleventh curtain is now two cubits (thirty-six inches) longer than all the others. The extra two cubits were allowed to trail on the ground at the back of the edifice, on the west side. This extra length provided for the boards on either side which were left exposed by the inner curtain. In this way the sides (which were made of boards) were completely protected by the outer curtain.

And you shall make a covering for the tent of rams' skins dyed red, and a covering of seals' skins above. (Exod. 26:14)

As a further protection for the precious fabrics of the tabernacle, there were two additional coverings of skin, which were spread over the roof and hung down at the sides. (According to rabbinical tradition, however, there was only one additional covering, made of rams' skins with patches of porpoise skin.) These skins, like the precious metals and fine fabrics used in furnishing the tabernacle, were among the booty taken from the Egyptians at the time of the Exodus. The Lord said, "I have already given you everything that I'm asking you for. Now you return it to Me, and you will see the blessing I will give you."

The rams' skins dyed red are a picture of our covering by the blood of Jesus Christ. Many denominations today refuse to talk about the blood of Christ. Yet in the Book of Revelation His blood is mentioned over and over again.

> You shall make the boards for the tabernacle of acacia wood standing up. Ten cubits shall be the length of a board, and a cubit and a half the breadth of each board. (Exod. 26:15-16)

Acacia is the same thing as shittim, the word used in the King James Version. The Lord's miraculous provision of acacia wood of the dimensions He specifies here has already been discussed, in connection with Exodus 25:5. A board 27 inches by 180 inches, or 15 feet, has to come from a good-sized tree. There are no acacia trees this large in the Holy Land today, nor have there been in modern history.

In giving these dimensions, the Lord is specifically demanding obedience. He says, "Don't ask me why. It's not for you to understand My ways, which are not your ways. That's how I want you to make it, Moses." And Moses doesn't ask why; he just obeys the Lord.

> Two tenons shall there be in each board, joined one to another: thus you shall make for all the boards of the tabernacle. And you shall make the boards of the tabernacle, twenty boards for the south side southward. And you shall make forty sockets of silver under the twenty boards; two sockets under one board for its two tenons, two sockets under another board for its two tenons. And for the second side of the tabernacle on the north side, there shall be twenty boards: and their forty sockets of silver; two sockets under one board, and two sockets under another board. And for the back part of the tabernacle westward you shall make six boards. And then two boards you shall make for the corners of the tabernacle in the hinder part. They shall be doubled beneath and in a like manner they shall be complete unto the top thereof unto the first ring: thus it shall be for them both; they shall be for the two corners. Thus there shall be eight boards and their sockets of silver, sixteen sockets; two sockets under the one board, and two sockets under another board. (Exod. 26:17-25)

The walls of the tabernacle were made of solid boards, placed vertically in position and joined by crosspieces at the top and at the bottom. The length of the boards (fifteen feet) was the height of the tabernacle. Tenons are projecting pegs which fit into sockets, and these tenons were "joined one to another" by being fixed onto a plate of metal. The sockets which received the tenons were on the bases or pedestals that kept the boards erect.

The north and south sides of the tabernacle were each made of twenty boards. Since each board was a cubit and a half wide, the length of the tabernacle was thirty cubits, or forty-five feet. The west side, which faced the Negev Desert and the Mediterranean Sea, contained only six boards, which would occupy a space of nine cubits. Yet it is certain that the width of the tabernacle was ten cubits, the same as the height. The one cubit still to be accounted for is found in verse 24, where the Lord says, "They shall be doubled beneath." This means that an additional board was to be fitted into each corner of the *inner* side of the west wall. These boards served as buttresses to strengthen the corners. Because they overlapped the last of the twenty boards on the north and south sides of the tabernacle, they added half a cubit to each end of the west wall.

> And you shall make bars of acacia wood: five for the boards of the one side of the tabernacle, and five bars for the boards of the other side of the tabernacle, and five bars for the boards of the side of the tabernacle, for behind the part westward. And the middle bar in the midst of the boards shall pass through from end to end. And now you shall overlay the boards with gold, you shall make their rings of gold for holders for the bars; and you shall overlay the holders with gold. (Exod. 26:26-29)

Along each of the three walls of the tabernacle were fixed three rows of bars. The central bar ran the entire length of the wall, but the top and the bottom rows were shorter. These bars fitted into gold rings, which were attached to the boards of the tabernacle. The rings and the bars served to hold the walls together, so that the tabernacle might not be shaken by the winds.

Remember that the tabernacle had to be constructed so that it could be dismantled at a moment's notice, because the people of Israel never knew when they were going to move. Everything about the tabernacle was portable and was made to fit together like a jigsaw puzzle, so that it could easily be taken apart and put back together. When the Lord lifted His pillar of cloud or fire, the people would dismantle the tabernacle and the Levites would carry it as the children of Israel marched, following the pillar of cloud (Jesus Christ) by day or the pillar of fire (the Holy Spirit) by night (Isa. 63:9-14).

> And you shall rear up the tabernacle according to the fashion thereof which has been shown to you in the mount. (Exod. 26:30)

This verse implies that more detailed directions were given to Moses than are recorded in this book. This supplementary instruction filled in any gaps which occur in the written account.

---

* A cubit is equal to eighteen inches.

19

The Holy of Holies and the Altar of Burnt Offering

(EXODUS 26:31—27)

Now the Lord gives Moses directions for making the veil that separates the holy of holies from the rest of the tabernacle.

And you shall make a veil of blue, purple, scarlet, and fine twined linen; with cherubim, the work of the skillful workmen, shall it be made. You shall hang it upon four pillars of acacia overlaid with gold, their hooks being of gold, upon four sockets of silver. You shall hang up the veil under the clasps, that you may bring in there within the veil the ark of the testimony. (Exod. 26:31-33a)

The Lord uses this term for the ark of the covenant because it contained the two tables of stone which had the Ten Living Words, the Decalogue, written upon them. The Decalogue is the testimony of God Himself, because it starts out, "I am the Lord thy God."

And the veil shall divide unto you between the holy place and the most holy, the holy of holies. You shall put the ark cover upon the ark of the testimony in the most holy place. (Exod. 26:33b-34)

The veil was held up by golden hooks attached to four wooden posts. The posts fitted into silver sockets similar to those placed under the boards.

The holy of holies formed a perfect cube, being ten cubits (fifteen feet) in height, length, and breadth.

Now the Lord tells Moses how He wants him to place the furniture in the tabernacle:

> You shall set the table outside the veil, and the candlestick over against the table on the side of the tabernacle toward the south: and you shall put the table on the north side. (Exod. 26:35)

The table of showbread was set on the north side of the tabernacle, 2½ cubits (almost four feet) from the wall. The candlestick was placed on the south side, the same distance from the wall. Between the two was the golden altar of incense.

> And you shall make a screen for the door of the tent, of blue, purple, and scarlet, and fine twined linen, the work of the weaver in colors. And you shall make for the screen five pillars of acacia, and overlay them with gold, and their hooks shall be of gold: and you shall cast five sockets of brass for them. (Exod. 26:36-37)

Instead of curtains for the entrance to the tabernacle, a special screen was made of material similar to that in the veil. No cherubim were embroidered on it, however, and the screen was supported by five pillars instead of four. This additional support was needed because the screen would be drawn aside so frequently, to allow the priests to enter.

When the high priest came into the tabernacle and prepared to enter the holy of holies, there was a specific order he had to follow in seeking the Lord. God is an orderly God, and when He commands that you are to enter in a certain way, He says there is no other way to follow. When Christ came into the world, He said there was only one way to enter in, and that was through Him. He said, "If you enter in any other way you're a robber and a thief."

The high priest would first approach the table of showbread, then come to the golden altar of incense, and then to the candlestick. He would be looking for the Lord in the showbread, in the candlestick, and in the altar of incense (which signified the prayers and the praise of the people of Israel). But the priest is not

186

going to find the Lord in any of those places, because He is at the mercy seat, in the holy of holies. The priest is going to have to make a commitment and enter into the holy of holies by faith. He has to have faith that he's going to be purified, sanctified, completely right with the Lord; because the minute he enters in, he's standing with holiness. He's totally unrighteous and unholy, but by his faith at that moment the Lord makes him righteous and holy.

Our Mishraic rabbis say that the high priest stands by the curtain before the holy of holies with a bucket of blood in one hand and a censer of incense in the other. The curtain is made without a seam or opening; but as the priest stands there in faith, the Lord translates him from one side of the curtain to the other side. If the man is not right with the Lord, he's going to drop dead the minute he is by that mercy seat, because the Lord looks into his heart.

The people of Israel were accustomed to tying a rope around the ankle of the high priest before he entered the holy of holies. If they failed to hear the bells tinkling on his garment after he went inside, they knew he was dead and they would drag him out by the rope. Nobody else could go in except the high priest's son, who was to become the next high priest.

The minute they heard the bells tinkling, the people of Israel would bow down and worship the Lord. They knew the high priest was still alive and well, and was interceding with the Lord for himself, for his family, and for them.

Chapter 27 begins with a description of the altar of burnt offerings—the altar where the people of Israel offered their sacrifices after they had first presented their sin offering. When God sent His Holy Spirit to consume the burnt offering, they knew they were forgiven sinners.

Our rabbis have made an acrostic of the Hebrew name for *altar,* making each letter the beginning of another word. The altar was the channel through which the people of Israel could seek reconciliation with God when they had become estranged by sin. Therefore the first letter signified the word for *forgiveness.* The

Lord would forgive them, and then they would forgive themselves. The Lord would forget their sin, and then they were to forget it. If they went back to the Lord saying, "Lord, forgive me for committing the same sin today that I committed yesterday," He would reply, "I'll forgive you of the sin you committed today, yes. But what sin did you commit yesterday?" God is true to His Word, and He says, "I forgive you of your sin and I forget it."

The second letter in the Hebrew word for *altar* stands for *gratitude*. The minute the people saw the Holy Spirit descend and consume the burnt offering, they knew they had received forgiveness from the Lord and they felt the spirit of gratitude, humility, contrition.

The next letter stands for the *blessing* from the Lord, which the people received by being true to the teachings around the altar. There they learned that man earns nothing for himself, but that the divine blessings of grace, love, and mercy come from God. And if a man finds all these in God and Jesus Christ after he himself has been forgiven, he becomes a blessing to his fellowman. The last letter of the word *altar* in Hebrew stands for *life everlasting* and the things that abide forever: truth, righteousness, and holiness.

The Old Testament altar, therefore, is a very beautiful picture of Jesus Christ and of the everlasting life found in Him. The Lord told Moses how to make this altar:

> And you shall make an altar of acacia wood, five cubits long, five cubits broad; the altar shall be foursquare: and the height thereof shall be three cubits. You shall make the horns of it upon the four corners thereof: the horns thereof shall be of one piece with it: and you shall overlay it with brass. (Exod. 27:1-2)

Brass denotes sin and this was the altar where the sinner would be released from his sin. Sin has power to keep us in bondage, in oppression, in depression unless we go to Jesus and say, "Lord, forgive me of my sin." Jesus said, "I am the way, the truth, and the life. If you seek My way, My life, and My truth, the truth shall set you free—free from the power of sin and from the bondage of sin."

The altar, including the horns, was made of one piece. It was foursquare, and the horns, one in each corner, were pointed at the top. The sacrifice was placed on the altar, but the blood was put upon the horns, so that it would always be lifted up. Jesus Christ said, "If I be lifted up, I will draw all mankind unto Me." He *was* lifted up on the cross, and by the sacrifice of His own body and His own blood, He entered into the holy of holies and justified you and me—made us just as if we had never sinned. Praise God!

When Josephus described the altar in the Second Temple, in the time of Jesus Christ, he said that the horns were to him the symbol of power, of glory, and of salvation. To the worshiper, these horns no doubt typified the might of God and His ability to protect those who resorted to His altar.

The protection against punishment promised by God to anyone clinging to the horns of the altar symbolized the protection given to those who come to the foot of the cross seeking forgiveness for their sins.

> And you shall make pans for it to receive its ashes, and shovels and basins and fleshhooks and firepans: all the vessels thereof you shall make of brass. And you shall make for it a grate of network of brass; and upon the net you shall make four brazen rings in the four corners thereof. And you shall put it under the ledge round the altar beneath, that the net may reach halfway up to the altar. You shall make staves for the altar, staves of acacia wood, and you shall overlay them with brass. The staves thereof shall be put into the rings, and the staves shall be upon the two sides of the altar, bearing it. (Exod. 27:3-7)

Everything is overlaid with brass, denoting sin: the shovels used for removing the ashes of the animals offered as burnt offerings; the basins which served as receptacles for the blood of the slain animals; the fleshhooks used for handling the flesh of the sacrifices; and the firepans in which the burning coals were carried from the altar of burnt offerings to the altar of incense.

This transfer of coals gives us a picture of what's happening in the sacrifice. After the Holy Spirit comes down and consumes your burnt offering, you know you're a forgiven sinner. The coal that the high priest takes from the altar of burnt offering and brings to the altar of incense is your prayer of praise and thanksgiving to the Lord for forgiveness, redemption, salvation.

Halfway around the altar there ran a ledge which, according to Hebrew tradition, was made of copper and was eighteen inches wide. This ledge rested upon a brazen grating which was 2½ feet high. Attached to the grating were rings that made it possible for the altar to be carried. The high priest stood on the narrow copper ledge as he watched the fire of the Holy Spirit come down and consume the burnt offering. You'd better believe that the priest's heart was right with the Lord as he witnessed the miracle taking place; if it hadn't been, the fire could have consumed him, too.

> Hollow with planks you shall make it: as it has been shown you in the mount, so they shall make it. (Exod. 27:8)

The altar consisted of wooden planks covered with metal, so that the inside was hollow. In Exodus 20:24, God commanded Moses to make an altar of earth unto Him. Wherever the tabernacle was erected, a mound of earth equal in dimensions to the hollow of the altar was heaped up, and the casing of the altar was set over it.

> You shall make the court of the tabernacle: for the south side southward there shall be hangings for the court of fine twined linen an hundred cubits long for one side. The pillars thereof shall be twenty, their twenty sockets of brass; the hooks of the pillars and their fillets shall be of silver. And likewise for the north side in length there shall be hangings of an hundred cubits long, and the pillars thereof twenty, their twenty sockets of brass; the hooks of the pillars and their fillets of silver.

> And for the breadth of the court on the west side shall be hangings of fifty cubits: their pillars ten, their sockets ten. And the breadth of the court on the east side eastward shall be fifty cubits. The hangings for the one side of the gate shall be fifteen cubits: their pillars three and their sockets three. And for the other side shall be hangings of fifteen cubits: their pillars three, and their sockets three. And for the gate of the

court shall be a screen of twenty cubits, of blue, purple, and scarlet, and fine twined linen, the work of the weaver in colors: their pillars four and their sockets four. All the pillars round about the court shall be filleted with silver; their hooks of silver, their sockets of brass.

The length of the court shall be an hundred cubits (150 feet) and the breadth fifty everywhere, and the height five cubits of fine twined linen, and their sockets of brass. (Exod. 27:9-18)

The court was an enclosure without a roof. It marked off the limits of the sanctuary, and only Israelites who were ritually clean could enter the court. To be made ritually clean, a man had to fast, pray, and abstain from the marital relationship. He had to obtain forgiveness of sin by bringing in his guilt offerings. Then he had to be immersed in water (baptized). After that, he was ritually clean and could enter the court.

The material used for the enclosure was fine twined linen, and the length was 150 feet. Fine twined linen, like the ritual of purification required for entering the court, is a picture of the purity of Jesus Christ. The linen hangings were supported by twenty pillars set 7½ feet apart. Since the height of the hangings was 7½ feet, the spaces created by the pillars were square. The pillars were connected by narrow strips (fillets) of silver binding material.

The court was twice as long as it was broad, having twenty pillars along its length and ten along its breadth. On the east side the hangings extended only fifteen cubits (22½ feet) from each corner. The open space left in the middle, measuring twenty cubits, or thirty feet, was filled in by a screen made of the same fabric as the hangings of the tabernacle.

The phrase, "the breadth fifty everywhere" (verse 18) implies that the dimensions of the court were fifty cubits by fifty cubits. For 115 years the rabbis argued over the meaning of this phrase. They finally arrived at the conclusion that the court was fifty cubits (seventy-five feet) square. Yet the Lord says in the same verse that "the length of the court shall be an hundred cubits." The way I see it, in the light of Jesus Christ, is that the phrase "fifty every where" was a reference to Pentecost, the day when God would pour out His Holy Spirit everywhere. Being a former rabbi, however, I'm not going to argue with the other rabbis.

> All the instruments of the tabernacle in all the service thereof, and all the pins thereof, and all the pins of the court, shall be of brass. (Exod. 27:19)

The instruments of the tabernacle are the tools that were used in setting up the tent, such as hammers for driving the pins into the ground. The word used here for "tabernacle" includes the court as well as the holy place and the holy of holies. Once again, everything "shall be of brass," because this is the place where sin would abound. But it is also the place where grace would abound that much more, as the Lord removed the sins of the people.

> And you shall command the children of Israel, that they bring unto you pure olive oil beaten for the light, to cause the lamp to burn continually. In the tent of meeting outside the veil, which is before the testimony, Aaron and his sons shall set it in order to burn from evening to morning before the Lord: it shall be a statute for ever throughout their generations on behalf of the children of Israel. (Exod. 27:20-21)

The light was to be kept burning in the sanctuary day and night with pure olive oil, which was used for sacred purposes. The first drops of oil obtained when olives are gently pounded in a mortar are of the purest quality, and that was the only kind of oil that was to be used.

Because no sunlight fell into the sanctuary, there always had to be one light burning outside the veil—in the holy place, not in the holy of holies. In synagogues today, the light of the sanctuary is represented by a lamp that burns perpetually before the ark where the Scriptures are kept.

The rabbis interpret the light as a symbol of Israel, whose mission it was to be a light to the world and to the heathen people surrounding them until the Messiah came; then He would be the light to all nations of the world. And all the nations would rally about Him and He would be the ensign, the banner of love, over all people. Praise God! Once in a while, we rabbis hit upon a truth.

It was to be the nightly duty of Aaron and his heirs to remove the burnt wick, replace it with a fresh one, and then fill the lamp with oil and relight it. The Lord says this duty will be a statute unto the children of Israel forever.

When the Maccabees, approximately 165 years before the birth of Christ, cleansed and rededicated the temple after it had been desecrated by the Syrians under Antiochus Epiphanes, there was enough oil for the lamp to burn only a few hours. They prayed to God for a miracle, and those few drops of oil lasted for nine days as the temple was rededicated and sanctified, and the people of Israel came back to the Lord. The festival of Hanukkah, celebrating the rededication of the temple, is a holiday still observed among Jews today.

20

The Priestly Garments

(EXODUS 28)

After God had finished giving Moses instructions for building the sanctuary, He told him what to do about the men who were to serve as priests. The sacred office was reserved for Aaron, his sons, and their descendants forever. Exodus 28 describes the garments to be worn by the priests when ministering in the sanctuary. These garments distinguished the priest from the lay Israelites and reminded him that he must make holiness the constant guide of his life. The vestments themselves were holy, and they contributed to the sense of awe with which the people of Israel regarded the service of the sanctuary.

The garments were to be worn by the priests *only* when they were discharging their holy function. And they were not to be worn by the high priest on the Day of Atonement. When he went into the holy of holies on that day, he had to wear a simple linen garment without seams—a garment of the type Jesus wore when He went to the cross as our sacrifice.

> And you bring unto you Aaron your brother, and his sons with him, from among the children of Israel, that he may minister unto Me in the priest's office, even Aaron, Nadab, Abihu, Eleazar, and Ithamar, Aaron's sons. (Exod. 28:1)

195

The Lord says that Aaron *may* minister—in other words, He will permit him to minister—to Him. The priest's first duty is to minister to the Lord. This comes before his ministry to the people.

> And you shall make holy garments for Aaron thy brother for splendor and for beauty. (Exod. 28:2)

These garments would remain intact from the first high priest to the last high priest—from the time of Aaron until the year A.D. 70, when Titus invaded Jerusalem, destroyed the temple, and killed two million Israelites. Those garments would fit tall priests and short priests. They would never show oil stains from the anointing or blood stains from the sprinkling of the blood. They were sanctified, holy garments because they were covered by the oil of the Holy Spirit and divinely protected by the shed blood of Jesus Christ.

> You shall speak unto all those who are wise hearted, whom I have filled with the spirit of wisdom, that they may make Aaron's garments to sanctify him that he may minister unto Me in the priest's office. (Exod. 28:3)

Wisdom is one of the gifts of the Holy Spirit, and whatever gifts a man possesses are endowments from God. Notice that the Lord said, "I have *filled* them with the spirit of wisdom. I have specifically chosen these particular men, and I have endowed them with extraordinary skill for this special occasion to make these garments. They'll come to you and offer their artistic skill for that purpose."

When the high priest did not have his garments on, he was not a high priest; he was an ordinary human being like you and me. But when he was in the garments of the high priest, he *was* the high priest. The man who wore the priestly garments was never pure and holy, but he was sanctified by the garments for ministry in the office of high priest.

> And these are the garments they shall make: a breastplate, an ephod, a robe, a tunic of checkered work, a mitre, and a girdle: they shall make holy garments for Aaron thy brother, and his sons, that he may minister unto Me in the priest's office. And they shall take the gold, the blue, the purple, the

scarlet, and the fine linen. And they shall make an ephod of gold, of blue, and of purple, of scarlet, and fine twined linen, the work of the skillful workmen.

It shall have two shoulder-pieces joined at the ends thereof, that it may be joined together. And the skillfully woven band which is upon it wherewith to gird it on shall be like the work thereof of the same piece, of gold, of blue, purple, scarlet, and fine twined linen. (Exod. 28:4-8)

The ephod was a short, close-fitting coat worn around the body under the arms and having straps over the shoulders to keep it in place. The ephod ended at the waist in an artistically woven band, or girdle. To indicate the intimate connection between the high priest and the sanctuary, the ephod was made of the same material as the curtain and the veil of the tabernacle. In addition, gold threads were woven into the material as a symbol of the royalty of God and of the high priest's position as the spiritual head of the community.

And you shall take two onyx stones and grave on them the names of the children of Israel: six of their names on one stone, the six names that remain on the other stone according to their birth. With the work of an engraver in stone, like the engravings of a signet, shall you engrave the two stones according to the names of the children of Israel; you shall make them to be enclosed in settings of gold. And you shall put the two stones upon the shoulder-pieces of the ephod to be stones of memorial for the children of Israel. (Exod. 28:9-12a)

The onyx stones which served as buttons for the shoulder straps of the ephod were engraved with the names of the twelve sons of Jacob, who gave their names to the tribes of Israel. The names of the six oldest sons, beginning with Reuben, were on the right shoulder; those of the six younger sons, ending with Benjamin, on the left. The left stone contained the name of Joseph rather than those of his sons, Ephraim and Manasseh. The engraver had to have a special endowment of wisdom from the Lord to do the engraving on these stones, because onyx is very hard to work with.

197

These stones were called "stones of memorial," not because they were to remind the Lord that He was to remember the people of Israel, but because they were to remind the people of Israel of their unity of descent. They must not say, "We can't love one another," because they're bound together by a common ancestry—as are all the peoples of the earth. We all came from Noah, so we're not to abhor one another or to be intolerant of one another; we are to love one another.

And Aaron shall bear their names before the Lord upon his two shoulders for a memorial. (Exod. 28:12b)

The high priest, as the representative of the entire community, was supposed to bear the children of Israel before God on his shoulders always, just as Jesus, our high priest, bears us upon His shoulders before God always.

And thou shalt make sockets of gold, and two chains of pure gold at the ends. Of wreathen work shalt thou make them, and fasten the wreathen chains to the settings. You shall make a breastplate of judgment, the work of the skillful workmen. Like the work of the ephod you shall make it; of gold, blue, purple, scarlet, and fine twined linen, you shall make it. Foursquare it shall be and doubled; a span shall be the length thereof, and a span the breadth thereof. And you shall set in it settings of stones, even four rows of stones. A row of carnelian, topaz, and carbuncle shall be the first row. The second row shall be diamond, sapphire, and emerald. The third row hyacinth, agate, and amethyst. The fourth row beryl, onyx, and jasper. They shall be enclosed in gold in their settings. And on these stones shall be written the names of the tribes of Israel. And the stones shall be according to the names of the children of Israel, twelve, according to their names, like the engravings of a signet; every one according to his name they shall be for the twelve tribes.

And you shall make upon the breastplate plaited chains of wreathen work of pure gold. You shall make upon the breastplate two rings of gold and you shall put the two rings upon the two ends of the breastplate. And you shall put the two wreathen chains of gold in the two rings at the ends of the breastplate. And the other two ends of the two wreathen chains you shall put in the two settings, and you shall put them on the shoulder-pieces of the ephod in the forepart thereof.

And you shall make two rings of gold, and you shall put them upon the two ends of the breastplate in the border thereof, which is in the side of the ephod inward. And two other rings of gold you shall make, and shall put them on the two sides of the ephod underneath, toward the forepart thereof, over against the other coupling thereof, above the curious girdle of the ephod. And they shall bind the breastplate by the rings thereof unto the rings of the ephod with a lace of blue, that it may be above the curious girdle of the ephod, and that the breastplate be not loosed from the ephod.

And Aaron shall bear the names of the children of Israel in the breastplate of judgment upon his heart, when he goes in unto the holy place, for a memorial before the Lord continually. (Exod. 28:13-29)

To emphasize the close relationship between the high priest and the holy of holies, the breastplate was to be made of the same material as that used in the ephod. The piece of cloth used to make it was a cubit in length and half a cubit in width. When this cloth was doubled, it formed a pouch nine inches square and open on all sides except the bottom.

The breastplate was set with twelve precious stones, each engraved with the name of a tribe of Israel. The stones were arranged in gold settings in four rows of three stones each, in the manner shown below:

Row 1: A carnelian (ruby), a topaz (yellowish green in color) and a carbuncle (red garnet).

Row 2: A diamond, a sapphire, and an emerald.

Row 3: A hyacinth (a clear, yellow stone), an agate (a red, opaque stone), and an amethyst.

Row 4: A beryl (green to yellow in color), an onyx, and a jasper (bright green).

Like the onyx stones on the shoulder-pieces of the ephod, these stones were to be "a memorial before the Lord continually."

Two chains of pure gold attached the breastplate to two rings placed on the lower part of the shoulder-pieces of the ephod. Threads of blue, representing God's *shekinah* glory (the Holy Spirit), tied the rings together, so that the breastplate was kept firmly in place on the breast of the high priest.

The high priest was supposed to intercede constantly for his people. But he was busy, so the stones on his heart represented his silent and continuous prayer to God on behalf of the entire nation of Israel. The twelve tribes needed lifting up constantly, just as *we* need to be constantly lifted up before the Lord. Praise God that we have a better high priest than Aaron—one who is always interceding for us, with our names upon His heart. His name is Jesus Christ.

The breastplate was called the "breastplate of judgment" because it contained the Urim and the Thummim, by means of which the high priest was to seek the judgment of God on questions affecting the welfare of the nation. [In the New Testament, Paul speaks of the "breastplate of righteousness" (Eph. 6:14) because we took on the righteousness of Jesus; but the breastplate worn by the high priest in Old Testament times was the breastplate of judgment.] The Urim and the Thummim were eight-sided stones, in which were set semiprecious stones (called "the lights and the perfections").

When the Urim and the Thummim were cast in the name of the Lord, these semiprecious stones would start to radiate, and the Lord would give His answer through His computer system—the twelve precious stones on the breastplate of judgment, representing the twelve tribes of Israel. The Lord would light up different stones as He brought forth the answer.

In the time when there was no judge over Israel, the people went before the Lord and asked, "Shall we go up and fight the enemy?" And the Lord lit up the stone engraved with the name of Judah, to indicate that the tribe of Judah was to do the fighting (Judg. 1:1-2).

And you shall make the robe of the ephod all of blue. And there shall be an hole in the top of it, in the midst thereof: it shall have a binding of woven work round about the hole of it, as it were the hole of an habergeon, that it be not rent. And beneath, upon the hem of it, you shall make pomegranates of blue, and of purple, and of scarlet, round about the hem thereof; and bells of gold between them round about: a golden bell and a pomegranate, a golden bell and a pomegranate, upon the hem of the robe round about. And it shall be upon Aaron to minister: and his sound shall be heard when he goeth in unto the holy place before the Lord, and when he cometh out, that he die not. (Exod. 28:31-35)

The robe worn by the priest was a long garment called "the robe of the ephod" because the ephod was worn over it. The high priest's robe had sleeves, but the robes of the other priests might have been sleeveless; we're not certain. The garment was seamless and was woven entirely of blue thread—the color of the Holy Spirit. The tallith, or prayer shawl, still worn by the people of Israel, has on it 613 fringes representing the 613 laws of Israel. These fringes are white signifying the purity we receive through Jesus. The fringe was also a reminder of all the commandments of the Lord (Num. 15:38-39).

Like the robe worn by Jesus, the high priest's robe was woven in one piece and had an opening only at the top. Since the priest had to put it on over his head, the opening was strengthened by means of a woven binding, to prevent the material from tearing.

The hem of the robe was adorned with seventy-two golden bells and seventy-two pomegranates woven of blue, purple, and scarlet material. Because it has many red seeds, the pomegranate represents sin. The purpose of the bells was discussed in connection with Exodus 26:36-37.

You shall make a plate of pure gold and grave upon it, like the engravings of a signet, HOLY TO THE LORD. You shall put on it a thread of blue; it shall be upon the mitre of the high priest, upon the forefront of the mitre it shall be. And it shall be upon Aaron's forehead, that Aaron may bear the iniquity committed in the holy things, which the children of Israel shall hallow even in all their holy gifts; and it shall always be upon his forehead, that they may be accepted before the Lord. You shall weave the tunic in checkerwork of fine linen, and you shall make the mitre of fine linen, and you shall make the girdle of the work of the weaver in colors. (Exod. 28:36-39)

The plate was made of pure gold, the same material used in the holy of holies. It was two fingers in depth and extended across the forehead of the high priest. The inscription, HOLY TO THE LORD, not only proclaimed the spiritual ideal of which the sanctuary was a concrete emblem; it also marked the dedication of the high priest to the service of God, and crystallized the aim and the purpose of his service. He was to remember always that he *was* holy to the Lord and that he bore the iniquity of the people of Israel.

The high priest of Israel was a picture of the perfect High Priest who would come into the world in fulfillment of the prophecy given in Isaiah 53—a High Priest who would bear our sins, our transgressions, and our iniquities, and by whose stripes we would be healed.

The gold plate was kept in position on the forehead of the high priest by threads of blue which attached it to the linen mitre. The linen symbolized the purity and the holiness of the priest and of Jesus. The high priest who succeeded Aaron came to office just by virtue of being the eldest living son of Aaron—without an oath, and regardless of whether he was right with God. But the Lord had a greater priesthood in mind, a greater covenant—Jesus Christ. In speaking about Jesus, the Lord said, "Thou art a priest forever after the order of Melchizedek" (Ps. 110:4).

As high priest, Aaron bore the iniquity of the people of Israel into the holy of holies. Jesus did the same thing for you and me. When He had borne our iniquity—all the sin, all the transgression, all the iniquity of the world—in His body on the cross, He brought it into the holy of holies.

Jesus died on Friday evening, and because the sabbath was

coming in, the job of wrapping His body could not be finished. He was wrapped only to the neck, and His face was covered with a cloth. When the sabbath was over, Mary went to the tomb to finish wrapping the body. But instead of Jesus' body she found an empty shell. Apostolic tradition says this was like an empty cocoon weighing ninety pounds. Then Jesus spoke to her; and when she recognized Him, He said a strange thing: "Don't cling to me, for I am not yet ascended to My Father" (John 20:17). He said this because He had not yet entered into the holy of holies and presented His blood as a sacrifice unto the Lord. Therefore, unholiness could not come in contact with holiness.

> And for Aaron's sons you shall make them tunics, you shall make for them girdles, and head attire you shall make for them for splendor and for beauty. (Exod. 28:40)

The ordinary priests were to have a coat, or tunic, and a girdle similar to those worn by the high priests, but no breastplate. And instead of a mitre and the gold plate saying HOLY TO THE LORD, they were to wear caps upon their heads.

> You shall put them upon Aaron your brother, and upon his sons with him; and you shall anoint them, and consecrate them, and sanctify them, that they may minister unto Me in the priest's office.
>
> And you shall make them linen breeches to cover the flesh of their nakedness; from the loins even unto the thighs they shall reach. And they shall be upon Aaron, and upon his sons, when they go into the tent of meeting, or when they come near unto the altar to minister in the holy place; that they bear not iniquity and die. And it shall be a statute for ever unto him and unto his seed after him. (Exod. 28:41-43)

The Lord specified that the priests were to wear breeches under their robes, so that when they bent over to worship the Lord they would not expose themselves and bear iniquity. Don't ever think the Lord isn't concerned about the smallest detail that concerns you. He says that not even a sparrow will fall out of the sky unless He ordains it (Matt. 10:29).

JESUS IN EXODUS

The priesthood, the altar, and the offering were the means provided by God for the people of Israel to find salvation until the coming of Jesus Christ. They were saved by grace, just as we are; don't think that the Israelites were not saved. But then our Savior became the sacrifice—the sin offering, the guilt offering, the burnt offering—for you and me. He became all things—everything we need.

21

Consecration of the Priests

(EXODUS 29)

This is the thing that you shall do unto them to hallow them, to minister unto Me in the priest's office. (Exod. 29:1a)

The Lord is still speaking to Moses, the true high priest of God. Moses appeared with Jesus on the mount of transfiguration as the representative of the true priesthood, the Melchizedek priesthood—because he was right before the Lord.

In this verse God repeats the words used in the first verse of Exodus 28: "minister unto *Me* in the priest's office." All ministers are priests unto God, and our first ministry is to *Him*. The people are always out there to be ministered to; but unless we minister to God first, we are powerless to do anything for them. The Lord is our source of life; He gives us the authority to go out and act in His name.

The Lord constantly reminds Israel that the battle is not theirs, but His. "I'm the one who has gone before you, and I have given you the victory. If you trust Me, it's yours. Stand and see the salvation of the Lord." And again He says, "Be still and know that I am God. You're not the burden-bearer; I am. Give Me the burden; give Me the circumstance. Let Me carry it for you." And He does, if we release it unto Him; that's all we need to do.

Take one young bullock, two rams without blemish, unleavened bread, cakes unleavened mingled with oil, wafers unleavened spread with oil: of fine wheaten flour you shall make them. You shall put them in one basket and bring them in the basket, with the bullock and the two rams. (Exod. 29:1b-3)

The bullock was for the sin offering; one ram was for the burnt offering, and the other was the ram of consecration for the high priest and the priests. The unleavened bread is a picture of the sacrament that we call Communion. When Jesus celebrated the Last Supper with His disciples on the night of the Passover, He picked up a piece of unleavened bread and said, ''Take and eat; this is My body which is broken for you.'' The oil that was spread upon the unleavened bread and the cakes was the oil of the Holy Spirit.

And Aaron and his sons you shall bring unto the door of the tent of meeting, and you shall wash them with water. (Exod. 29:4)

The priests must at this point have prepared themselves and made atonement for their own transgressions. Now they are to be baptized for their consecration. The baptism was performed in the court of the sanctuary, and the priest's entire body had to be immersed in water. That's why I can make the statement that we Jews were the first Baptists.

John the Baptist incurred the wrath of the Pharisees by baptizing every day of the year instead of at one time during the year, on the Day of Atonement. Orthodox Jews still baptize only on the Day of Atonement, on Yom Kippur. And baptism is usually by immersion, although if a synagogue is not too affluent it can be done by sprinkling. After the candidate is cleansed of sin by baptism, he brings his sacrifice for atonement to the Lord.

When Jesus was baptized by John, it was not because He needed to be cleansed of sin, but in order to fulfill all righteousness (Matt. 3:15), so that we may be righteous in Him. We are to follow in His footsteps, and to fulfill all the righteousness which He has granted us, by being baptized if it is within our means and our power. As Christians, we will not have the power to overcome unless we have gone to death with Him in the waters of baptism and have risen with Him into a new life.

When David wrote in Psalm 24 that the Lord desires clean hands and a pure heart, he was showing us a picture of baptism. Clean hands and a pure heart were essential qualifications for the priests, just as they are for anyone who would draw near to God. God asks us to trust Him in all things and to remain clean constantly, inside and out.

> You shall take the garments, and put upon Aaron the tunic, and the robe of the ephod, and the ephod, and the breastplate, and gird him with the skillfully woven band of the ephod. You shall put the mitre upon his head, and put the holy crown upon the mitre. Then you shall take the anointing oil, and pour it upon his head, and anoint him. (Exod. 29:5-7)

If I were the high priest, I would panic at this point and say, "You're going to mess up the whole outfit!" The oil had to cover the priest from the top of his head to the bottom of his toes—but because the garments were anointed and miraculously protected by the Holy Spirit, they never got stained. The anointing oil made the garments holy; and unless the high priest had on the anointed garment, he himself was not under the anointing of the Holy Spirit. The only time he was a high priest was when he was wearing the garments anointed by the Lord through Moses.

> And you shall bring his sons, and put tunics upon them. And you shall gird them with girdles, Aaron and his sons, and bind head attires on them. And they shall have priesthood by a perpetual statute: and you shall consecrate Aaron and his sons. (Exod. 29:8-9)

"A perpetual statute" meant that the priesthood was forever restricted to the house of Aaron until God, in the fullness of time, would bring in the perfect priesthood of Christ Jesus.

> You shall bring the bullock before the tent of meeting; and Aaron and his sons shall lay their hands upon the head of the bullock. (Exod. 29:10)

By laying their hands upon the bullock, the priests signified that their own sin, transgression, and iniquity were passing to the bullock, which was the sin offering. Jesus said that believers "shall lay hands on the sick and they shall recover" (Mark 16:18). Here we see that hands can pass on sin, transgression, and iniquity as well as healing.

You shall kill the bullock before the Lord at the door of the tent of meeting. (Exod. 29:11)

The slaying of the sacrificial animal did not have to be done by a priest. The ritual which God describes here is that which normally accompanied the sacrifice of a sin offering.

And you shall take of the blood of the bullock, and put it upon the horns of the altar with your finger, and pour out all of the remaining blood at the base of the altar. (Exod. 29:12)

This bullock, the sin offering, now bore all the sin, transgression, and iniquity of the priests. Just as its blood was lifted up by being placed on the horns of the altar, our sin was lifted up with Jesus on the cross. By presenting His blood, His sacrifice at the throne of grace, He saved each and every one of us, even before we knew Him. And just as the blood of the sin offering was poured at the base of the altar, the blood of Jesus was spilled at the foot of the cross—your altar and my altar. Praise God!

And you shall take all of the fat that covers the inwards, the lobe above the liver, the two kidneys, and the fat that is upon them, and you shall make them smoke upon the altar. But the flesh of the bullock, its skin, and its dung, you shall burn with fire outside the camp: it is a sin offering. (Exod. 29:13-14)

The sin offering had to be taken outside the camp of Israel; Jesus was taken outside the city of Jerusalem to be crucified. He fulfilled all the requirements for the sacrifice.

You shall also take the one ram; and Aaron and his sons shall lay their hands upon the head of the ram. You shall slay the ram, and you shall take its blood, and dash it round about against the altar. And now you shall cut the ram into its pieces, wash its inwards and its legs, and put them with its pieces and its head. And you shall make the whole ram smoke upon the altar. It is a burnt offering unto the Lord. And it is a sweet savour, an offering made by fire unto the Lord. (Exod.

208

29:15-18)

After the sin offering (the bullock) had brought purification from sin, the burnt offering (the ram) symbolized communion with God, as He sent His Holy Spirit down to consume it. We are now at peace with God, and He is at peace with us. He just made us right by accepting our sin, our transgression, and our iniquity. If we have any sinful thoughts remaining, He removes them from our minds as we commune with Him while the offering sends up its "sweet savour unto the Lord."

The brain is where the enemy attacks, where sin first comes in. First you look and see; then you may want to touch and feel—whether it's gold, flesh, or anything else. Communion with God while the offering burned brought peace to the man who offered the sacrifice. Jesus gives us the peace that passes understanding, because He frees us not only from our sin but even from the temptation to sin. This is the greatest freedom of all, and to obtain it we have only to call upon His name.

> And you shall take the other ram; and Aaron and his sons shall lay their hands upon the head of the ram. (Exod. 29:19)

This is the consecration sacrifice, and everything that preceded it has been preparing the priests for this rite of induction. They've been cleansed of their sin; they're in close communion with God. Now they will be inducted into His service. In this rite the Lord is saying, "I just gave you a complete washing; from this point on, you are to remain clean."

> Then you shall kill the ram, take of its blood, put it upon the tip of the right ear of Aaron, and upon the tip of the right ear of his sons. (Exod. 29:20a)

You and I always hear three voices in our lives: that of the enemy, that of our flesh, and—lastly and very rarely—the voice of God. The blood of the ram of consecration was placed on the right ear of Aaron and his sons to indicate that, from this point on, their right ear was to hear only the Lord's voice, so that they would be able to distinguish between what was true and what was false. You and I are high priests unto the Lord, and by the blood of Jesus we are to hear only the voice of God.

The blood was also to be placed
> Upon the thumb of their right hand, and upon the great toe of
> their right foot. (Exod. 29:20b)

The hands that performed the duties connected with the priesthood were to be clean hands; they were not to get stained with sin. The blood of the sacrifice on the thumb of the right hand symbolized the consecration of the priest's hand to remain righteous in God's service. Then the right foot was anointed with the blood to remind the priests to walk in the path of righteousness, that they might not stumble or fall.

God told the people of Israel, "You are a kingdom of priests unto Me. There is not one of you who is not a priest, who is not holy. I have made you holy because I am holy." In a kingdom of priests, the consecration of the ear, the hand, and the foot is extended to every member of the kingdom. Christ gave us that extension by His blood. First He justified us; then He sanctified us, made us holy; then He consecrated us. So we're in the same position as the high priest. Our hands are to perform the righteousness connected with the priesthood God gave us, and our feet are to stray neither to the left nor to the right, but are to remain in the Way.

> And dash the blood against the altar round about. (Exod.
> 29:20c)

The blood of the sin offering and the blood of the burnt offering have already been mingled at the base of the altar. Now the blood of the consecration is added. When we bring our sin before God, the blood of the Lamb without sin or blemish, Jesus Christ, makes us just as if we had never sinned (justifies us), puts us in communion with Him, and then consecrates us. Praise God!

> And you shall take of the blood that is upon the altar and of the
> anointing oil, and sprinkle it upon Aaron, and upon his
> garments, and upon his sons and upon the garments of his
> sons with him that he and his garments shall be hallowed and
> his sons and his sons' garments with him. (Exod. 29:21)

It wasn't bad enough that the priestly garments had to be covered completely with oil; now they were going to be messed up with blood. But by God's miracle, the blood and the oil only consecrated and sanctified the garments; they never stained them. This is a picture of what the blood of Jesus does for you and me. We're made holy by the blood of Jesus and by the oil and the power of the Holy Spirit.

> And you shall take of the ram the fat and the fat tail, the fat that covers the inwards, the lobe of the liver, the two kidneys, and the fat that is upon them, and the right thigh; for it is a ram of consecration: and one loaf of bread, one cake of oiled bread, and one wafer out of the basket of the unleavened bread that is before the Lord: And you shall put the whole in the hands of Aaron and in the hands of his sons; and they shall wave them for a wave offering before the Lord. (Exod. 29:22-24)

The wave offering signified that Aaron and his sons were now invested as priests, with authority to bring sacrifices unto the Lord. It is called a "wave offering" because the priests turned the offering to all four parts of heaven and earth as a symbol that it was offered to the God who is the Lord of heaven and earth. "The earth is the Lord's and all the fullness thereof" (Ps. 24:1). As the priest waved the offering before the Lord, from north to south and then from east to west, he made the sign of the cross. In all these instructions, the Lord keeps giving a picture of the coming of Jesus Christ.

> And you shall take them from their hands and make them smoke on the altar for a burnt offering, for a sweet savour before the Lord; an offering made by fire unto the Lord. And you shall take the breast of Aaron's ram of consecration, and wave it for a wave offering before the Lord: and it shall be your portion. (Exod. 29:25-26)

Moses, as the priest who was officiating at this consecration service, was allowed by the Lord to have as his portion the breast that was waved before the Lord. Even today, the people of Israel are not allowed to eat of the breast or the thigh; these portions are reserved for the priests. The thigh is forbidden because the Lord smote Jacob upon his thigh. From that day on, Jacob's limp reminded him that he had met the Lord face-to-face. As you know, all the best steaks—New York cut, porterhouse, T-bone—come from the thigh. The only steaks lay Israelites are allowed to eat are rib steaks.

> And you shall sanctify the breast of the wave offering, and the thigh of the heave offering, which is waved and which is heaved up, of the ram of consecration, even of that which is for Aaron, and of that which is for his sons. (Exod. 29:27)

The heave offering was the priests' portion. It is what you and I give when we present our tithes to the Lord. Bear in mind that we are not doing God a favor to give Him back ten percent of the trust He gave us. Tithing is a privilege that He allows us. So we don't give our tithe to Him with any strings attached; we *heave* it up and say, "Here, Lord, it's Yours in the first place. I thank You for giving me the other ninety percent. The United States Government requires twenty percent, and You're asking only ten; You're giving it to me wholesale."

> And it shall be for Aaron and his sons as a due forever from the children of Israel: for it is a heave offering. (Exod. 29:28a)

Since the priests and Levites were to live by faith, the heave offerings brought in by the people of Israel were assigned to them by the Lord as their portion. Later on, when the Promised Land was apportioned to the people of Israel, the tribe of Levi did not receive an inheritance. The Lord said, "You'll have to trust Me. I've shown you that My credit is good. Your inheritance is with Me." I can't think of a better way to have my inheritance than in the Lord Jesus Christ—and He says He made me, and made you, joint heirs with Him.

> And it shall be a heave offering from the children of Israel of the sacrifices of their peace offerings, even their heave offering unto the Lord. (Exod. 29:28b)

So the heave offering is also the peace offering. Let's review the order of offerings: After the blood of the *sin offering* has been placed on the horns of the altar to make atonement for your sins and the Lord has consumed the *burnt offering* to let you know that you are forgiven, you bring in a *peace offering,* because He's made peace with you and you've made peace with Him. And a portion of that peace offering is heaved before the Lord and becomes the *heave offering,* the priests' inheritance from God.

And the holy garments of Aaron shall be for his sons after him, to be anointed in them, and to be consecrated in them. Seven days shall the son that is priest in his stead put them on, even he who comes into the tent of meeting to minister in the holy place. (Exod. 29:29-30)

These consecrated garments would pass from father to son until the priesthood went out of existence seventy years after the birth of Christ (see Numbers 20:25-28).

And you shall take the ram of consecration and seethe its flesh in the holy place. And Aaron and his sons shall eat of the flesh of the ram, and the bread that is in the basket, at the door of the tent of meeting. They shall eat those things wherewith the atonement was made, to consecrate and to sanctify them. (Exod. 29:31-33a)

The priests were to eat the meat of the ram of consecration, and the unleavened bread. The unleavened bread had to be made as a cake and broken, because it symbolized the breaking of the body of Jesus. "This is My body which is broken for you" (1 Cor. 11:24).

But a stranger shall not eat thereof, because they are holy. (Exod. 29:33b)

This warning has a New Testament parallel in Paul's first letter to the Corinthians:

Whoever shall eat this bread and drink this cup of the Lord unworthily shall be guilty of the body and blood of the Lord.

For he that eats and drinks unworthily, eats and drinks damnation to himself, not discerning the Lord's body. For this cause many are weak and sickly among you, and some have died. (1 Cor. 11:27, 29-30)

The body and blood of the Lord Jesus Christ are holier than any of the sacrifices made on the altar of burnt offerings. If we take communion unworthily, we are risking sickness and even death.

And if any of the flesh of the consecrations, or of the bread, remains unto the morning, then you shall burn the remainder with fire: it shall not be eaten, because it is holy.

And you shall do unto Aaron, and to his sons, according to all that I have commanded you: seven days you shall consecrate them. And every day you shall offer the bullock of sin offering besides the other offerings for atonement: and you shall do the purification upon the altar, when you make atonement for it, and you shall anoint it, to sanctify it. Seven days you shall make atonement for the altar, and sanctify it. (Exod. 29:34-37a)

This process of sanctification and consecration was to be repeated for seven days, to take the garbage and sin out of the life of Aaron and his sons. Then atonement had to be made for the altar, because it was made out of gold that came from Egypt. When the atonement had been made, the altar was to be anointed with oil and blood to sanctify it.

Thus shall the altar be most holy: whatsoever toucheth the altar shall also be holy. (Exod. 29:37b)

If any unholy person came in contact with the altar, he would die. Only after the high priest had been sanctified and consecrated to the Lord could he come into the holy of holies.

Now this is that which you shall offer upon the altar: two lambs of the first year day by day continually. (Exod. 29:38)

To keep judgment from coming upon Israel, sacrifice is going to have to be made for the nation continually—every day two lambs under one year old.

The one lamb you shall offer in the morning; and the other lamb you shall offer at dusk. (Exod. 29:39)

The Lord says, "I forgive their sin, transgression, and iniquity in the morning; but by the time evening comes, they have committed a few hundred additional sins. So you'll offer one lamb in the morning and one at dusk, before the sun sets."

Now here's a strange part:

With the one lamb a tenth part of an ephah of fine flour mixed with the fourth part of a hin of beaten oil; and the fourth part of a hin of wine for a drink offering. (Exod. 29:40)

The Lord is always pointing to the communion that we celebrate today. So here He's saying, "I will not accept a sacrifice unless you bring in that unleavened bread (standing for the body of Christ), the oil of the Holy Spirit, and the drink offering (wine, which stands for the blood of Christ).

And the other lamb you shall offer at dusk. You shall do thereto according to the meal offering of the morning, and according to the drink offering thereof, for a sweet savour, an offering made by fire unto the Lord. It shall be a continual burnt offering throughout all of your generations at the door of the tent of meeting before the Lord: where I will meet with you, to speak there unto you. (Exod. 29:41-42)

Our continual burnt offering nowadays is Jesus, and it is through Him that we can meet with God and hear Him speak to us.

And there I will meet with the children of Israel, and the tent shall be sanctified by My glory. (Exod. 29:43)

The Lord says, "By My *shekinah* glory, by My Spirit, the tent itself will be sanctified."

And I will sanctify the tent of meeting and the altar: Aaron also and his sons will I sanctify, to minister to Me in the priest's office. And I will dwell among the children of Israel, and will be their God. (Exod. 29:44-45)

There's the gospel of the Old Testament: "I will dwell." The Hebrew word for "dwell" is *shekinah*. The Lord says, "My glory, My presence will be in the midst of Israel. My Holy Spirit will be among the children of Israel and I will be their God."

And they shall know that I am the Lord their God, that brought them forth out of the land of Egypt, that I may *shekinah* among them. I am the Lord their God. (Exod. 29:46)

Praise God that it is so!

22

To Worship the Lord

(EXODUS 30—31)

You shall make an altar to burn incense upon: of acacia wood
you shall make it. (Exod. 30:1)

The purpose of this altar was for burning incense, which
signifies the prayers and praise of God's people. The Lord says, "I
want the prayers, I want the praise of My people. I inhabit the
praises of My people" (Ps. 22:3). His throne of grace and glory is
right where we are thanking Him and praising Him. The more we
gripe, the farther away He gets. The more we praise, the more He
sits enthroned upon our praise.

A cubit shall be the length thereof, and a cubit the breadth
thereof; foursquare shall it be. And two cubits shall be the
height thereof: the horns thereof shall be of one piece with it.
And you shall overlay it with pure gold, the top thereof, the
sides thereof round about, and the horns thereof; and you shall
make unto it a crown of gold round about. And two golden
rings you shall make for it under the crown thereof, upon the
two ribs thereof, upon the two sides of it you shall make them;
they shall be for places for staves wherewith to bear it. You
shall make the staves of acacia wood, and overlay them with
gold. And you shall put it before the veil that is by the ark of

the testimony, before the ark cover that is over the testimony, where I will meet with you. (Exod. 30:2-6)

The altar of incense was not inside the holy of holies, but was about halfway between the altar of burnt offerings and the holy of holies. After the sin offering and the burnt offering and the peace offerings had been made, the prayers and praise of the forgiven sinners had to go up before the priest could enter into the holy of holies.

And Aaron shall burn thereon incense of sweet spices. (Exod. 30:7a)

This incense that was to be burned before the Lord was to be a mixture of different types of incense, which would produce a distinctive fragrance. The Lord says, "I want all different types of incense to be burned together: Presbyterian, Methodist, Baptist, Hebrew. When the incense of every denomination comes up to me all mixed together, it'll be a sweet savour unto the Lord."

Every morning when he dresses the lamps, he shall burn it. And when Aaron lights the lamps at dusk, he shall burn incense upon it, a perpetual incense before the Lord throughout all of your generations. You shall offer no strange incense thereon, nor burnt offering, nor meal offering; and you shall pour no drink offering thereon. (Exod. 30:7b-9)

Don't go to the Lord with lip service. He says, "Don't bother to bring any strange incense unto Me. I'm not going to accept it. I have very good eyes, and I can look into your heart and know what you're thinking. So don't bother to give Me lip service; save your time and My time." (That's the new paraphrased edition, the gospel according to Mike.)

And Aaron shall make atonement upon the horns of it once in the year with the blood of the sin offering of atonement: once in the year shall he make atonement upon it throughout your generations: it is most holy to the Lord.

And the Lord spoke unto Moses, saying, When you take the sum of the children of Israel according to their number, then they shall give every man a ransom for his soul unto the Lord, when you number them; that there be no plague among them, when you number them. This they shall give, every one that passes among them that are numbered, half a shekel after the shekel of the sanctuary: (a shekel is twenty gerahs:) half a shekel for an offering unto the Lord. (Exod. 30:10-13)

The Lord says, "I will ransom you; I will buy you back." Again, it's a picture of our redemption through Jesus Christ, who bought us by His body and His blood. And the Lord says, "When I number you, if you want to stand up and say, 'As for me and my house, this day we will choose the Lord' (Josh. 24:15), you can bring in half a shekel." (Half a shekel is only thirty cents.) The Lord says, "Is your life, your eternal life and salvation worth thirty cents to you? Then give it to Me. I don't need your thirty cents; I need your obedience. I demand your obedience and your love. I have a right to demand it, because I am the Lord your God who took you up out of your bondage, out of all the garbage and the filth you were living in."

This ransoming process took place when the Israelites were being numbered—and I praise God that we are numbered with the elect. From the beginning of time, God knew we would come to Him and accept the sacrifice of our Savior. So we were destined. I can't say "predestined" because God, knowing all things, knew that in the fullness of time we would say, "Yes, Lord, I do accept the sacrifice. I invite Jesus into my heart as my personal Savior, as my redeemer, as my sacrifice."

Every one that passes among them that are numbered, from twenty years old and upward, shall give the offering of the Lord. (Exod. 30:14)

The age of accountability that the Lord is revealing here is twenty years. Under the age of twenty, a person is not held accountable.

The rich shall not give more, and the poor shall not give less than the half shekel, when they give the offering of the Lord to make atonement for your souls. And you shall take the atonement money from the children of Israel, and shall appoint it for the service of the tent of meeting; that it may be a memorial for the children of Israel before the Lord to make

219

atonement for your souls. (Exod. 30:15-16)

The silver of the shekels was used for the bases of the pillars of the sanctuary, and also for the hooks to keep the boards together. And the Lord says, "When I look upon it, it is a memorial forever." The brass used in the tabernacle denoted sin and the silver denoted redemption. So now the Lord says, "You have been redeemed. As long as this silver stands in My tabernacle, there is your redemption before Me and also before your own eyes." Every person who has paid his shekel can say, "I have a part in the sanctuary of God, and He is part of me."

In later ages, the half shekel became a tax levied on the people of Israel annually for maintaining the public service of the temple. Thus the daily worship was carried on by all the people of Israel and not by a few rich donors. In this way the people would always be making atonement for their sins.

In specifying that the rich were not to give more than half a shekel, or the poor to give less, the Lord was trying to teach us that rank and wealth are of no importance to Him—that He's no respecter of persons (Acts 10:34). The small size of the ransom required by the Lord taught that each individual's contribution to the community is just a fragment and that, for any complete work to be achieved on behalf of the sanctuary, the efforts of all—the high and the low, the rich and the poor alike—are required. Half a shekel—thirty cents—was just a small token. But the Lord wanted obedience through that token.

And the Lord spoke unto Moses, saying, You shall also make a laver of brass, and the base thereof of brass, wherein to wash: and you shall put it between the tent of meeting and the altar, and you shall put water therein. (Exod. 30:17-18)

According to Hebrew oral tradition, the only people of Israel who had brass were the women, who used it for their mirrors. And when the women brought the brass mirrors to Moses to be used in the tabernacle, he refused to accept them, because they were given by women rather than men. But the Lord said, "Take them. I'm no respecter of persons, and the women have made a greater sacrifice by giving their mirrors to Me than any man will ever make."

And Aaron and his sons shall wash their hands and their feet
thereat: when they go into the tent of meeting, they shall wash
with water, that they die not; or when they come near to the
altar to minister, to cause an offering made by fire to smoke
unto the Lord. So they shall wash their hands and their feet,
that they die not. (Exod. 30:19-21a)

They cannot come in and minister to the Lord unless they're
washed clean of their sin. If they haven't been washed and baptized
before they go into the tent of meeting, they'll die.

And it shall be a statute for ever to them, even to Him and to
His seed throughout their generations. (Exod. 30:21b)

The "Him" that God is speaking about is Jesus.

Moreover, the Lord spoke unto Moses, saying, You shall also
take unto you the chief spices, of flowing myrrh five hundred
shekels, of cinnamon half so much, even two hundred and
fifty, of sweet calamus two hundred and fifty, of cassia five
hundred, after the shekel of the sanctuary, and of olive oil an
hin. You shall make it an holy anointing oil, a perfume
compounded after the art of the perfumer: it shall be an holy
anointing oil. And you shall anoint therewith the tent of
meeting and the ark of the covenant, and the table and all the
vessels thereof, and the candlestick and the vessels thereof,
and the altar of incense, and the altar of burnt offering with all
the vessels, the laver and the base thereof. And you shall
sanctify them, that they may be most holy: whatsoever
touches them shall be holy.

You shall anoint Aaron and his sons, and sanctify them that
they may minister unto Me in the priest's office. And you
shall speak unto the children of Israel, saying, This shall be an
holy anointing oil unto Me throughout all of your generations.
Upon the flesh of man shall it not be poured, neither shall you
make any like it, according to the composition thereof: it is
holy and it shall be holy unto you. Whoever compounds any
like it, or whoever puts any upon a stranger, shall be cut off
from his people.

And the Lord said unto Moses, Take unto you sweet spices,

stacte, and onycha, and galbanum; sweet spices with pure frankincense; of each there shall be a like measure of weight. You shall make of it incense, a perfume after the art of the perfumer, seasoned with salt pure and holy. (Exod. 30:22-35)

The Lord would not accept the incense unless it had salt in it. Salt is not corrupt. Honey and sugar ferment and become corrupt; salt remains pure. This is why Jesus told you and me, "You are the salt of the earth (Matt. 5:13). Through your witness, through your testimony, they will know that I am alive."

You shall beat some of it very small and put it before the testimony [before the ark of the covenant] in the tent of meeting, where I will meet with you: it shall be unto you most holy. And the incense which you shall make according to the composition thereof, you shall not make it for yourselves: it shall be unto you holy for the Lord. Whoever shall make like unto that, to smell thereof, he shall be cut off from his people. (Exod. 30:36-38)

The incense was to be brought into the holy of holies with the blood to make atonement for the sins of Israel. But that was before Jesus became our atonement on the cross of Calvary. Praise God for the perfect work He did for us there, taking care once and for all, of the complex ritual of atonement.

He shall take [at the expense] of the congregation of the Israelites, two male goats for a sin offering, and one ram for a burnt offering. And Aaron shall present the bull as the sin offering for himself, and make atonement for himself and for his house [the other priests]. He shall take the two goats and present them before the Lord at the door of the tent of meeting. Aaron shall cast lots on the two goats; one lot for the Lord, the other lot for Azazel *or* removal. And Aaron shall bring the goat on which the Lord's lot fell, and offer him as a sin offering. But the goat on which the lot fell for Azazel, *or* removal, shall be presented alive before the Lord to make atonement over him, that he may be let go into the wilderness for Azazel (for dismissal).

Aaron shall present the bull as the sin offering for his own sins, and shall make atonement for himself and for his house [the other priests]; and shall kill the bull as the sin offering for himself. He shall take a censer full of burning coals of fire from off the [bronze] altar before the Lord, and his two hands full of sweet incense beaten small, and bring it within the veil [into the holy of holies]. And put the incense on the fire [in the censer] before the Lord, that the cloud of the incense may cover the mercy seat that is upon [the ark of] the testimony, lest he die. He shall take the bull's blood, and sprinkle it with his finger on the front [the east side] of the mercy seat, and before the mercy seat he shall sprinkle of the blood with his finger seven times.

Then shall he kill the goat of the sin offering, that is for [the sins of] the people, and bring its blood within the veil [into the holy of holies], and do with that blood as he did with the blood of the bull, and sprinkle it on the mercy seat and before the mercy seat. Thus he shall make atonement for the holy place, because of the uncleanness of the Israelites, and because of their transgressions, even all their sins; and so shall he do for the tent of meeting, that remains among them in the midst of their uncleanness. There shall be no man in the tent of meeting when the high priest goes in to make atonement in the holy of holies [within the veil] until he comes out and has made atonement for his own sins and those of his house [the other priests] and of all the congregation of Israel. And he shall go out to the altar [of burnt offering in the court] which is before the Lord, and make atonement for it, and shall take some of the blood of the bull and of the goat and put it on the horns of the altar round about. And he shall sprinkle some of the blood on it with his fingers seven times, and cleanse it and hallow it from the uncleanness of the Israelites.

And when he has finished atoning for the holy of holies and the tent of meeting and the altar [of burnt offering], he shall present the live goat; And Aaron shall lay both his hands upon the head of the live goat, and confess over him all the iniquities of the Israelites, and all their transgressions, all their sins; and he shall put them upon the head of the goat [the sinbearer], and send him away into the wilderness by the hand of a man who is timely (ready, fit). The goat shall bear upon himself all their iniquities, carrying them to a land cut off (a land of forgetfulness *and* separation, not inhabited)! And the man leading it shall let the goat go in the wilderness.

Aaron shall come into the tent of meeting and put off the linen garments which he put on when he went into the holy of holies, and leave them there; And he shall bathe his body with water in a sacred place, and put on his garments, and come forth, and offer his burnt offering and that of the people, and make atonement for himself and for them. And the fat of the sin offering he shall burn upon the altar. (Lev. 16:5-25 TAB)

The Lord spoke unto Moses, saying, Behold, I have called by name Bezaleel the son of Uri, the son of Hur, of the tribe of Judah. (Exod. 31:1-2)

When God calls you and me, He always calls us by our name. He knows our name; He knows every hair upon our head.

And I have filled him with the Spirit of God in wisdom, and in understanding, and in knowledge, and in all manner of workmanship, that he will be able to devise skillful works, to work in gold, and in silver, and in brass. And in cutting of stones, for setting, and in carving of wood, to work in all manner of workmanship. And I, behold, I have appointed with him Aholiab, the son of Ahisamach, of the tribe of Dan: and in the hearts of all those that are wise hearted I have put My wisdom, that they may make all that I have commanded you. (Exod. 31:3-6)

Notice that Bezaleel, a man to whom God gave His great gift, was of the tribe of Judah. From this tribe would come Jesus Christ, the Savior of the world, who was called "the Lion of the tribe of Judah." Aholiab, strangely enough, was a member of the tribe of Dan—the tribe to which Judas Iscariot belonged. But God did not give Aholiab the gift of the Holy Spirit, although He placed His wisdom in his heart. These two chosen men, together with other wise-hearted artisans, were to make everything that God had shown Moses on the mount:

The tent of meeting, the ark of the covenant, the ark cover that is thereupon, all the furniture of the tent itself, the table and its vessels, the pure candlestick with all its vessels, and the altar of incense, and the altar of burnt offering with all its vessels, the laver and its base, the plated garments, the holy garments for Aaron the priest, and the garments of his sons, to minister in the priest's office, and the anointing oil, and the incense of sweet spices for the holy place: according to all that I have commanded you they shall do.

And the Lord spoke unto Moses, saying, Speak also unto the children of Israel, saying, Verily (truly) you shall keep My sabbaths: for it is a sign between Me and you throughout your generations; that you may know that I am the Lord your God who sanctifies you. (Exod. 31:7-13)

The word *sabbath* means "desistance." The Lord does not specify the seventh day as the day of desistance. Although it was on the seventh day that He desisted from further creative activity, He says only that we are to desist from work one day a week and commit that day unto Him. It makes no difference whether it's Sunday, Monday, Tuesday, Wednesday, Thursday, Friday, or Saturday. Any day that you set aside to the Lord is your day of sabbath, your day of desistance. He will accept it (see Romans 14:5-6).

Although the construction of the tabernacle was of the highest importance, it was not permitted to supersede the divinely ordained sabbath. The sabbath was to be observed, even though God Himself had commanded the tabernacle to be brought into being. Observance of the sabbath by the people of Israel was a constantly recurring acknowledgment of God as the Creator of the universe. It would be an open denial of God for any of the people of Israel to desecrate the sabbath, even in the construction of the tabernacle. Furthermore, such a desecration would contradict the essential purpose of the sanctuary itself: the sanctification of Israel's life in the service of God. God told the children of Israel, through Moses, "I am the Lord who sanctifies you. I am the one who brings you to the point that you may go out and be My missionaries in the heathen world, showing that there is a God who is alive, who is well, who loves, who forgives, who understands.'' By means of the sabbath, all the world may come to recognize that it is God who sanctifies Israel, and that He provides Israel with the means of becoming a holy people.

> You shall keep the sabbath therefore; for it is holy unto you; every one that profanes it shall surely be put to death: for whoever does any work therein, that soul shall be cut off from among his people. Six days shall work be done, but the day of sabbath is a day of solemn rest, holy to the Lord: whoever does any work in the sabbath, he shall surely be put to death. (Exod. 31:14-15)

The Lord says, ''I will supply your needs in the six days that you work; but you are to set aside one day for Me. On the day of desistance, you are not to go out and do anything which creates income or money.''

The penalty for profaning the sabbath was death. The reason for this extreme punishment is that the man who profanes the sabbath is denying the trustworthiness of God and is rebelling against God's authority. The message comes through to us, as it came to the people of Israel through the prophet Samuel: ''Rebellion is as the sin of witchcraft; stubbornness is as the sin of idolatry'' (1 Sam. 15:23).

> Therefore the children of Israel shall keep the sabbath, to observe the sabbath throughout their generations, for a perpetual covenant. It is a sign between Me and the children of Israel for ever: for in six days the Lord made heaven and earth, and on the seventh day He ceased from work and He desisted. (Exod. 31:16-17)

The sabbath was recognized throughout the ancient world as the peculiar and distinctive festival of the Hebrew people. It was more than a day of rest; it was a day of worship, praise, and thanksgiving unto the Lord. We Christians are recognized as a peculiar people by our observance of Sunday as our day of sabbath—our day of worship, praise, and thanksgiving, and the day when we remember the resurrection of our Lord Jesus Christ.

And He gave unto Moses, when He had made an end of speaking with him upon Mount Sinai, the two tables of the testimony, tables of stone, written with the finger of God (Exod. 31:18)

Thus Moses received the Decalogue, the Ten Living Words, the Ten Logos, "written with the finger of God." This expression indicates both the sanctity of the tables of stone—that they came from a divine source, from God Himself—and the importance of the message, not just for the people of Israel, but for all mankind. When Jesus came into the world, He said, "I have not come to break the commandments, but to fulfill them" (Matt. 5:17). And He did fulfill them, for you and for me. Praise God that He did! We could never do it for ourselves.

23

The Golden Calf

(EXODUS 32—33)

When the people saw that Moses had delayed to come down from the mount, the people gathered themselves together unto Aaron, and they said unto him, Up! What are you sitting down for? Get up! Make us gods who shall go before us; for as for this Moses, the man that brought us up out of the land of Egypt, we know not what has become of him. (Exod. 32:1)

The Israelites knew for a certainty who had brought them up out of Egypt. They had spent one year seeing God perform miracle after miracle in their behalf; they had seen His judgment upon the idolatry of Egypt; and still they made the statement, "We don't know what's become of this man who brought us up out of the land of Egypt. Get up! Make us a god we can see."

Sometimes we Christians do the very same thing: we fail to trust the living Lord. We have seen miracle upon miracle, we have seen God move by His Spirit, we have seen people healed, delivered, saved, yet we say, "We want a god we can see and touch, one who will go before us. We can't see this God who's in heaven. We've got to take Him by faith, and we don't have that kind of faith."

The children of Israel made their demand of Aaron, the high priest of Israel, the one who stands between God and the people,

JESUS IN EXODUS

the one who will make atonement for their sin. But instead of putting up an argument and saying, ''I cannot sin against my Lord and my God,''

Aaron said unto them, Break off the golden earrings, which are in the ears of your wives, of your sons, and of your daughters, and bring them unto me. (Exod. 32:2)

As part of the idolatrous practices they picked up in Egypt, the sons were wearing earrings. Sounds like the twentieth century, doesn't it?

And all the people broke off the golden earrings which were in their ears, and brought them unto Aaron. And he received them at their hand, and he fashioned it with a graving tool, and he made it a molten calf: and they said, This is your god, O Israel, which brought you up out of the land of Egypt. (Exod. 32:3-4)

After all they had seen! After crossing the Red Sea, with the wall of water on their left and on their right! After they had heard God speak with their own ears: ''I am the Lord thy God. I'm the One who brought you up out of Egypt, out of bondage, out of slavery. I am the One who has delivered you. I am the One who has healed you, who has saved you.'' Yet they forgot all about that, and they worshiped a golden calf. And in speaking of a golden calf as their god, they committed the one unforgivable sin: blaspheming God's Holy Spirit. The minute we take the glory away from the Lord and give it to Satan or to idolatry, we are committing blasphemy against the Holy Spirit. And Jesus Himself said that this is the one unforgivable sin (Matt. 12:31).

And when Aaron saw it, he built an altar before it; and Aaron made proclamation, and said, Tomorrow shall be a feast unto the Lord. (Exod. 32:5)

''That way we can play both ends against the middle. We'll still remember the Lord our God, but we will worship this golden calf at the same time.'' Does that sound kosher? No, it would be impossible.

So they rose up early in the morning, and offered burnt

offerings, and brought peace offerings; and the people sat down to eat and to drink, and they rose up to make merry. (Exod. 32:6)

"They rose up to make merry" means that they took off their clothing and had the biggest sex orgy in history. And of course, the Lord knew what was taking place. He even knew the words that the people used.

The Lord said unto Moses, Go, get yourself down; for your people, which you brought up out of the land of Egypt, have dealt corruptly. They have turned aside quickly out of the way which I commanded them: they have made a molten calf, and have worshiped it, and have sacrificed unto it, and said, This is your god, O Israel, which brought you up out of the land of Egypt. (Exod. 32:7-8)

The Lord had already commanded, "You shall have no other god except Me." They knew they were sinning against Him.

And the Lord said unto Moses, I have seen this people, and, behold, it is a stiffnecked people: now therefore let Me alone, that My wrath may wax hot against them, and that I may consume them; and I will make of you a great nation. (Exod. 32:9-10)

The Lord was offering Moses the opportunity to become the father of a new nation of Israel. He told him, "I will still keep My promise to Abraham, to Isaac, and to Jacob; but these people I will wipe out right now, in one instant. Stand aside. Let My wrath wax hot against them, and that's it. They're destroyed: spiritually, physically, for all eternity."

Many leaders would have seized the opportunity to advance themselves by playing power politics with God. But this is the Moses who gave up the kingdom of Egypt to be accounted as one of the abominable Hebrew slaves, because he knew they belonged to God. So instead of taking the opportunity to glorify himself, he interceded for the Israelites and thereby glorified God (see Hebrews 11:24-26).

And Moses besought the Lord his God, and said, Lord, why does Your anger wax hot against Your people that You have

brought forth out of the land of Egypt with great power, and
with a mighty hand? (Exod. 32:11)

"They're not *my* people, Lord; they're *Your* people," Moses
was saying. God had just referred to the Israelites as "your
people" (the people of Moses). Moses now reminds God that they
are His people, and then he appeals both to the mercy and to the
glory of the Lord.

Wherefore should the Egyptians speak saying, For evil did
He, the Lord God, bring them forth to slay them in the
mountains, to consume them from the face of the earth?
(Exod. 32:12a)

And now Moses prays a positive intercessory prayer. He doesn't
say, "If it be Thy will, Lord." He knows where he stands with
God—and we should know where we stand with our Lord, with
our Savior and our Deliverer. Moses' prayer shows that he trusts
the mercy of God, the graciousness of God, the loving-kindness
and forgiveness of God. So he says to the Lord,

Turn from Your fierce anger, and rescind this evil against
Your people. (Exod. 32:12b)

If the word in your Bible is "repent," change it, because God is
not a man that He should repent (1 Sam. 15:29).

Moses now reminds the Lord of His promises to Abraham,
Isaac, and Israel. He uses the name *Israel* rather than *Jacob*,
because *Jacob* means supplanter. He was a conniver, deceiver,
liar, cheat. God had to work with him for twenty years to bring him
forth as *Israel*, the one who was born again, the one whose name
means he is a ruler with God.

Remember Abraham, Isaac, and Israel, Your servants, to
whom You did swear by nobody else but Yourself and You
did say unto them, I will multiply your seed as the stars of
heaven, and all this land that I have spoken of will I give unto
your seed, that they shall inherit it for ever.

And the Lord regretted the evil which He said He would do
unto His people. (Exod. 32:13-14)

The Almighty God permitted Himself to be entreated by Moses'
prayer.

And Moses turned and went down from the mount, with the two tables of the testimony in his hand: tables that were written on both their sides; on the one side and on the other were they written. And the tables were the work of God, and the writing was the writing of God, graven upon the tables. (Exod. 32:15-16)

On his way down from Sinai, Moses met Joshua. Joshua had been standing part way up the mountain. (Remember that this is Mount Horeb, although the summit is called *Sinai*.)

And when Joshua heard the noise of the people as they shouted, he said unto Moses, There is a noise of war in the camp. And he [Moses] said, It is not the voice of them that shout for mastery, neither is it the voice of them that cry for being overcome: but the noise of them that sing do I hear.

And it came to pass, as soon as he came nigh unto the camp, that he saw the calf, and the dancing: and Moses' anger waxed hot, and he cast the tables out from his hands, and he broke them beneath the mount. And he took the calf which they had made, and he burnt it with fire, and ground it to powder, and strewed it upon the water, and made the children of Israel drink of it. (Exod. 32:17-20)

Moses' anger waxed hot, and he broke the tables containing the covenant that God had made with Israel. Yet it was not anger that caused Moses to shatter the tables. Our rabbis wrote in the Talmud that he who breaks anything in anger is as if he were an idolater. Anger is selfish and blind, and is a purely emotional reaction against any injury received.

It was a feeling of moral indignation that swept over Moses at this point—the feeling that sometimes comes over us when we see a great wrong being committed. Anger is always provoked by something that injures *us*, but indignation can be aroused by an outrage against justice and right. Such a feeling of indignation filled Moses when he saw the people that had been at Sinai dancing before a golden calf. A mob guilty of such base ingratitude to God was, he felt, unworthy of the divine Words, the Ten Logos of God; so he broke the tables.

233

Then he ground the golden calf to powder and strewed it upon the water. Deuteronomy 9:21 tells us that "the water" was a brook which descended out of the mountain. To the Hebrews, strewing something upon water is still a symbol of perfect annihilation. Moses then made the children of Israel drink the water containing their own sin, their own corruption. Then Moses went right to the source, to Aaron.

> And Moses said unto Aaron, What did this people do unto you, that you have brought such a great sin upon them? And Aaron said, Let not the anger of my lord wax hot: you know the people, that they are always set on evil. (Exod. 32:21-22)

"You know how they are, Moses. They're always griping and complaining; they're always wanting to do evil. We took them out together, brother. You know what it's like." Aaron is passing the buck, wanting to blame somebody else.

> For they said unto me, Make us a god, which shall go before us: for this man Moses, the man that brought us up out of the land of Egypt, we know not what has become of him. And I said unto them, Whoever has any gold, let them break it off. So they gave it to me: then I cast it into the fire, and there came out this calf. (Exod. 32:23-24)

"I had nothing to do with it. I'm perfectly innocent. All I did was throw it in the fire, and out came the calf," Aaron said, pretending to be innocent of wrongdoing.

The Scripture has said that Aaron took the gold, melted it, and fashioned it with an engraving tool, and that he built an altar and declared a feast unto the Lord. Yet he says, "I did nothing."

The Lord says to His people constantly, "Repent; change your ways. Come to Me and ask for forgiveness of sin, and I'll always forgive you. But you have to open your mouth and *ask* for forgiveness of sin." If, instead of repenting when we are confronted with our sin, we pass the buck, we will remain guilty before God always. And Aaron passed the buck.

> And when Moses saw that the people had broken loose (for Aaron had let them loose for a derision among their enemies) then Moses stood in the gate of the camp, and said, Whoever

is on the Lord's side, let him come unto me. (Exod. 32:25-26a)

Moses is giving an altar call and an invitation: "Whoever is on the Lord's side, let him take a step right now before me, before the elders of Israel, and before God."

And all the sons of Levi gathered themselves together unto him. And he said unto them, Thus saith the Lord God of Israel, Put you every man his sword upon his side, and go to and fro from gate to gate throughout the whole camp, and slay every man his brother, and every man his companion, and every man his neighbor. And the sons of Levi did according to the word of Moses: and there fell of the people that day about three thousand men.

And Moses said, Consecrate yourselves today to the Lord, for every man has been against his son, and against his brother; that He, the Lord, may also bestow upon you a blessing this day. (Exod. 32:26b-29)

Moses is telling the Levites, who had been put in charge of the sanctuary, that they should lift up their hands and ask God to forgive them of the blood that was upon their hands—even though it was there because of a commandment from the Lord.

And it came to pass on the morrow, that Moses said unto the people, You have sinned a great sin: and now I will go up unto the Lord; perhaps I shall be able to make atonement for your sin. (Exod. 32:30)

He says, "I don't know. When I left the Lord, He was pretty angry. But I'll see if I can make atonement for your sin." Moses is going to intercede with God once again, and he will win God's forgiveness for the people. Intercessory prayer is the greatest privilege Jesus has given you and me. He said in His Word, "Pray for one another, that you might be healed" (James 5:16). As we pray for each other, the Lord heals us.

And Moses returned unto the Lord and said, O Lord God, this people have sinned a great sin. They have made themselves a god of gold. Yet now, if You will forgive their sin— (Exod. 32:31-32a)

235

And Moses stops right there; there's a big blank in the Hebrew. He waits upon the Lord; but when he doesn't get an answer from the Lord, he continues speaking:

If not, blot me, I pray You, out of Your book which You have written. (Exod. 32:32b)

Moses was willing to make a supreme sacrifice when he said, "Take me and my family and my name out of the Book of Life. I will stand as the atonement for the people of Israel."

Did you ever wonder why Moses was seen upon the Mount of Transfiguration? He was willing to lay down his life for his fellowman, just as Jesus laid down His life for you and me. He said, "Cast me to hell for all eternity, but spare the people of Israel." And Jesus said, "No man has greater love than this—that he would lay down his life for his fellow man" (John 15:13).

Then at last the Lord replied.

And the Lord said unto Moses, Whoever has sinned against Me, him will I blot out of My book of life. Now go, lead the people unto the place of which I have spoken unto you: and behold, my Angel—the Angel of the Lord—shall go before you. (Exod. 32:33-34a)

The Angel of the Lord, the Redeeming Angel, is Jesus the Christ. And God is saying, "Christ Himself will go before you."

In a footnote at page 831, the Amplified Bible has this to say about the Angel of the Lord:

"The Angel of the Lord," "of God," or "of His Presence," is readily identified as the Lord God (Gen. 16:11, 13; 22:11, 12; 31:11, 13; Exod. 3:1-6, etc.). But it is obvious that the Angel of the Lord is a distinct person in Himself from God the Father (Gen. 24:7; Zech. 1:12, 13; Exod. 23:20; etc.), as this verse shows. Nor does the Angel of the Lord longer appear after Christ came in human form. He must of necessity then be One of the three-in-one Godhead.

The Angel of the Lord is the visible Lord God of the Old Testament, as Jesus Christ was of the New Testament. Thus His Deity is clearly portrayed in the Old Testament. "There is a fascinating forecast of the coming Messiah, breaking

236

through the dimness with amazing consistency, at intervals from Genesis to Malachi, Abraham, Moses, the slave girl Hagar, the impoverished farmer Gideon, even the humble parents of Samson, had seen and talked with Him centuries before the herald angels proclaimed His birth in Bethelehem'' (Cambridge Bible).

Nevertheless, in the day when I visit I will visit their sin upon them. (Exod. 32:34b)

The Lord did not accept Moses' intercessory prayer at this point, but He says He will postpone the day of reckoning for the sake of Moses. The 603,550 people twenty years of age and older who participated in the iniquity of the golden calf had sinned beyond the point of no return. Even those who did not actively participate in the orgy had failed to go to the high priest and say, "Aaron, you can't make this golden calf. This is an abomination unto the Lord." Nobody wanted to get involved, and by their failure to get involved they committed the sin of omission. They were "accessories after the fact," as they say in courts of law. Therefore no member of that generation would be permitted to enter the Promised Land—except two, Caleb and Joshua. The people of Israel, led by the Angel of the Lord, would wander in the wilderness for the next forty years, until God brought into being a new generation which had not seen the golden calf.

All this is described in the New Testament Book of Hebrews:

Therefore, as the Holy Spirit says, Today, if you will hear His voice, Do not harden your hearts, as [happened] in the rebellion [of Israel] and their provocation and embitterment [of Me] in the day of testing in the wilderness, Where your fathers tried [My patience] *and* tested [My forbearance] and found I stood their test, and they saw My works for forty years. And so I was provoked (displeased and sorely grieved) with that generation, and said, They always err *and* are led astray in their hearts, and they have not perceived *or* recognized My ways *and* become progressively better *and* more experimentally *and* intimately acquainted with them. Accordingly I swore in My wrath *and* indignation, They shall

237

not enter into My rest.

[Therefore beware,] brethren; take care lest there be in any one of you a wicked, unbelieving heart which refuses to cleave to, trust in and rely on Him—leading you to turn away *and* desert *or* stand aloof from the living God. But instead warn (admonish, urge and encourage) one another every day, as long as it is called Today, that none of you may be hardened [into settled rebellion] by the deceitfulness of sin—[that is,] by the fraudulence, the stratagem, the trickery which the delusive glamor of his sin may lay on him. For we have become fellows with Christ, the Messiah, *and* share in all He has for us, if only we hold our first newborn confidence *and* original assured expectation [in virtue of which we are believers] firm *and* unshaken to the end.

Then while it is [still] called Today, if you would hear His voice, *and* when you hear it, do not harden your hearts as in the rebellion [in the desert, when the people provoked and irritated and embittered God against them]. For who were they that heard *and* yet were rebellious *and* provoked [Him]? Was it not all those who came out of Egypt led by Moses? And with whom was He irritated *and* provoked *and* grieved for forty years? Was it not with those who sinned, whose dismembered bodies were strewn *and* left in the desert? And to whom did He swear that they should not enter His rest, but to those who disobeyed—who had not listened to His word, and who refused to be compliant or be persuaded? So we see that they were not able to enter [into His rest] because of their unwillingness to adhere to *and* trust *and* rely on God—unbelief had shut them out. (Heb. 3:7-19 TAB)

And the Lord smote the people, because they made the calf, which Aaron made. (Exod. 32:35)

God held Aaron and the people responsible, because they had committed the unforgivable sin: blasphemy against His Holy Spirit.

And the Lord said unto Moses, Depart, go up from here, you and the people which you have brought up out of the land of

Egypt, unto the land which I swore unto Abraham, to Isaac,
and to Jacob, saying, Unto your seed will I give it: and I will
send My angel before you; and I will drive out the Canaanite,
the Amorite, the Hittite, the Perizzite, and Hivite, and the
Jebusite: unto a land flowing with milk and honey: for I will
not go up in the midst of you. (Exod. 32:35, 33:1-3a)

"My Holy Spirit will not go up in the midst of you. I will send
My Redeeming Angel, the pre-incarnate Christ Jesus, to go with
you; but My Holy Spirit will not go with you."

For you are a stiffnecked people: lest I consume you in the
way. (Exod. 33:3b)

"Unholiness cannot come in contact with holiness, and I am a
holy God. If My Holy Spirit is in the midst of you and you're still in
sin, I will consume you."

And when the people heard these evil tidings, they mourned:
and no man did put on himself his ornaments. (Exod. 33:4)

They decided, "Hey, we pushed our heavenly Father just a little
too far," so they left off all the idolatrous doodads they brought out
of Egypt to wear around their necks. They did the right thing for
once, because

As the Lord spoke to Moses, He had said, Say to the children
of Israel, You are a stiffnecked people. If I go in the midst of
you for one moment, I shall consume you. Therefore put off
your ornaments from you, that I may know what to do unto
you. (Exod. 33:5)

The Lord knows what He's going to do in advance, but He is
testing the people of Israel to see if they will be obedient. "Will
you sacrifice that heathen ornament unto Me?" He asks. "Even if
it's worth two million dollars, would you destroy it in obedience to
Me?"

And the children of Israel stripped themselves of their
ornaments from Mount Horeb onward.

Now Moses used to take the tent and pitch it outside the
camp, afar off from the camp, and he called it the tent of
revelation. And it came to pass that every one that sought the
Lord went out unto the tent of revelation which was outside

the camp. And it came to pass, when Moses went out to the tent, that all the people rose up and stood every man by his tent door, and looked after Moses until he was gone into the tent. And it came to pass that when Moses entered into the tent, the pillar of cloud [Jesus Christ] descended and stood at the door of the tent of meeting and the Lord spoke with Moses. And when all the people saw the pillar of cloud standing at the door of the tent, all the people rose up and worshiped, every man at his tent door. (Exod. 33:6-10)

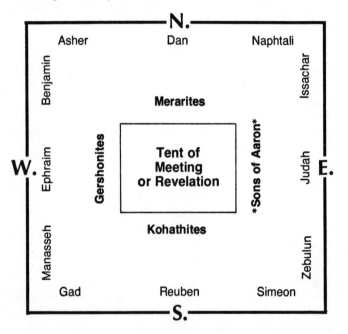

They rose up from a prostrate position. And when they stood up, they raised their hands and praised God that their intercessor was meeting with the Lord.

And the Lord spoke unto Moses face-to-face, as a man speaks unto his friend. And he returned unto the camp, but his minister Joshua, the son of Nun, a young man, departed not out of the tent. (Exod. 33:11)

Here's a miracle of miracles. The Lord kept Joshua, who was still a young man, in the tent of revelation in order to prepare his mind, his body, his spirit, and his soul to bring the people of Israel into the Promised Land forty years later. The Lord is constantly preparing you and me for the day of His coming. He constantly works in my life and in your life to get out the garbage. You can call it dross, chaff, or anything you want to—but it's still garbage. And He wants it out of us.

Now Moses said unto the Lord, Lord, You say unto me, Bring up this people. (Exod. 33:12a)

When Moses speaks to the Lord, he doesn't use fancy words and throw in a lot of "If it be Thy wills." He gets right to the point. And when you and I pray, the Lord wants us to get to the point and state our case. He says, "I heard you and I've already answered you—*if* you believe."

Moses continues,

And You have not let me know whom You will send with me. Yet You have said, I know you by name, and you have found grace in My sight. Now therefore, I pray You, if I have found grace in Your sight, show me now Your way, that I may know You, to the end that I may find grace in Your sight: and consider that this nation is Your people. (Exod. 33:12b-13)

Moses again reminds the Lord that the Israelites are *His* people, not Moses'. "You're the one that brought them up out of Egypt by all those miracles. You're the one who made all the promises to Abraham, Isaac, and Jacob. So don't call them *my* people and tell me that *I* brought them up." Moses not only reminds the Lord that the people of Israel are His people, His burden, His responsibility; he also reminds God of His statement that Moses had found grace in His sight. He appeals to the mercy and grace of the Lord—and God responds to him with love, mercy, and grace:

And the Lord said, My presence—My Holy Spirit—shall go with you and I will give you rest.

And he said unto Him, If Your presence does not go with me, carry us up not hence—don't even bother to take us to the

Promised Land. For how shall it be known that I have found grace in Your sight? Is it not in that You go with us? So we are distinguished, I and Your people, from all the people that are upon the face of the earth.

And the Lord said unto Moses, I will do this thing also that you have spoken: for you have found grace in My sight, and I know you by your name. (Exod. 33:14-17)

"Moses, Moses, I called you out of that burning bush."

Made bold by the Lord's answer to his intercessory prayer, Moses now begs the privilege of getting acquainted with the glory of God.

And he said, Show me, I pray You, Your glory. (Exod. 33:18)

Moses wants to psychoanalyze the Lord. "Lord, what are You made of? What are You? Who are You?" That is how intimate Moses was with God. Only one other man ever born on earth was as close to God as Moses, and that was Jesus Christ, who was God incarnate.

And He said, I will make all my goodness pass before you, and I will proclaim the name of the Lord before you. (Exod. 33:19a)

The name God is going to proclaim is *Jesus*. That's the true name that Moses can call upon, because all the power of the universe is tied up in that name. YHWH, the name that the German translator translated as "Jehovah," is an unpronounceable word in Hebrew. There's no such name as "Jehovah."

And I will be gracious unto whom I will be gracious, and I will show mercy on whom I will show mercy. (Exod. 33:19b)

The Lord now goes back to the great "I AM." "I am who I am; I am gracious unto whom I will be gracious; I will cause to be what I will cause to be. I'm the cause of all things. Nothing happens by accident, only by My divine will, My divine appointment. A sparrow will not fall out of the sky unless I ordain it. I know every hair on your head. I know every plan that you have devised."

And He said, You cannot see My face: for man shall not see Me and live. (Exod. 33:20)

This statement confirms the fact that the Lord with whom Moses had been communicating on Sinai and at the tent of revelation was Jesus Christ. Now he's speaking to God the Father. And no man has ever seen God and lived. The only way we can see God is through Jesus Christ, who said, "I and the Father are one (John 10:30). If you've seen Me, you've seen the Father, and there's no way to the Father except through Me" (John 14:6-10).

> And the Lord said, Behold, there is a place by Me, and you shall stand upon the rock. (Exod. 33:21)

"You can stand upon Jesus. You can see Me through the eyes of Jesus, and I will look at you through the eyes of Jesus." Praise God that we can see Him through the eyes of Christ, and that He not only sees us through the eyes of Jesus, He sees us *as* His beloved Son, Jesus Christ. He sees the Jesus *in* us. He does not see us as the sinners we are, because we have been purchased with the blood of Jesus Christ.

> And it shall come to pass, while My glory passes by, that I will put you in the cleft of the rock, and will cover you with My hand until I have passed by. And I will take away My hand and you shall see My back: but My face shall not be seen. (Exod. 33:22-23)

God Himself hid Moses in Jesus while His glory passed by. The glory of God is revealed in His eternal qualities, His eternal attributes. God's moral attributes consist of goodness revealed as love, mercy, and forgiveness. And God's divine demand upon us, as upon the people of Israel, is that we imitate Him by being loving, merciful, and forgiving. God said to the people of Israel, "You shall be holy; for I, the Lord your God, I am holy." Israel is not only to serve God but to imitate Him.

Man, being mortal, cannot imitate God's infinity, His omnipotence, or His eternity. That side of God's nature which is beyond human comprehension is also beyond human imitation. But we can know God's goodness, and we can imitate His mercy and forgiveness. God has just revealed Himself to Moses as a merciful and a forgiving God. Forgiveness is a divine attribute that we not only can imitate but *must* imitate. As you have been forgiven, so you are to forgive. If you hold a grudge, a resentment, or hatred toward anyone, don't expect God to forgive *you*.

Man is never nearer to God's divine quality of goodness than in his compassionate moments. God is compassionate toward us, and He wants us to show compassion to our fellowman. The Lord says to you and me, "Even as I am merciful, you be merciful" (Luke 6:36).

When God created man, He made him in His image and gave him His character; but because Adam and Eve disobeyed God, the image became tarnished and the character changed, and sin and death came into the world. In the fullness of time, Christ came to show us how we can imitate God in His divine attributes of mercy, forgiveness, and love. Jesus said, "I give you a new commandment. The way I have loved you is the way I want you to love one another" (John 13:34).

In our efforts to obey these divine demands, we can constantly appeal to the mercy of God, for His mercy endures forever (Ps. 136) and Jesus Christ is always interceding as our High Priest before God the Father: "Father, I have been in the same position these kids are in. I was tempted on all points as they are. Because I was divine, I remained without sin; but they're just mortal human beings. I bought them with My body and My blood, and I ask You now to forgive them." And as the Lord brings us under the conviction of the Holy Spirit and we appeal to His mercy, He is just and faithful to forgive us of our sin and to bring us back to the right path—to the truth, to the life.

The time we need to pray hardest is when we know we are sinning and yet we do not come under conviction. If we have become so hardened that we no longer hear the voice of the Lord, we are about to pass from grace into judgment.

If you're not having a trial, know that God is not dealing with you. The Lord says the trials of the righteous are many, because He's constantly going to test us, purify us, refine us, in order to bring us to the point where we become exact images of Jesus Christ. When we call ourselves by the name "Christian," we have professed to the Lord that we are little Christs. As Christians, we must recognize and accept the obligation the Lord placed on us when He said,

> If My people, which are called by My name shall humble themselves, and pray, and seek My face, and turn from their wicked ways; then will I hear from heaven, and will forgive their sin—their transgression, their iniquities—and will heal their land. (2 Chron. 7:14)

As a people and as a nation, we need to go to the Lord in intercessory prayer, appealing to His mercy, His love, His grace to heal our land. And if we do, our land will be healed—because He always keeps His Word.

Praise God that He has given His children the high calling! If God has called you to be like Jesus in all of your spirit, and if you have absolutely sold yourself to be His slave, He will take you at your word. He will wrap you up in a jealous love and will put on you such demands of obedience that He will not allow you to do things which He seems to let other good people do. Other Christians may push themselves forward, pull wires, and work schemes to carry out their plans; but you cannot. And if you attempt to, you will meet with such failure and rebuke from the Lord as to make you sorely penitent. Others can brag on themselves, on their work, on their success; but the Holy Spirit will not allow you to do any such thing. And if you begin it, He will lead you into some deep mortification that will make you despise yourself and all your good works.

Others will be allowed to accumulate great wealth; but God may supply your needs on a daily basis because He wants you to have something far better than gold—and that is a helpless dependence on Him. The Lord may let others be honored and put forward while He keeps you hidden away in obscurity, because He wants you to produce some choice fruit for His coming glory that can be brought forth only in the shade. God will let others be great, but He will keep you small. He will let others do a work for Him and get credit for it, but He will make you toil on without knowing what you are accomplishing. And then, to make your work still more precious, He will let others get the credit for what you have done. And all this

245

will make your reward ten times as great when Jesus comes.

The Holy Spirit will put a strict watch on you with a jealous love. He will rebuke you for wasting your time or for little words and feelings which never seem to distress other Christians. And He will not explain to you a thousand things about His dealings which may puzzle your reasoning. So make up your mind that God is sovereign and has a right to do as He pleases with His own. Settle it forever that you are to deal directly with the Holy Spirit and that He is to have the privilege of tying your tongue or chaining your hands or closing your eyes in ways that others are not dealt with.

When you are so possessed by the living God that you are in your secret heart delighted over this peculiar, personal, private, jealous guardianship and management of His Holy Spirit over your life, you will have found the vestibule of heaven in Jesus Christ.

24

The Broken Covenant Renewed

(EXODUS 34)

In response to Moses' intercessory prayer, God now tells him that He is ready to renew His covenant with the people of Israel.

And the Lord said unto Moses, Hew yourself two tables of stone like unto the first: and I will write upon the tables the words that were on the first tables which you did break. Be ready by the morning, and come up in the morning unto Mount Sinai, and present yourself there to Me on the top of the mount. And no man shall come up with you, neither let any man be seen throughout all of the mount; neither let the flocks nor herds feed before that mount. (Exod. 34:1-3)

The Lord tells Moses exactly what to do in preparation for this second meeting with Him on Sinai. "This time," He says, "no man shall go up to the mountain with you. You shall come up by yourself."

Following the Lord's instructions,

Moses hewed two tables of stone like the first; and Moses rose up early in the morning, and went up unto Mount Sinai, as the Lord had commanded him, and he took in his hand the two tables of stone. And the Lord descended in the cloud, and stood with him there, and proclaimed the name of the Lord.

(Exod. 34:4-5)

I believe that the Lord revealed to Moses the name of *Jesus*—a name he could call upon.

And the Lord passed by before him and proclaimed, The Lord, the Lord God, merciful and gracious, long-suffering, and abundant in goodness and truth, keeping mercy unto the thousandth generation, forgiving iniquity and transgression and sin, and that will by no means clear the guilty. (Exod. 34:6-7a)

In these verses, the Lord reveals thirteen distinct attributes of Himself to Moses and to mankind. The repetition "YHWH, YHWH God"—means, "I am the merciful God before a man commits his sin, and I am the same merciful and forgiving God *after* a man has sinned." Whatever change has to be made must take place in the heart of the sinner, not in the nature of God. Although He despises the sin, He loves the sinner.

The word *God* (which is in the Hebrew *El*) reveals the third attribute of God, His sovereignty. The Almighty Lord of the universe is not just the ruler of nature, but the ruler of mankind as well.

The fourth attribute of God is mercy. He says, "I am full of affectionate sympathy for human frailties. You can always appeal to My mercy. I am also a just and holy God, but don't ever appeal to My justice—because if you do, you're going to *get* justice." And I don't believe any one of us wants justice from God; we constantly want and need His mercy.

"My fifth attribute," the Lord says, "is graciousness. I am constantly consoling the afflicted and raising up the oppressed. All you have to do is call upon Me, appeal to My mercy and to My grace."

In man, the qualities of grace and mercy manifest themselves fitfully and occasionally, but in God they are permanent, inherent in His very nature. Therefore He alone can be spoken of as being merciful and gracious. "Mercy and grace shall surely follow me all the days of my life, and I shall dwell and praise and worship in the house of the Lord forever" (Ps. 23:6). Once I come to know

Him, He's never going to leave me alone. Praise God that, because of His divine attributes of mercy and grace, He will leave the ninety-nine sheep that are secure and will go out and bring back the one who strays.

The sixth attribute that God reveals is that He is long-suffering. The Hebrew means that He is slow to anger; He doesn't lose His cool. He says, "I don't hasten to punish the sinner. I afford him every opportunity to repent—to turn around and find his way back to Me." God brings us under conviction by His Holy Spirit, in order to give us every opportunity to come back to Him.

Abundant goodness is the seventh attribute of God. Jesus said, "I have come into the world to give you life and to give it to you more abundantly" (John 10:10). When the Lord says to Moses, "I am abundant in goodness," He means that He will grant us gifts and blessings beyond our just deserts, because the only thing we deserve is the cross. From the very foundations of the earth, Jesus went to the cross for you and me. He loved us before we even heard of Him, and He grants us gifts and blessings beyond our imagination.

"My eighth attribute," God says, "is truth." Jesus said, "I am the way, the truth, and the life" (John 14:6). And God reveals to Moses that He is eternally true to Himself. His plans are designed for the salvation of mankind, and His will is the only will that will be done. He is always calling man to salvation, and He will always reward those who are obedient to His will.

Loving-kindness precedes truth in God's revelation of Himself, both here and throughout all of Scripture. He's giving you and me a message: "Speak the truth by all means, but be quite sure that you speak the truth in love—because that's the way I speak to you." God always speaks to us in love—never in criticism or judgment. There is a day of judgment coming, but—praise God!—we will stand in that judgment with Jesus Christ, who has already paid the price for you and me by His body and blood.

Ninth, God reveals to Moses that He will keep mercy unto the thousandth generation. If you had an ancestor a thousand generations ago who knew God, God would keep mercy unto you.

And if this world lasts for another thousand generations before Christ comes again, He will show mercy to your descendants from this day forth because you love God and you love Jesus Christ. Praise God that He is so merciful, and that we can always appeal to His mercy!

God also says, "I will forgive. . . ." Forgiveness of iniquity, transgression, and sin makes up His tenth, eleventh, and twelfth attributes. Isaiah 53 tells us that Jesus took our sin, transgression, and iniquity with Him to the cross.

The Hebrew word translated *iniquity* means "sins committed from an evil disposition," and an evil disposition is something we're born with. So the Lord is saying that He will bear with indulgence the failings of man, and by forgiveness will restore him to his original purity—to the soul that God gave man when He made him in His image and in His likeness.

The Lord also forgives *transgression*—any willful, deliberate sin, which is always rebellion against God. If you disobey a sign which says "Do not trespass," or if you disobey God's commandment not to steal, that is transgression, deliberate rebellion against God. And God has already revealed that rebellion is as the sin of witchcraft (1 Sam. 15:23).

Sin, as distinct from iniquity and transgression, is that sin which was imparted to us by our father Adam, and it is also shortcomings due to heedlessness and error. It's not willful and deliberate, but it comes upon us suddenly.

God's thirteenth attribute seems very strange in light of the first twelve. He says He will not allow the guilty to pass unpunished. Yet we are all guilty. So God has provided a perfect sacrifice for you and me—a Lamb without blemish, Jesus Christ, to bear our punishment for us. But there's still something that we have to do. We must come to Jesus and say, "Lord, I ask You to forgive me of my sin." In his Pentecost sermon, Peter told the crowd to repent (change their ways) and be baptized in the name of Jesus for the remission of their sins. And then, he told them, they would receive a special gift from the Lord—the gift of the Holy Spirit (Acts 2:38). But those who refuse to repent and to ask for forgiveness of sin can never be pardoned. When the Lord says, "I will by no means clear the guilty," He means that they will remain guilty unless they come to Him and ask for forgiveness of sin.

Although God is merciful, gracious, and forgiving, He will never blot out the eternal and unbridgeable distinction between light and darkness, between good and evil. God cannot and will not leave repeated wickedness and obdurate persistence in evil entirely unpunished. Hebrews 10:26 says that if we willfully and deliberately keep on sinning, after we have once received the truth, there will no longer be any sacrifice left to atone for our sins. If we persist in deliberately sinning, God says we will pass from grace into judgment. But praise God for His patience! We usually give up on our neighbors after two weeks, or on our loved ones after two days—and we go to see a lawyer about an injunction or a divorce. But praise God that He doesn't divorce us after two days or two weeks, or two years!

Because God's mercy cannot destroy His justice, the sinner must suffer the consequences of his misdeeds if he remains a sinner. The unfailing and impartial consequences of sin are not vindictive punishments by God, but are remedies intended to bring the sinner back to salvation. If a man continues to sin, he's going to get chastised. The Lord might start out by spanking him like a little baby. But then the spanking is going to get harder, and then finally the Lord will take out a big club and hit him over the head just as we would hit a jackass to get his attention.

But God works with the sinner, as He did with Jacob. He worked with Jacob for twenty years to bring him to the point where He could change his name from *Jacob* (conniver) to *Israel* (prince of God). The Lord gave him four wives and thirteen children who were always fighting and squabbling. When Jacob would come home from work and walk into that tent, it was sheer bedlam. But the Lord was dealing with him. And when Jacob was on his deathbed, he could say, "I wait for Thy salvation, O Lord."

Most of us misinterpret the last part of Exodus 34:7, largely because the translators of the King James Version misunderstood the Hebrew. It says that God is

251

Visiting the iniquities of the fathers upon the children, and upon the children's children, unto the third and to the fourth generation. (Exod. 34:7b).

This law relates only to the *consequences* of sin. When God pardons a sinner, He forgives his guilt and removes his sinfulness, but He does not always remit the penalty for his sin. Jesus paid the penalty for our sin—the penalty of death. But if we continue to sin, our children, grandchildren, great-grandchildren, and possibly great-great-grandchildren will suffer for our sins. If you take a drink every night, your children are probably going to drink, too. You'll pass that sin on to your children. If you smoke, it's likely that they'll be smokers. And if you drive ninety miles an hour on the freeway, that's the way they're going to drive. The Lord will allow those who hate Him, who are His enemies, to visit their sins upon their children unto the third and fourth generation.

But compare this consequence of the permissive will of God with the mercy God shows to the descendants of those who love Him—unto the *thousandth* generation! Where sin abounds, it's only to the third and fourth generation; but where love and grace abound, it's to the thousandth generation.

The message God is giving us here is that, even though a person or an entire family is at enmity with God, He will divinely intervene in the third or fourth generation to arrest that heritage of evil. But He says, "I will allow you in the meantime to visit your iniquities upon your own children. You'll do it yourself; you don't need any help from Me. All I'm trying to do is to help you come to salvation, to deliverance, to healing. If you trust Me, if you believe Me, if you belong to Me, I'll supply all of your needs according to My riches in glory" (Phil. 4:19).

When Moses found out what God's attributes are—that He is merciful, gracious, kind, long-suffering—he could hardly wait until the Lord got through speaking to appeal to His mercy on behalf of Israel.

And Moses made haste, and bowed his head toward the earth, and worshiped. (Exod. 34:8)

Then Moses, who had offered himself as the atonement for

Israel's sin (Exod. 32:32) and had been the intercessor for Israel ever since they left Egypt, addressed God the Father and said, "Lord, You just spoke about grace."

If I have found grace in Your sight, O Lord, let my Lord I pray You, go in the midst of us. (Exod. 34:9a)

(Remember that God had said, "My Holy Spirit will not go with you, lest I consume you in a moment—because unholiness can never come in contact with holiness.")

. . . for it is a stiffnecked people. (Exod. 34:9b)

("Lord, I agree with You there. You gave us the right name; we *are* stiffnecked.")

And pardon our iniquity and our sin and take us once again to Your inheritance. (Exod. 34:9c)

And the Lord responded to Moses' appeal to His mercy and grace by renewing the conditions and the covenant that He had made with Israel before the iniquity of the golden calf. In renewing the covenant, however, the Lord still speaks of the people of Israel as Moses' people, not His:

And He said, Behold, I make a covenant: before all your people I will do marvels—miracles—such as have not been wrought in all the earth, nor in any nation: and all the people among which you are shall see the work of the Lord that I am about to do with you: that it is tremendous. Observe that which I am commanding you this day: behold, I drive out from before you the Amorite, the Canaanite, the Hittite, the Perizzite, the Hivite, and the Jebusite. (Exod. 34:10-11)

Some of the conditions of the covenant are reviewed in the verses that follow. These are largely a repetition of commandments which have been discussed in connection with their first appearance.

Exodus 34:12-17 repeats God's warning that the children of Israel must not allow their worship of Him to be corrupted by the nations already dwelling in the land of Canaan—the nations God has promised to drive out before them.

Take heed to yourself, lest you make a covenant with the inhabitants of the land where you do go, lest they be a snare for you in the midst of you. You shall break down their altars, dash in pieces their pillars, and cut down their Asherahs. (Exod. 34:12-13)

The word translated "groves" in the King James Version means *Asherahs*—wooden poles made in the shape of the male sex organ, which these heathen tribes worshiped.

For you shall bow down to no other gods: for the Lord, your God, whose name is Jealous, is a jealous God. (Exod. 34:14)

Let's retranslate that verse: "For the Lord, whose name is Righteously Indignant, is a righteously indignant God." God is the only one in the universe who has the right to become righteously indignant—because only He is righteous. And He says, "If I do become righteously indignant, look out! Then you're in trouble."

Lest you make a covenant with the inhabitants of the land, and they the people of Israel go astray after their gods, and sacrifice to their gods, and call upon them, and eat of their sacrifice; and you take of their daughters for your sons, and their daughters go astray after their gods, and make your sons go astray after their gods. You shall not make for yourself molten gods. (Exod. 34:15-17)

Exodus 34:18-26 repeats some of the instructions given in Exodus 22 and 23 concerning the worship of the true God.

The feast of unleavened bread you shall keep. Seven days you shall eat unleavened bread, as I commanded you, at the appointed time in the month of Abib: for in the month of Abib you came out from Egypt. (Exod. 34:18)

The Feast of Unleavened Bread, or the Passover, is to be kept as a remembrance of the night before the Exodus. That was the night the Angel of Death passed over the houses of the Israelites, sparing their firstborn sons, when he saw the sign of the cross made in blood over the lintel of the door and on each doorpost. The salvation from death bought by the blood of a lamb on Jewish homes that night is, of course, symbolic of the salvation bought for all races by the blood of Jesus Christ, the Lamb of God.

All that opens the womb is mine; of all your cattle you shall sanctify the males, the firstlings of an ox or sheep. But the firstling of an ass you shall redeem with a lamb: if you will not redeem it, then you shall break its neck. All the firstborn of your sons you shall redeem. And none shall appear before me empty. (Exod. 34:19-20)

When the Lord said, "None of you shall appear before me empty," He was saying that when we appear at the throne of grace we're not to come in empty-handed, with our arms outstretched, saying, "Daddy, I need, I want, give me." Instead, we are to enter in with a song of praise and thanksgiving. We are to have a song on our lips, worshiping and praising God for all the blessings He has already given us. We don't deserve any of them, but He has given them to us anyway.

Six days you shall work, but on the seventh day you shall rest: in plowing time and in harvest time you shall rest. You shall observe the feast of weeks, even the firstfruits of wheat harvest, and the feast of ingathering at the turn of the year. Three times in the year shall all your males appear before the Lord God, the God of Israel. (Exod. 34:21-23)

The Feast of Ingathering is more commonly called the Feast of Tabernacles, and it is a picture of the time when Jesus Christ will come and tabernacle with His people for a thousand years.* He is the true tabernacle of God. For a discussion of the Feast of Weeks (Pentecost), see comments at Exodus 23:16-17.

For I will cast out nations from before you, and I will enlarge your borders: neither shall any man covet your land, as long as you remain obedient unto Me by going up to appear before the Lord your God three times in a year. (Exod. 34:24)

"If you remain in obedience to Me, nobody will covet your land. I am your divine protection." This promise has a message for every Christian nation today.

You shall not offer the blood of My sacrifice with leaven; neither shall the sacrifice of the feast of the passover be left until the morning. (Exod. 34:25)

This verse explains why Jesus—the Passover Sacrifice without leaven (sin)—said on the cross, "Father, into Thy hands I commend My spirit" (Luke 23:46). Unlike you and me, He had the power to give up His spirit voluntarily. When He had finished the work of salvation for mankind, He released His spirit into the Father's hands. God ordained that His body would be taken down from the cross before the sun set on that Passover Friday, because the sacrifice could not be left until morning.

> The choicest of the fruits of your land you shall bring into the house of the Lord your God. (Exod. 26a)

The Lord says, "I want the best of that which I have given you. It is I who gave it to you, so now you bring the best unto Me and see if I will not open the windows of heaven and bless you out of your imagination" (Mal. 3:10). We like to rationalize and say, "Well, I give God ten percent of what's left of my income after the government takes its twenty percent." But God is asking for ten percent right off the top. He says, "That belongs to Me, because the other ninety percent is mine also. You're my steward, and I gave it to you as a trust. If you return that ten percent to Me off the top, I will bless you and your income will stretch where I purpose it to stretch." Praise God!

God concludes the conditions for the renewal of His covenant with the repetition of the very strange commandment of Exodus 23:19 from which all the Jewish dietary laws came:

> You shall not seethe a kid in its mother's milk. And the Lord said unto Moses, Write these words: for after the tenor of these words I have made a covenant with you and with Israel. (Exod. 34:26b-27)

God's covenant was with Moses first, and then with Israel. Israel was saved because Moses interceded for them.

> And he was there with the Lord forty days and forty nights: neither did he eat bread, nor drink water. And he wrote upon the tables the words of the covenant, the ten words. (Exod. 34:28)

In the Hebrew the Ten Commandments are still called the Ten Living Words. And when the Loving Word came, He fulfilled them all for us.

The day Moses descended from Sinai after his second forty-day meeting with God is the day that is observed by the Hebrew people as the Day of Atonement.

> And it came to pass, when Moses came down from Mount Sinai with the two tables of testimony in his hand, when he came down from the mount, that Moses did not know that the skin of his face shone and sent forth beams when he talked with Him. (Exod. 34:29)

Because Michelangelo misunderstood this verse, his statue of Moses has two horns upon his head. The Hebrew word means "beams," but he translated it as "horns." The beams were rays of the Holy Spirit which shone from Moses' face and from his head.

> And when Aaron and all the children of Israel saw Moses, behold, the skin of his face also sent forth beams; and they were afraid to draw nigh unto him. And Moses called unto them; and Aaron and all the rulers of the congregation returned unto him: and Moses spoke to them. And afterward all the children of Israel came nigh: and he gave them in commandment all that the Lord had spoken with him in Mount Sinai. Now when Moses had done speaking with them, he put a veil on his face. (Exod. 34:30-33)

The people could not stand to look on Moses' face. The Holy Spirit was so heavy upon him that they were slain under His power. Therefore Moses covered his face with a veil.

> But when Moses went in before the Lord that he might speak with Him, he took the veil off until he came out. (Exod. 34:34a)

See the beauty of that picture. When Moses went in to speak to the Lord, he took the veil off so that he could speak face-to-face with Jesus—God the Son.

> And he came out and spoke unto the children of Israel that which the Lord commanded. And the children of Israel saw the face of Moses, that the skin of Moses' face sent forth beams, and Moses put the veil upon his face again, until he went in to speak with Him. (Exod. 34:34b-35)

_____
* See the author's *Next Visitor to Planet Earth*.

25

Building the Tabernacle and Robing the Priests
(EXODUS 35—39:31)

And Moses assembled all the congregation of the children of
Israel together and said unto them, These are the words which
the Lord our God has commanded, that you should do them.
Six days shall work be done, but on the seventh day there shall
be to you a holy day, a sabbath of solemn rest unto the Lord:
whoever does any work therein shall be put to death. You
shall kindle no fire throughout your habitations upon the
sabbath day.

And Moses spoke unto all the congregation of the children
of Israel, saying, This is the thing which the Lord
commanded, saying, Take you from among the people of
Israel an offering unto the Lord: whoever has a willing heart,
let him bring it, which is the Lord's offering: gold, silver,
brass, blue, purple, scarlet, fine linen, and goats' hair, and
rams' skins dyed red, and seals' skins, and acacia wood, and
oil for the light, spices for the anointing oil, for the sweet
incense, and onyx stones, and stones to be set for the ephod,
and for the breastplate. (Exod. 35:1-9)

The Lord says, "I want this tabernacle to represent Me, but if
you have a willing heart I also want it to be a part of you. In that

way, you will be a part of Me.''

Let every wise hearted man among you come, and make all that the Lord has commanded. (Exod. 35:10)

Here the Lord is saying, ''I have prepared the hearts of certain men among you and have filled them with the spirit of wisdom and the spirit of knowledge. Let them now, if they have willing hearts, come forward. I will not bring them forward; they must come forward of their own accord. When they do, they are to make all that I have commanded'':

The tabernacle, its tent, its covering, its clasps, its boards, its bars, its pillars, its sockets, the ark, the staves thereof, the ark cover, the veil of the screen, the table, its staves, and all its vessels, and the showbread. The candlestick also for the light, its vessels, and its lamps, and the oil for the light. And the altar of incense, and its staves, the anointing oil, the sweet incense, the screen for the door at the door of the tabernacle. The altar of burnt offering, with its grating of brass, its staves, all its vessels, the laver and its base. (Exod. 35:11-16)

The laver, where the priests washed their hands, their faces, and their feet before going in to minister unto the Lord, was a picture of the Word. The priests would be cleansed by the Word. Later on, when Solomon built the temple in Jerusalem, he replaced the laver with a brazen sea, to allow for full immersion.

The hangings of the court, the pillars thereof, and their sockets, the screen for the gate of the court, the pins of the tabernacle, and the pins of the court, and their cords, the plated garments for ministering in the holy place, the holy garments for Aaron the priest, and the garments of his sons, to minister in the priest's office.

And all the congregation of the children of Israel departed from the presence of Moses. And they came, every one whose heart stirred him up, and every one whom his spirit made willing, and they brought the Lord's offering for the work of the tent of the meeting and for all the service thereof, and for the holy garments. And they came, both men and women, as many as were willing hearted, and brought their nose rings, their earrings, their signet-rings, their girdles, all jewels of gold: even every man that brought an offering brought gold unto the Lord. And every man, with whom was found blue, purple, scarlet, fine linen, goats' hair, rams' skins dyed red, seals' skins, brought them. Every one that did set apart an offering of silver and brass brought the Lord's offering: and every man, with whom was found acacia wood for any work of the service, brought it. And all the women that were wise hearted, who had the wisdom of the Holy Spirit, did spin with their hands, and they brought that which they had spun, the blue, the purple, the scarlet, and the fine linen. And all women whose heart stirred them up in wisdom spun the goats' hair. The rulers brought the onyx stones, and the stones to be set, for the ephod, and the breastplate; and spice, and oil for the light, and for the anointing oil, and for the sweet incense. And the children of Israel brought a freewill offering unto the Lord, every man and woman, whose heart made them willing to bring for all the work which the Lord had commanded by the hand of Moses to be made.

And Moses said unto the children of Israel, See, the Lord has called by name Bezaleel the son of Uri, the son of Hur, of the tribe of Judah. (Exod. 35:17-30)

Judah means "praise," and God wanted a man who was of the tribe of praise—the tribe from which would come the Lion of Judah, to whom all the praises of the earth would come.

And he has filled him with the spirit of God—the Holy Spirit—in wisdom, and in understanding, and in knowledge, and in all manner of workmanship; to devise skillful works, to work in gold, and in silver, and in brass, and cutting of stones for setting, and carving of wood for working all manner of skillful workmanship. And He has put in his heart that he may teach, both he and Aholiab, the son of Ahisamach, of the tribe of Dan. (Exod. 35:31-34)

Judah was the leading tribe of Israel; Dan, next to Benjamin, was the smallest of the tribes. Our rabbis interpret God's selection of these two men as signifying that the great and the small should be united and that, in God's eyes, both are equal.

Them He has filled with wisdom of heart, to work all manner of workmanship, of the craftsman, the skillful workman, and of the weaver in colors, in blue, and in purple, and scarlet, in fine linen, and of the weaver, even of them that do any workmanship and those that devise skillful work. (Exod. 35:35)

Through His Holy Spirit, the Lord gave these two men wisdom, knowledge, understanding to bring forth that which He placed in their minds and hearts. But from that day until the present, there have been no famous Jewish painters or sculptors. This is because the rabbis interpret the second commandment ("You shall not make any graven image or any likeness of anything that is in heaven above or in the earth beneath, or in the water under the earth") as prohibiting any work in plastic art. The rabbis speak of God as the incomparable artist, and of His whole creation as a process of unfolding total, complete beauty.

According to Hebrew teachers and rabbis of all generations, the greatest art is not that of self-expression but that of self-control. Thus the master artist in Judaism is the one who is able to control himself and his passions. The man who fashions himself into a sanctuary is a temple of the living God, the Holy Spirit. And this is what the Talmud says God meant man to be.

One of the saddest phenomena of our age is the misuse of art for the perversion of youth. Here is what is written in the Talmud: "Art is a divine gift and must be divinely used." When the Hebrew spirit prevails over the Greek spirit, art is stripped of pagan sensuality, so that the beauty of God, untarnished by anything barbaric, is revealed in all artistry. Because God took these men from the tribes of Judah and Dan and filled them with His Holy Spirit, they were able to bring forth the beauty that He wanted in His tabernacle.

God planned every detail of the tabernacle, because it was the place where His people could come to worship Him in spirit and in truth. And He was always there to be found if anyone desired Him enough to leave his tent, walk the fifty yards or so to the tabernacle, and go in and seek Him. God says, "I will dwell in the midst of you." So the tabernacle was always placed in the center of the encampment and was called "the camp of the *shekinah* glory of God"—the camp of the Holy Spirit.

> Bezaleel and Aholiab shall work, and every wise hearted man, in whom the Lord has put His wisdom, His understanding, to know how to work all the work for the service of the sanctuary, according to all that the Lord had commanded. And Moses called Bezaleel and Aholiab, and every wise hearted man, in whose heart the Lord had put wisdom, even every one whose heart stirred him up to come to the work to do it. (Exod. 6:1-2)

God gave Moses at that particular moment the discernment to know whom He had chosen for the work and into whose heart He had put His wisdom.

And now we see the fulfillment of God's commandment to Moses that the people of Israel are to give liberally for the construction of His tabernacle.

> They received of Moses all the offering, which the children of Israel had brought forth for the work of the service of the sanctuary, wherewith to make it. And they brought yet unto him freewill offerings every morning. (Exod. 36:3)

After they had brought what the Lord had asked for, the Spirit moved them to give even more. In addition to our tithes—that first ten percent off the top—the Lord wants our offerings. We Christians often fail to participate in the ministry to the poor, the widow, and the orphan. God is very much concerned about that ministry. He says, "Whatever you do unto the least of any one of these, you've done unto Me" (Matt. 25:40).

> And all the wise men, that wrought all the work of the sanctuary, came every man from his work which they worked; and they spoke unto Moses, saying, The people bring much more than enough for the service of the work, which the Lord commanded to make. (Exod. 36:4-5)

The picture given here is completely opposite to the condition described by Malachi, the last prophet whom the Lord sent to

Israel. God's message to the people of Israel through Malachi was, "You have robbed Me in your tithes and in your offerings" (Mal. 3:8). At this point, however, Israel is giving *more* than God had asked for.

> And Moses gave commandment, and they caused it to be proclaimed throughout the camp of Israel, saying, Let neither man nor woman make any more work for the offering of the sanctuary. So the people were restrained from bringing. For the stuff they had was sufficient for all the work to make it, and it was too much. (Exod. 36:6-7)

That's a beautiful commitment. The people had to be *restrained* from bringing unto the Lord. They were being blessed because they were giving, and the more they gave, the more the Lord blessed them. What a pity that the people of Israel soon lost that generous spirit!

The balance of chapter 36, and all of chapter 37, virtually duplicate information given in chapters 26 and 27. See discussion of those chapters for comments on the content of these parallel chapters.

The thirty-eighth chapter of Exodus sees the fulfillment of God's commandments to Moses concerning the altar of burnt offering, the laver, and the court: the completion of the tabernacle and all of its furnishings.

> And he made the altar of burnt offering of acacia wood: five cubits was the length thereof, and five cubits the breadth; it was foursquare; and three cubits the height. He made the horns thereof upon the four corners of it; the horns thereof were of one piece with it; and he overlaid it with brass. (Exod. 38:1-2)

This altar was covered with brass because it would receive the sin offering, the guilt offering, the blood from which would be placed on the horns at all four corners of the altar. The symbolism of this lifting up of the blood was discussed at Exodus 27:1-2.

> And he made all the vessels of the altar, the pots, the shovels, the basins, the fleshhooks, and the firepans: all the vessels thereof he made of brass. He made for the altar a grating of

network of brass under the ledge round it beneath reaching halfway up. He cast four rings for the four ends of the grating of brass, to be holders for the staves. And he made the staves of acacia wood, and overlaid them with brass. He put the staves into the rings on the sides of the altar, wherewith to bear it. He made the altar hollow with planks.

And he made the laver of brass, and the base thereof of brass, of the mirrors of the serving women that did service at the door of the tent of meeting. (Exod. 38:3-8)

The great sacrifice made by the women of Israel in giving away their mirrors was discussed at Exodus 30:17-18.

And he made the court: for the south side southward the hangings of the court were of fine twined linen, a hundred cubits: their pillars twenty, their brazen sockets twenty; the hooks of the pillars and their fillets were of silver. For the north side the hangings were a hundred cubits, their pillars twenty, their brazen sockets twenty; the hooks of the pillars and their fillets of silver. For the west side were hangings of fifty cubits, their pillars ten, and their sockets ten; the hooks of the pillars and their fillets of silver. The east side eastward was fifty cubits. The hangings for the one side of the gate were fifteen cubits; their pillars three, and their sockets three. And so for the other side: on this hand and that hand by the gate of the court were the hangings fifteen cubits; their pillars three, and their sockets three. (Exod. 38:9-15)

The only way to enter the court was through that one doorway, or gate, on the east end of the tabernacle. I believe the three pillars on each side of the gate represented the Trinity: Father, Son, and Holy Spirit. At that door were always stationed members of the tribe of Judah, not Levi. Judah is the tribe of praise, so the people would enter the court through praise. Jesus said, "I am the Door; this is the only way to enter in."

All the hangings of the court round about were of fine twined linen. (Exod. 38:16)

Fine twined linen represents purity. When the high priest entered the court on the Day of Atonement, he could not wear his priestly robes but was clothed with just a simple garment of fine twined linen. When Christ went to the cross, He had on a simple linen garment, signifying His purity. He did not go to the cross as our High Priest, but He became our High Priest after He had presented His body and His blood as the sacrifice for you and me. And we are made as pure as Jesus Christ by His righteousness, not by yours and mine. We have no righteousness of our own.

And the sockets for the pillars were of brass; the hooks of the pillars and their fillets of silver; and the overlaying of their capitals of silver; and all the pillars of the court were filleted with silver. The screen for the gate of the court was the work of the weaver in colors, of blue, purple, and scarlet, fine twined linen: and twenty cubits was the length, and the height in the breadth was five cubits, answerable to the hangings of the court. Their pillars were four, their sockets of brass four; their hooks were of silver and the overlaying of their capitals and their fillets of silver. And all the pins of the tabernacle, and of the court round about, were of brass.

These are the accounts of the tabernacle, even the tabernacle of the testimony as they were rendered according to the commandment of Moses for the service of the Levites, by the hand of Ithamar, the son of Aaron the priest. And Bezaleel the son of Uri, the son of Hur, of the tribe of Judah, made all that the Lord commanded Moses. And with him He put Aholiab, the son of Ahisamach, of the tribe of Dan, a craftsman, a skillful workman, a weaver of colors in blue, purple, scarlet, fine linen.

All the gold that was used for the work in the work of the sanctuary, even the gold of the offering, was twenty-nine talents, seven hundred and thirty shekels, after the shekel of the sanctuary

The silver of them that were numbered of the congregation was a hundred talents, and a thousand seven hundred and threescore and fifteen shekels, after the shekel of the sanctuary: a beka—half a shekel—a head, after the shekel of the sanctuary for every one that passed over to them that are numbered, from twenty years old and upward, for six hundred and three thousand and five hundred and fifty men. And the hundred talents of silver were for casting the sockets of the sanctuary, and the sockets of the veil: a hundred sockets for a hundred talents, a talent for a socket. And of the thousand seven hundred and seventy-five shekels he made hooks for the pillars, and overlaid their capitals, and made fillets for them.

And the brass of the offering was seventy talents, two thousand and four hundred shekels. And therewith he made the sockets to the door of the tent of meeting, the brazen altar, the brazen grating for it, and all the vessels of the altar, and the sockets of the court round about, the sockets for the gate of the court, and all the pins of the tabernacle, and all the pins of the court round about. (Exod. 38:17-31)

Since each adult male contributed half a shekel and the silver weighed 301,775 shekels, the total census of the men of Israel was 603,550, as reported also in Numbers 1:46.

In addition to the silver, the brass that was offered weighed about three tons, and the gold alone would be worth fifteen to twenty million dollars in the world today. All for a little tabernacle 75 by 150 feet to be erected in the wilderness! When the Lord said, "I will permit you to despoil the Egyptians," He certainly kept His word. He sent Mrs. Goldberg, Mrs. Levine, and Mrs. Silverman to knock on the doors of the Egyptians and say, "Give me your gold, your silver, your brass, your raiment, your linen—everything you have." And they found favor in the eyes of the Egyptians (Exod. 11:3). Instead of seeing the abominable Hebrew people and slamming the door in their faces, those Egyptians saw the Lord and gave of their riches. So the Israelites left Egypt with great wealth, which they used for the tabernacle that they built unto the Lord.

God made His tabernacle small for two reasons. One of these was that He knew who would enter in and who would not, and He made it just large enough to accommodate the true believers. The second reason was that the children of Israel had to carry it around; it had to be a portable sanctuary. The pillars of cloud and fire led the Israelites through the wilderness in circles—including forty laps around Mount Edom. Since they didn't learn their lesson the first time around, He ran them around again and again and again. Because they never learned to trust God, 603,548 of them died in the wilderness, but He brought their children into the Promised Land.

Another lesson the Israelites failed to learn was to confess their sins to God instead of passing the buck to someone else. Aaron passed the buck when he made that golden calf, and even Moses passed the buck to the people of Israel when he struck the rock because he lost his temper. Because he failed to surrender that temper to the Lord, God would not hear his intercessory prayer. If Moses had said, "Lord, I did it again; I lost my temper. Forgive me," God would have permitted him to enter the Promised Land. But instead He said, "You have failed to glorify me in the eyes of Israel; therefore you shall not enter in (Num. 20:12). But because you have been my servant and my friend and I have spoken to you face-to-face, I'll take you up on Mount Nebo and show you the Promised Land." So Moses had to wait fourteen hundred years for the coming of Christ before he entered in and stood on the Mount of Transfiguration with Jesus and Elijah.

Chapter 39 describes the vestments of the priests, which God had shown Moses how to make. These were sanctified garments, which fitted every high priest and lasted from the time of Aaron until A.D. 70, when the last high priest wore them.

> Now of the blue, of the purple, of scarlet, they made plated garments for ministering in the holy place, and they made the holy garments for Aaron; as the Lord commanded Moses. And he made the ephod of gold, blue, purple, and scarlet, fine twined linen. They did beat the gold into thin plates, and cut it into threads, to work it into the blue, into the purple, into the scarlet, into the fine linen, the work of the skillful workmen. They made shoulderpieces for it, to join it together; at the two ends it was joined together. And the skillfully woven band that was upon it, wherewith it was girded on, was of the same

268

piece and the like work thereof; of gold, blue, purple, and scarlet, fine twined linen, as the Lord commanded Moses.

They wrought onyx stones enclosed in settings of gold, graven with the engravings of a signet according to the names of the children of Israel. He put them on the shoulderpieces of the ephod to be stones of memorial for the children of Israel; as the Lord commanded Moses. (Exod. 39:1-7)

The names of the children of Israel were always to be lifted up before the Lord by the high priest—not because the Lord was in danger of forgetting them, but because we need to intercede for one another.

He made the breastplate, the work of the skillful workmen, like the work of the ephod: of gold, blue, purple, and scarlet, and fine twined linen. (Exod. 39:8)

The blue of the Holy Spirit, the scarlet of Jesus Christ, the purple of God the Father, and the purity of the fine twined linen were woven all together.

It was foursquare; they made the breastplate double: a span was the length thereof, a span the breadth thereof, being doubled. And they set in it four rows of stones: a carnelian, a topaz, and a carbuncle was the first row. The second row, a diamond, a sapphire, and an emerald. The third row, a hyacinth, an agate, and an amethyst. And the fourth row, a beryl, an onyx, and a jasper: they were enclosed in settings of gold in their settings. And the stones were according to the names of the children of Israel, twelve, according to their names, like the engravings of a signet, every one according to his name for the twelve tribes. And they made upon the breastplate plaited chains of wreathen work of pure gold. (Exod. 39:9-15)

In addition to bearing the names of Israel on his shoulders, the high priest also wore them on his breastplate. It was called the "breastplate of judgment" because it contained the Urim and the Thummim. (See discussion at Exodus 28:13-30.)

And they made two settings of gold, and two gold rings; and put the two rings in the two ends of the breastplate. And they put the wreathen chains of gold in the two rings on the ends of the breastplate. And the other two ends of the two wreathen chains they put on the two settings, and put them on the shoulderpieces of the ephod in the forepart thereof. They made two rings of gold and put them on the two ends of the breastplate, on the edge thereof, which was toward the side of the ephod inward. They made two other rings of gold, and put them on the two shoulderpieces of the ephod underneath in the forepart thereof, close by the coupling thereof, above the skillfully woven band of the ephod. They did bind the breastplate by the rings thereof unto the rings of the ephod with a thread of blue, that it might be upon the skillfully woven band of the ephod, and that the breastplate might not be loosed from the ephod; as the Lord commanded Moses.

Now he made the robe of the ephod of woven work, all of blue. There was a hole in the robe in the midst thereof, as the hole of a coat of mail, with a binding round about the hole, so that it should not be rent. They made upon the skirts of the robe pomegranates of blue, purple, scarlet, fine twined linen. They also made bells of pure gold, and put the bells between the pomegranates upon the skirts of the robe, round about between the pomegranates: a bell and a pomegranate, a bell and a pomegranate, upon the skirts of the robe round about it to minister in; as the Lord commanded Moses. (Exod. 39:16-26)

The significance of the bells was discussed in the comments on Exodus 26:36-37.

And they made tunics of fine linen of woven work for Aaron, and for his sons, and a mitre of fine linen, the goodly head attires of fine linen, and linen breeches of fine twined linen, and a girdle of fine twined linen, and blue, purple, and scarlet, the work of the weaver in colors; as the Lord commanded Moses.

And they made the plate of the holy crown of pure gold, and wrote upon it a writing, like the engravings of a signet, which said, HOLY UNTO THE LORD. And they tied unto it

270

a thread of blue, to fasten it upon the mitre above; as the Lord commanded Moses. (Exod. 39:27-31)

To get a clear idea of the appearance of the high priest, look at a picture of Pope Paul as he celebrates the mass at St. Peter's Basilica. His attire is an exact copy of the biblical description of the priestly garments.

26

The Lord Is in His Holy Temple!

(EXODUS 39:32—40)

Thus was finished all the work of the tabernacle of the tent of
meeting: and the children of Israel did according to all that the
Lord commanded Moses, so did they.

They brought the tabernacle unto Moses, the tent, all of its
furniture, its clasps, its boards, its bars, its pillars, its sockets,
and the covering of rams' skins dyed red, the covering of
seals' skins, and the veil of the screen, the ark of the
covenant, the staves thereof, and the ark cover—the mercy
seat—the table, all the vessels thereof, and the showbread,
the pure candlestick with the lamps thereof, even the lamps to
be set in order, and all the vessels thereof, and the oil for the
light, and the golden altar, the anointing oil, the sweet
incense, and the screen for the door of the tent, the brazen
altar, its grating of brass, its staves, and all its vessels, the
laver, and its base, the hangings of the court, its pillars, its
sockets, and the screen for the gate of the court, the cords
thereof, the pins thereof, and all the instruments of the service
of the tabernacle, of the tent of meeting, the plated garments
for ministering in the holy place, the holy garments for Aaron
the priest, and the garments of his sons, to minister in the

priest's office. (Exod. 39:32-41)

There were two different garments: the plated garments for Aaron for ministering in the holy of holies, and the holy garments for his sons to minister in the priest's office.

> According to all that the Lord commanded Moses, so the children of Israel did all the work. Moses saw all the work, and, behold, they had done it as the Lord had commanded, even so they had done it: and Moses blessed them in the name of the Lord. (Exod. 39:42-43)

Moses expressed his thanks to the workmen and the people of Israel by invoking his blessing upon them. The time had been short, the task arduous; but the laborers had been fired by the Holy Spirit. He gave them the enthusiasm and the zeal to complete joyfully the work they had undertaken. Moses did not pronounce his blessing at the *beginning* of the work, because he realized that beginnings are easy. The people of Israel, he knew, were always willing to start something; but the tabernacle was one of the few projects that they completed. Moses withheld his blessing until it was finished, because completions are rare.

Hebrew oral tradition says that Moses composed Psalm 90—a psalm which is repeated by the people of Israel for all occasions of praise and thanksgiving. The concluding words of this prayer of Moses are, "Establish Thou also upon us the work of our hands; yea, the work of our hands, establish Thou it." Moses was invoking the blessings of God upon all that the Lord had given them the privilege of bringing forth for His tabernacle.

> And the Lord spoke unto Moses, saying, On the first day of the first month you shall rear up the tabernacle of the tent of meeting. (Exod. 40:1-2)

The first day of the first month was April 14, the time of Passover.

> You shall put therein the ark of the testimony, and screen the ark with the veil. (Exod. 40:3)

The separation between God and His people lasted until Christ Jesus came into the world. By His death, He opened that veil screening the holy of holies and made it possible for all believers to enter in with boldness and confidence.

>And you shall bring in the table, and set in order the bread that is upon it; then you shall bring in the candlestick, and light the lamps thereof. You shall set the golden altar for incense before the ark of the testimony, and put the hanging to the door of the tabernacle. And you shall set the altar of burnt offering before the door of the tabernacle of the tent of meeting. You shall set the laver between the tent of meeting and the altar, and you shall put water therein. You shall set up the court round about, and hang up the screen of the gate of the court. You shall take the anointing oil, and you shall even anoint the tabernacle and all that is therein, and shall hallow it, and all the furniture thereof: and it shall be holy. Then you shall anoint the altar of burnt offering and all of its vessels, and sanctify the altar: and the altar shall be most holy. You shall anoint the laver and its base, and sanctify it. (Exod. 40:4-11)

The entire tabernacle had to be anointed with oil, representing the Holy Spirit, before it would be holy. When God gives *us* His Holy Spirit, He brings us up from the level of redemption (represented by silver) to the level of sanctification and the purity of gold.

>And you shall bring Aaron and his sons unto the door of the tent of meeting, and you shall wash them with water. (Exod 40:12)

Moses, the true high priest, was also the first baptizer. Aaron and his sons didn't wash themselves; Moses washed them with water.

>And you shall put upon Aaron the holy garments, and anoint him, and sanctify him; that he may minister unto Me in the priest's office. Now you shall bring his sons, and put tunics upon them. And you shall anoint them, as you anointed their father, that they may minister unto Me in the priest's office: and their anointing shall be unto them for an everlasting priesthood throughout their generations. Thus did Moses: according to all that the Lord commanded him, so did he.

And it came to pass in the first month in the second year, on the first day of the month, that the tabernacle was reared up. And Moses reared up the tabernacle, laid its sockets, and set up the boards thereof, and put in all the bars thereof, and reared up its pillars. And he spread the tent over the tabernacle, and put the covering of the tent above upon it; as the Lord commanded Moses.

He took and put the testimony into the ark. (Exod. 40:13-20a)

Moses was the only man who was ever able to come in contact with the ark of the covenant and live. At the Lord's command, Moses took the testimony of God—the stone tablets on which God had written the Ten Commandments—and placed them in the ark,

And set staves upon the ark, and put the ark cover upon the ark; and he brought the ark into the tabernacle, and set up the veil of the screen, and he screened the ark of the testimony of the Lord; as the Lord commanded Moses.

And he put the table in the tent of meeting on the side of the tabernacle northward, outside the veil. He set a row of bread in order upon it before the Lord; as the Lord had commanded Moses. (Exod. 40:20b-23)

When Moses was with God on Mount Sinai, the Lord had showed him the heavenly tabernacle. Now Moses is setting it up exactly as he saw it there.

And he put the candlestick in the tent of meeting, over against the table, on the side of the tabernacle southward. And he lighted the lamps before the Lord; as the Lord commanded Moses. (Exod. 40:24-25)

According to Hebrew oral tradition, Moses didn't actually light the lamps himself. He just stood there and said "Lord, You have commanded me to light these lamps, and now I ask You to send down Your Holy Spirit to do it." And the Holy Spirit came and lit the lamps. From that point on, it was Aaron's duty to keep them lit with an overflowing oil of the Holy Spirit. The Jewish historian, Josephus, wrote that the lamp in the temple went out when Christ was born—for Jesus said, "I am the light of the world" (John

8:12). The Hebrew people still look upon Josephus as a traitor because, in writing about Jesus Christ, he came to know and to love Him, and he became a completed Jew. I'm sure that God Himself revealed Christ to Josephus. As Jesus said, "No man comes unto Me unless My Father brings him" (John 6:65).

He—Moses—put the golden altar in the tent of meeting before the veil: and he burnt thereon the incense of sweet spices; as the Lord commanded Moses.

And he put the screen to the door of the tabernacle. The altar of burnt offering he set at the door of the tabernacle of the tent of meeting, and he offered upon it the burnt offering and the meal offering; as the Lord commanded Moses. (Exod. 40:26-29)

The meal offering, or cereal offering, was unleavened bread, which signified the broken body of Christ. Moses was carrying out every function of the high priest and performing the first sacrifice.

He set the laver between the tent of meeting and the altar, and put water therein, wherewith to wash. And Moses and Aaron and his sons washed their hands and their feet thereat: when they went into the tent of meeting, and when they came near unto the altar, they washed, as the Lord commanded Moses. And he reared up the court round about the tabernacle and the altar, and set up the screen of the gate of the court. So Moses finished the work. (Exod. 40:30-33)

As Moses finished the court, something very strange happened.

Then a cloud covered the tent of meeting, and the glory of the Lord filled the tabernacle. (Exod. 40:34)

The Lord now signified by His presence that Jesus was there, and He said, "I am well pleased with what you have done. You've followed My commandments exactly by perfect obedience."

And Moses was not able to enter into the tent of meeting, because the cloud abode thereon, and the glory of the Lord filled the tabernacle. And whenever the cloud was taken up from over the tabernacle, the children of Israel went onward throughout all of their journeys: but if the cloud was not taken up, then they journeyed not till the day that it was taken up.

JESUS IN EXODUS

For the cloud of the Lord was upon the tabernacle by day, and there was fire therein by night, in the sight of all the house of Israel, throughout all their journeys. (Exod. 40:35-38)

The cloud was Jesus Christ. He ascended in a cloud, and He will return in a cloud (Acts 1:11). The fire that was seen on the tabernacle at night and did not consume it or burn it was the fire of the Holy Spirit. By means of the cloud and fire, God led His children in the wilderness for forty years.

When the reading of any of the five books of the Pentateuch (which we Jews call the *Torah*) is completed in the synagogue, it is customary for the congregation to exclaim, ''Be strong, be strong, and let us strengthen one another!'' This is an echo of the ancient words repeated by Hebrew warriors before going into battle: ''Be of good courage and let us prove strong for our people and for the city of our God'' (2 Sam. 10:12). When used in the synagogue, the words ''be strong'' mean to carry out the teaching contained in the book just completed.

In the Book of Exodus, we have seen the people of Israel in Egypt. We saw the spiritual contrast between Israel and Egypt. The Israelites went into Egypt believing in God, but only one tribe remained faithful to the Lord, and that was the tribe of Levi. The other eleven tribes said, ''This God is not going to deliver us. That's just tradition, something our fathers told us to give us hope. It's a bunch of baloney; let's forget it.'' The tribe of Levi maintained that God gave His Word and that He will always keep His Word.

Then we saw the ten plagues that preceded the Exodus, and we saw the Exodus itself. God took twelve tribes, a bunch of rabble-rousers and made of them a congregation of peoples, a people called unto Himself. His promise to them was, ''I shall be your God and you shall be My people. I am holy; therefore I shall make you holy.''

We studied the Decalogue, the Ten Living Words given on Mount Sinai to show man forever how to live with God, his Father, and how to live with his fellowman. We talked about the vertical relationship described in the first five commandments (called "statutes"), which tell us how to get along with God. And we discussed the horizontal relationship described in the last five Logos (called "ordinances"), which show us how to get along with one another.

Through the Ten Commandments, the world outside of Israel came to know for the first time that there was a God of freedom. Every heathen god is a god of oppression, depression, condemnation. For the first time in the history of man, there was revealed a God of freedom who said, "There is no condemnation in Me." The message is still the same today. There is no condemnation in Christ Jesus (Rom. 8:1). Remember that. Condemnation comes from the enemy. Christ Jesus has freed us all.

Christ came into the world as the Revelation of the Ten Living Words, fulfilling all the commandments of God for you and me. But then, because we couldn't understand even ten instructions, He reduced them to two and gave them to us wholesale. He said, "If you love the Lord your God with all your heart, soul and mind, and love your fellowman as yourself, you have fulfilled all the law and all the prophets" (Matt. 22:37-40).

Jesus also said, "The commandment I give you is a brand new one, but it really shouldn't shock you, because I've tried to tell it to you throughout all the Old Testament and all the New Testament: the way I have loved you is the way I want you to love one another (John 13:34). And I have loved you unto the point of death."

Praise the Lord that He has loved us unto the point of death and unto eternal life!

――――― ―――――

Dr. Esses has been selected to appear in the 1976-77 edition of *Community Leaders and Noteworthy Americans*. He has also been selected to appear in the 1977-78 edition of *Who's Who in America* and *Who's Who in Religion*.

Bibliography

The Amplified Bible. Grand Rapids, Mich.: Zondervan Publishing House, 1965.

The Babylonian Talmud, tr. under the editorship of Rabbi Dr. I. Epstein. London: Soncino Press, 1936-38.

Dummelow, J.R., ed. *A Commentary on the Holy Bible* by various writers. London: Macmillan, 1909.

Freeman, James M. *Manners and Customs of the Bible*. Plainfield, N.J.: Logos International, 1972.

Ginzberg, Louis. *The Legends of the Jews*. 7v. Philadelphia: Jewish Publication Society of America, 1909-66.

Hastings, James, ed. *Dictionary of the Bible*. Rev. ed. New York: Scribners, 1963.

Henry, Matthew. *Commentary on the Whole Bible*. 6v. Old Tappan, N.J.: Revell, n.d.

Henry Matthew. *Logos Commentary on the Bible*, by Matthew Henry and Thomas Scott. 3v. Plainfield, N.J.: Logos, n.d.

The Interlinear Greek-English New Testament. The Nestle Greek Text with a Literal English Translation, by Alfred Marshall. Grand Rapids, Mich.: Zondervan, 1958.

The Interpreter's Bible. 12v. New York: Abingdon, 1952-57. 4v. and supplementary volume.

The Interpreter's Dictionary of the Bible. Nashville, Tenn.: Abingdon, 1962-76.

Josephus, Flavius. *The Works of Flavius Josephus*. Tr. by William Whiston. 4v. Grand Rapids, Mich.: Baker Book House, 1974.

The Living Bible. Paraphrased. Wheaton, Ill.: Tyndale House, 1971.

Midrash Rabbah, tr. . . . under the editorship of Rabbi Dr. H. Freedman and Maurice Simon. 10v. London: The Soncino Press, 1939.

Smith, William, ed. *A Dictionary of the Bible*. Hartford, Conn.: S.S. Scranton, 1868.

The Torah: The Five Books of Moses: A New Translation of the Holy Scriptures According to the Masoretic Text. Philadelphia: The Jewish Publication Society of America, 1962.